Bolingbroke G-BPIV has represented examples of the Blenheim in both its Mk IV and I guises for more than three decades. All images Key Publishing, unless stated

Forgotten No More

It is difficult to overestimate the importance of the Bristol Blenheim to the RAF when it first entered service. Flying a fast, modern, monoplane medium bomber was a step change for a generation of airmen who had previously flown open cockpit biplanes. The Blenheim was to Bomber Command what the Hawker Hurricane was to Fighter Command.

Yet unlike the legendary fighter, the Blenheim tends to be overlooked in the history books. In its night fighter guise – especially when equipped with airborne radar, which it helped pioneer – it merits a mention as 'also flown during the Battle of Britain'. But its participation in the Battle of France, the early bombing raids and 'Circuses' – and especially in the anti-shipping campaigns – are less well covered.

Part of the reason why is that many who flew in Blenheim squadrons in the early years of the war did not survive to write their down their experiences. Losses were extremely high. Subsequent variants of the Blenheim did nothing to address the fact that it was hopelessly outclassed and outgunned by the time it went to war. It remained in service because there was nothing better until the mid-war years, by when the tide of the war was beginning to turn in favour of the Allies. It disappeared from frontline service relatively quickly.

Another factor was the absence of Blenheims after the war; of the nearly 5,400 that rolled out of British factories, not one was kept for posterity. Finland continued to fly them into 1958 and had the foresight to preserve an example built by Valtion. It is thanks to Canadian production as the Bolingbroke – a Blenheim in all but name – that the aircraft was reintroduced to the UK in the 1970s. The painstaking restoration to airworthy condition of a Bolingbroke airframe marked a revival in interest in the aircraft, and those who flew, serviced and built them. Operating from Duxford, Cambridgeshire, G-BPIV initially represented long-nosed Mk IVs, before a Mk I cockpit section was fitted.

Attempting to condense the Blenheim story into just over 100 pages is a difficult proposition. I would like to thank both Jim Winchester and Jon Lake, whose help and contributions made that process considerably easier.

David Willis
September 2025

COVER ART BY ANTONIS KARIDIS
Bristol Blenheim IV P4852 of 82 Squadron, 2 Group, RAF Bomber Command attacks and sinks U-31 during a reconnaissance of Heligo Bight in March, 1940. The vessel was the first U-boat sunk by an aircraft during World War Two and the first dispatched by the RAF. Original art commissioned by Key Publishing.

ISBN: 978 1 83632 180 4
Editor: David Willis
Senior editor, specials: Roger Mortimer
Email: roger.mortimer@keypublishing.com
Cover Design: Steve Donovan
Design: SJmagic DESIGN SERVICES, India
Advertising Sales Manager: Sam Clark
Email: sam.clark@keypublishing.com
Tel: 01780 755131
Advertising Production: Becky Antoniades
Email: Rebecca.antoniades@keypublishing.com

SUBSCRIPTION/MAIL ORDER
Key Publishing Ltd, PO Box 300, Stamford, Lincs, PE9 1NA
Tel: 01780 480404
Subscriptions email: subs@keypublishing.com
Mail Order email: orders@keypublishing.com
Website: www.keypublishing.com/shop

PUBLISHING
Group CEO: Adrian Cox
Publisher: Steve O'Hara

Published by
Key Publishing Ltd, PO Box 100, Stamford, Lincs, PE9 1XQ
Tel: 01780 755131
Website: www.keypublishing.com

PRINTING
Precision Colour Printing Ltd, Haldane, Halesfield 1, Telford, Shropshire. TF7 4QQ

DISTRIBUTION
Seymour Distribution Ltd, 2 Poultry Avenue, London, EC1A 9PU
Enquiries Line: 02074 294000.

CONTENTS

Bristol and the Blenheim

The Blenheim Family

Blenheim

For nearly a third of a century, the public has been able to see a Blenheim in the air. The aircraft was built as a Bolingbroke IV-T but has been flown in several schemes representing Blenheims of different squadrons. It is seen during its time as Z5722 of 68 Squadron, a night fighter unit. Its existence has helped keep the exploits of Blenheim crews alive for generations born after the war.

The Blenheim embodied many firsts and completed many pioneering wartime missions. However, the rapid advance of military aircraft in the late-1930s made it nearly obsolete at the start of the conflict and, sent out unescorted, its squadrons suffered heavy losses.

It was one of the first multi-role combat aircraft, produced in both bomber and fighter variants. It served with every wartime RAF air command, with the exception of Transport Command, and in every theatre of war, and was produced in four countries. In Britain, sub-contractors built more than Bristol Aeroplane Company, which built 1,014 of the aircraft. Rootes Securities at its factories in Speke, Liverpool and Blyth Bridge in Staffordshire produced 3,422, while Avro at Chadderton in Lancashire added at least 1,000 (with five more unconfirmed). Total production in the UK and abroad amounted to more than 6,200 aircraft.

SERVICE INTRODUCTION

The true prototype of the Blenheim, Type 142M K7033, first flew on June 25, 1936. The Type 142M was very similar to the Type 142 *Britain First* ordered by Viscount Rothermere, except that the wing was raised to a mid-position, allowing a bomb bay to be incorporated and a bomb-aimer's position provided in the nose. A dorsal turret with a single 0.303in (7.7mm) Lewis gun was installed. With the extra equipment and only slightly more powerful 840hp (626kW) Bristol Mercury VIII engines, performance slipped from the spritely Type 142 and – apart from range – would not improve with later versions.

Being more sophisticated than the previous generation of biplane bombers, with higher speeds and then novel features such as a retractable undercarriage, landing flaps and variable-pitch propellers, there was a high accident rate once deliveries to the squadron

began. Early Mercury engines were also prone to sudden stoppage.

The Blenheim was first issued to 114 Squadron at RAF Wyton in Huntingdon during March 1937. Five more RAF Bomber Command squadrons were equipped with the new bomber by the end of the year and a further 11 during 1938. RAF Fighter Command began receiving the Mk IF fighters from October 1938. The Mk IF was a simple conversion of the bomber, with a gun pack mounted under the fuselage containing four fixed forward-firing Browning 0.303in (7.7mm) machine guns. During the era of the eight-gun single-seat monoplane, it was far from ideal, but it was available in quantity and helped bolster Britain's air defences. By September 1939, about 1,000 Blenheims had been delivered to the RAF. As well as equipping home-based squadrons, Blenheims were also serving with commands in Egypt, India and Singapore.

BLENHEIM VCS

Although the Blenheim's performance was impressive for 1936, it became increasingly obsolescent in the face of faster foreign fighters and improved anti-aircraft defences. RAF Bomber Command would lose 745 Blenheims before they were superseded by de Havilland Mosquitoes in late 1942. A Mk I of the Fighter Interception Unit, based at RAF Ford in West Sussex, made the first successful night-time interception using air-to-air radar on May 11, 1940, but as new equipment arrived – notably Bristol's Beaufighter – Fighter Command soon relegated its Mk IFs to night-fighting duties, where they had reasonable success. RAF Coastal Command used the Blenheim primarily as a fighter, flying both defensive patrols and bomber escort missions.

Three RAF Blenheim pilots were awarded the Victoria Cross. Each flew in a different theatre of war. Wing Commander Hughie Edwards of 105 Squadron, Bomber Command, led a daring low-level attack on the German port of Bremen on July 4, 1941. Wing Commander Hugh Malcolm led 18 Squadron on numerous raids in Libya, before being killed in an unescorted attack on a fighter airfield on December 4, 1942. All the Blenheim Vs on the raid failed to come back.

Squadron Leader Arthur Scarf made a solo attack on a Japanese airfield after his own base in Thailand was bombed and the rest of 62 Squadron's Blenheims were destroyed or damaged. Badly wounded by fighter attacks, Scarf brought his aircraft and crew back, crash-landing on an airfield in Malaya before succumbing to his injuries.

EXPORTS

Even before the Blenheim had entered RAF service, it had attracted export interest. Finland's Valtion company acquired a licence

A trio of Blenheim IVs from the first production batch of the variant built by Bristol, originally ordered as Mk Is but completed to the later standard when the contract was changed. The complex shape of the aircraft's nose was a compromise that provided the navigator/bomb aimer with more room while giving the pilot an adequate forward view.

One of the Blenheim's least remembered contributions to victory was the role it played in expanding the aircraft industry under the 'shadow scheme', whereby factories involved in manufacturing items for other industries built aviation components or assembled whole aircraft. The Blenheim was one of the first types produced under the scheme. More than half of the Blenheims built were produced at two Rootes Securities factories, while Bristol at Filton (seen here) and Avro produced around 1,000 each.

to build the type at Tampere. They bought 18 new and 24 ex-RAF Mk Is, which saw action in the Winter War of 1939-40 with the Soviet Union. From 1940, an additional 45 Mk IIs and ten Mk IVs were built without a licence and used against the USSR during the Continuation War, and against German forces in Finland in the brief Lapland War of 1945. Finland would play a significant role in the Blenheim story and was the last country to fly the type; some remained in service as late as 1958.

Neutral Turkey ordered 20 Mk Is before the war and ten more were delivered in 1940. Three Mk IVs and 17 Mk Vs were supplied from RAF stocks in the Middle East in 1943. While they were not involved in combat operations, they remained in service until 1948. Yugoslavia took 20 Mk Is and manufacturer Ikarus AD began licence production of 50 more at Zemun outside Belgrade. Only 16 were completed before

The Blenheim IV was the most numerous of all the variants built. Bomber Command had begun the process of upgrading from its Mk Is by the outbreak of war, but the new variant offered little more and was slightly slower than the aircraft it replaced. While the original Blenheim was faster than most of the fighters it would encounter when it entered service, by the time the Mk IV appeared a new generation meant the bomber could not rely on its speed to protect it, while defensive armament was far from adequate.

the factory and uncompleted airframes were sabotaged to keep them out of German hands. Romania ordered 40 Blenheims in 1939, but they wound up fighting for the 'other' side, principally during the German invasion of the Soviet Union. Numbers dwindled, although they were augmented by few former Yugoslavian examples. By August 1944, the few remaining were relegated to transport duties. Portugal acquired three Blenheim Vs intended for service in North Africa that landed on their territory while in transit from south England to Gibraltar. Later, Britain supplied 24 more Mk IVs in exchange for basing rights in the Azores.

LONG NOSES

The major version was the Blenheim IV with a completely revised, longer nose giving the navigator/bomb-aimer more room. Many had

By the time it entered production the Blenheim V was hopelessly outclassed for operations over Europe and the majority of the aircraft were sent to North Africa and the Middle East. Originally designed for close air support, experience demonstrated that fighter-bombers were more effective supporting troops on the ground and it was instead built as a light bomber, a mission that other, better designs could undertake. Nevertheless, many Blenheim Vs were usefully employed as bombers, while others flew coastal patrols.

BLENHEIMS COMPARED

Blenheim	Mk I	Mk IV	Mk V
Length	39ft 9in (12.12m)	42ft 7in (12.98m)	43ft 11in (13.39m)
Wingspan	56ft 4in (17.17m)	56ft 4in (17.17m)	56ft 1in (17.09m)
Height	12ft 10in (3.91m)	12ft 10in (3.91m)	12ft 10in (3.91m)
Empty weight[1]	8,100lb (3,674kg)	9,791lb (4,411kg)	11,000lb (4,990kg)
Max T/O weight[1]	12,250lb (5,670kg)	14,400lb (6,532lb)	17,000lb (7,711kg)
Max speed	285mph (459kph)	266mph (428kph)	260mph (418kph)
Service ceiling	32,000ft (9,754m)	31,500ft (9,601m)	31,000ft (9,449m)
Range	1,125 miles (1,810km)	1,460 miles (2,350km)	1,600 miles (2,575km)
Powerplants[2]	VIII 840hp (626kW)	XV 925hp (690kW)	25/30 950hp (708kW)

Notes: [1] Weights did vary slightly between individual aircraft, which had an impact on performance; [2] Bristol Mercury variant and rating

Nearly all Blenheims and Bolingbrokes were powered by the Bristol Mercury, a nine-cylinder, air-cooled, single-row, piston radial engine. The Mk VIII, XV, XVI, XX, 25 and 30 were all used to power various versions of the aircraft. Around 21,000 Mercuries were built.

an under-nose blister with rearwards-firing 0.303in (7.7mm) Brownings. Twin Brownings were also fitted in the dorsal turret of many Mk IVs, doubling the defensive armament that could be brought to the rear quadrant, although in many cases it was still inadequate. All these changes increased weight and reduced speed to a full 40mph (64kph) below that of the Type 142, although the additional fuel tanks in the wings improved range.

From November 1939, Mk IVs were built by Fairchild Aircraft of Canada, the first 18 as the Type 149 Bolingbroke I with British-standard measurements and fittings. The American-standard Bolingbroke IV with Mercury XV engines and many equipment changes, intended for coastal reconnaissance and bombing, became the first major production version built in Canada. The IV-W was powered by Pratt & Whitney R-1535s in case delivery of Mercuries was interrupted, but only 14 were produced. The 457 Bolingbroke IV-Ts were navigation and gunnery trainers and played a significant role in the training of pilots and crews for the British Empire. Canadian production ended in November 1943. Eight Royal Canadian Air Force squadrons used the type between July 1940 and September 1945 in coastal patrol, anti-submarine, photographic and training roles. Some were deployed to the Aleutian Islands, a combat theatre in 1942-43, and they attacked submarines on at least one occasion.

The most overlooked version of the aircraft is the Type 160 Blenheim Mk V. While it was designed for either the ground support mission with a four-gun pack and armour plate or as a high-altitude bomber with a glazed nose, production concentrated on the latter variant. The prototype, known as the Bisley I, flew for the first time on February 24, 1941. Apart from the redesigned nose section it was similar to the Mk IV and the new name was quickly dropped by the time it entered production. Rootes built 942 of them up to mid-1943, although by then the Blenheim was obsolete. The Mk V served overseas, but was generally not popular with its crews, although many were supplied by the RAF to other operators.

FORGOTTEN NO MORE

In general, the Blenheim gained a reputation as the 'forgotten bomber' as more effective, better later types received much of the glory. No complete, British-built Blenheims survived to be preserved. The only example of a European-built Blenheim on display today is Mk IV BL-200, one of the prized exhibits at the Aviation Museum of Central Finland. It is one of the aircraft built by Valtion.

It was through the efforts of Graham Warner and his team at Duxford, Cambridgeshire, that an airworthy 'Blenheim' graces the skies today. Back in 1987, a Bolingbroke IV airframe was lovingly restored back to flying condition, but unfortunately the aircraft was wrecked in a crash soon afterwards. A second restoration was completed in 1993 and since then the aircraft (G-BPIV) has worn various colour schemes to represent many wartime RAF squadrons that flew Blenheims. The original long nose of the aircraft was eventually replaced with that of a Blenheim I that had spent much of the post-war period as a car, making the aircraft the only representative of 'short nose' variants. As of late 2025, it wears the colours of a Fighter Command Mk IF of 23 Squadron. The operation of this single aircraft over more than 30 years has done much to highlight the role played by the Blenheim and its aircrews. It is a fitting tribute to those who flew the aircraft, particularly during the dark, early days of the war.

The Blenheim and Bolingbroke quickly disappeared from RAF and RCAF service at the end of the war. Many Canadian aircraft were sold for scrap or even the fuel left in their tanks, their hulks slowly deteriorating over the years. In the 1960s, interest in these hulks began to rise and many of the Bolingbrokes currently on display in museums in Europe and North America were painstakingly restored from such remains.

The Bristol Story Part One

From Boxkites to the Blenheim

The Bristol & Colonial Aeroplane Company grew out of a business making buses and trams to became one of Britain's most important aircraft manufacturers. The formative years saw both success and failure, but more importantly Bristol attracted talented engineers, designers and pilots who would go on to achieve great things for both the company and the nation, as Jim Winchester outlines.

The founder of what would one day be Bristol Aerospace, Sir George White, is not as well known as some of Britain's other pioneers, perhaps as he was not an engineer or pilot. Born in Bristol into a working-class family, he became a pioneer in the field of electric trams and founded a stockbroking company. He was elected president of the Bristol Stock Exchange in his 20s and was also chairman of the Imperial Tramway Company. He was associated with Bristol Royal Infirmary and other local institutions, being made a baronet in 1904.

By 1908, the Bristol tramway was extended to Filton, in the north of the city. The Bristol Tramways and Carriage Co (BT&CC) began building buses in two facilities at Filton, inaccurately known as the 'Tram Sheds'. This site was to become home to one of Britain's largest aircraft factories.

While in France doing business with a local tram manufacturer in 1909, Sir George visited the Wright Brothers school at Pau and became very enthusiastic about aviation. One of the reasons was that he could see that the crowds that flying exhibitions attracted could generate great custom for tramways.

MANUFACTURING AND TRAINING

In February 1910, Sir George told BT&CC shareholders that he wanted to build aeroplanes. Three days later they registered four similar company names: British & Colonial Aeroplane Company Ltd, with a capital of £25,000; the Bristol Aeroplane Company Ltd; the Bristol Aviation Company Ltd; and the British & Colonial Aviation Company Ltd. The latter three were holding companies established with a capital of just £100 each.

As one of its first acts the Bristol & Colonial Aeroplane Company booked a stand at the Olympia Aero Show in London, although it did not have anything yet to display. Having acquired the rights from Société Zodiac in France to build the biplane designed by Gabriel Voisin, one was quickly imported and was exhibited as the Bristol & Colonial Zodiac.

After the show it was taken to Brooklands in Surrey for flight trials, but unfortunately it was underpowered, the wings had insufficient camber and it refused to leave the ground. The Bristol-Zodiacs in production at Filton were abandoned and the licence cancelled. Bristol was without any aeroplanes to make. The company quickly turned to another existing French design and began producing it in a modified form as the Boxkite.

As the Boxkite was essentially an unlicensed copy of the 1909 Farman biplane, the French firm rightly

The British & Colonial Aeroplane Company had been building aircraft for more than a quarter of a century before the first flight of the Blenheim. Like most companies, many of its designs progressed no further than the drawing board, while among those that flew, few made it into production.

Production under way at the British & Colonial Aeroplane Company facility at Filton in January 1911, with Boxkites at the rear.

sued. Bristol's defence was that it had made so many improvements that it was essentially a new type, although in truth its changes mainly amounted to some new metal fittings. The case was thrown out and the Boxkite was sold in large numbers for the time.

The British & Colonial Flying School was established at Larkhill, Wiltshire, and at Brooklands, and was soon busy teaching private and military budding aviators. An estimated 80% of British pilots trained by the outbreak of war in August 1914 had graduated from the Bristol schools.

Flying training quickly became half of the company's business and was to remain important for it into the 1950s. Other schools were set up in Spain, Italy and – following a demonstration of a Prier monoplane before the Kaiser – at Halberstadt in Germany. This operated until the outbreak of war, so Bristol can also lay claim to have trained many of the initial pilots on both sides of the conflict.

A new factory was opened at Brislington in South Bristol, which completed the final six Boxkites. The bus business was evicted from the Filton sheds and their assembly moved to the new site.

The company's first monoplanes were the Challenger-Low machines of 1911, which used wing-warping rather than ailerons and refused to fly. More successful designs came from Pierre Prier, the first person to fly from London to Paris non-stop in April 1911 and an instructor at the Blériot school at Hendon, north of the capital, and from the Romanian Henri Coandă. He joined the company in January 1912 and would

become its chief designer. Bristol-Prier and Bristol-Coanda monoplanes would begin to establish the company's reputation for design and engineering quality.

Bristol's best design of the period was the Scout, which stemmed from work started by Coandă and completed by Frank Sowter Barnwell and Harry Busteed in early 1914. It became one of the first single-seat fighters used by the Royal Flying Corps (RFC) and Royal Naval Air Service (RNAS), with 374 built.

WAR-TIME PRODUCTION

When war broke out in August 1914, the War Office insisted that Bristol build other manufacturers' designs. The Royal Aircraft Factory B.E.2, designed by Geoffrey de Havilland in 1911, was the preferred type, even

The Bristol Boxkite was one of the most successful of the early designs and around 78 were built. Officially, the aircraft was the Bristol Biplane, but it was universally known as the Boxkite.

though it was approaching obsolescence. The government-supplied drawings for the B.E.2 left a lot to be desired, with Bristol's draughtsmen spending a lot of time to bring them up to an acceptable standard. Many modifications were called for during production. This resulted in an adaptable workforce that had intimate knowledge of the aircraft, with the result that Bristol-built B.E.2s were said to be the best of those made by any contractor. Orders came in frustratingly small batches, although they did add up to 1,079 examples by the time production ended.

With the government managing aircraft design, there was little for Bristol's designers to do. Coandă returned to Romania, eventually becoming its minister for science. In late 1914, Barnwell left to join the RFC and flew in France with 12 Squadron, which operated a mixed bag of different types. Frustrated by losses to superior German aircraft, the generals sent him back to Bristol, where he arrived in August 1915 to take up the position of chief designer. Barnwell hired Leslie George Frise, who would go on to introduce many innovations within the company.

Together they worked on the twin-engined T.T. (Twin Tractor) two-seater for local defence. Unavailability of RAF 4a engines resulted in the design being modified as the T.T.A in January 1916, but although two were flown it was not accepted for service. The Admiralty had a separate requirement for an escort and anti-Zeppelin fighter. Bristol offered the F.3A, based on the T.T.A, but this was not built. The pair recovered from these setbacks to create one of the best aircraft of the era, the F.2 Fighter. In its original form and using defensive tactics, the Fighter came off second best in air combat, but used aggressively in its refined F.2B form it became the mount of many aces. More than 5,300 were built, a small proportion of them in the United States, and would serve with the RAF into the early 1930s.

The speed advantage of monoplanes was obvious despite a prejudice against them following pre-war accidents. Frank Barnwell designed the M.1, which flew in July 1916. Its impressive performance, including a top speed of 130mph (209kph), earned it the nickname 'Bullet', but the distrust of monoplanes

Pierre Prier standing next to the Bristol Prier P-1 No. 46 at Larkhill, Wiltshire, in July 1911. He had joined the firm in the previous month, having received his French pilot's licence (number 169) on August 9, 1910.

Bristol Priers of the British & Colonial Flying School at Larkhill. Pilot training was an important role for the company in the early days of aviation.

lingered and only 125 were built, most serving as trainers or in theatres of war away from the Western Front.

RFC pilot Cyril Frank Uwins joined the company in October 1916. He would make the maiden flight of almost every Bristol aircraft that followed up to the Type 170 Freighter in 1946. Sir George White died suddenly on November 22, 1916, aged 62. His son, also George but known by his middle name, Stanley, inherited the baronetcy. He was managing director of the firm from 1911 until his death in 1964, steering it through two world wars and the challenges of the post-war eras. It is said that more than £500,000 was put into the company before Bristol's backers got a penny back, but in the long term it proved to be a wise investment.

PEACE, UPGRADES AND ENGINES

After the war, Bristol's business was precarious; it managed to keep going by modifying existing aircraft, rather than mass producing new models. The company constructed numerous new types, but produced fewer than five examples of most

Work on the Bristol Scout was started by Henri Coandă and completed by Frank Barnwell and Harry Busteed in early 1914. These examples are Scout Cs operated by the Royal Naval Air Service. When Bristol began retrospectively allocating design numbers to its aircraft, the Scout C became the Type 1.

and only one of several. The Bulldog fighter was its one true success story of the 1920s.

Following the cancellation of all wartime contracts in early 1919, Bristol had little work. The tramways side of the business stepped in to fill the gap in manufacturing, with orders for buses to replenish the Bristol city fleet. Vans and tankers on Bristol chassis were also built at Filton and the company made luxury car bodies for Siddeley Motors. The aircraft business itself was saved by an order for 215 upgrades of F.2Bs into the Mk II variant, also called the 'J-Type'.

Acquisition of the bankrupt Cosmos Engineering aeroengine business at the government's insistence proved invaluable to the company in the medium and long-term. Along with it came Alfred Hubert Roy Fedden, later to be responsible for engines that played not only a significant role for Bristol but also for the British aircraft industry. Fedden's Jupiter radial became a standard in the 1920s and more than 7,000 were built and installed in over 260 different types of aircraft.

By far the most successful design to emerge from Bristol during World War One was the F.2 Fighter. A3303 was the prototype F.2A, powered by a 190hp Rolls-Royce Falcon, but the definitive version was the F.2B.

PROTOTYPES

During the inter-war years, Bristol tried everything from lightplanes to fighters, bombers and airliners, many of which failed to attract orders. The Type 30 Babe of 1919 was an attempt to build a single-seater private aeroplane and the result was Bristol's smallest aircraft. Finding a reliable, low-powered engine for the design proved difficult, and the two Babe biplanes built seldom flew – and the Babe III monoplane not at all.

Civil aviation activity was permitted again in May 1919 after the lifting of the wartime ban. The company civilianised the F.2 Fighter in various configurations, first as company runabouts, then for commercial use as the Tourer, which sold to several governments and some early airlines.

A more fully developed version of the Tourer was the Type 36 Seely, obsequiously named for the then Under-Secretary of State for Air, who resigned before it had even flown. Entered in an Air Ministry competition for a light civil aircraft, it failed to win. It was rebuilt in 1923 as the Type 85 and was used by the Royal Aircraft Establishment (RAE) at Farnborough, Hampshire, on engine and supercharger trials.

May 1919 saw the debut of the Barnwell-designed F.2C, a proposed replacement for the F.2B Fighter, but the RAF was happy with the original to undertake the colonial policing role and had little in the way of finance to buy new aircraft. Four examples of the F.2C, later known as the Badger, were

built. Barnwell, famously an erratic pilot, crashed one and it was never rebuilt. Another attempt at a 'Brisfit' replacement was the Type 78 of 1923. Stability problems saw it rebuilt as the Type 84 Bloodhound. Only four were produced and they helped prove the reliability of the Jupiter engine, clearing the way for its adoption as standard by Imperial Airways.

On February 9, 1920, the Bristol & Colonial Aeroplane Company became the Bristol Aeroplane Company, one of the four names it had registered during its foundation a decade earlier. The original capital of £100 was raised to £1m. One of the reasons for this change was to reduce the firm's tax obligations by winding down the original company.

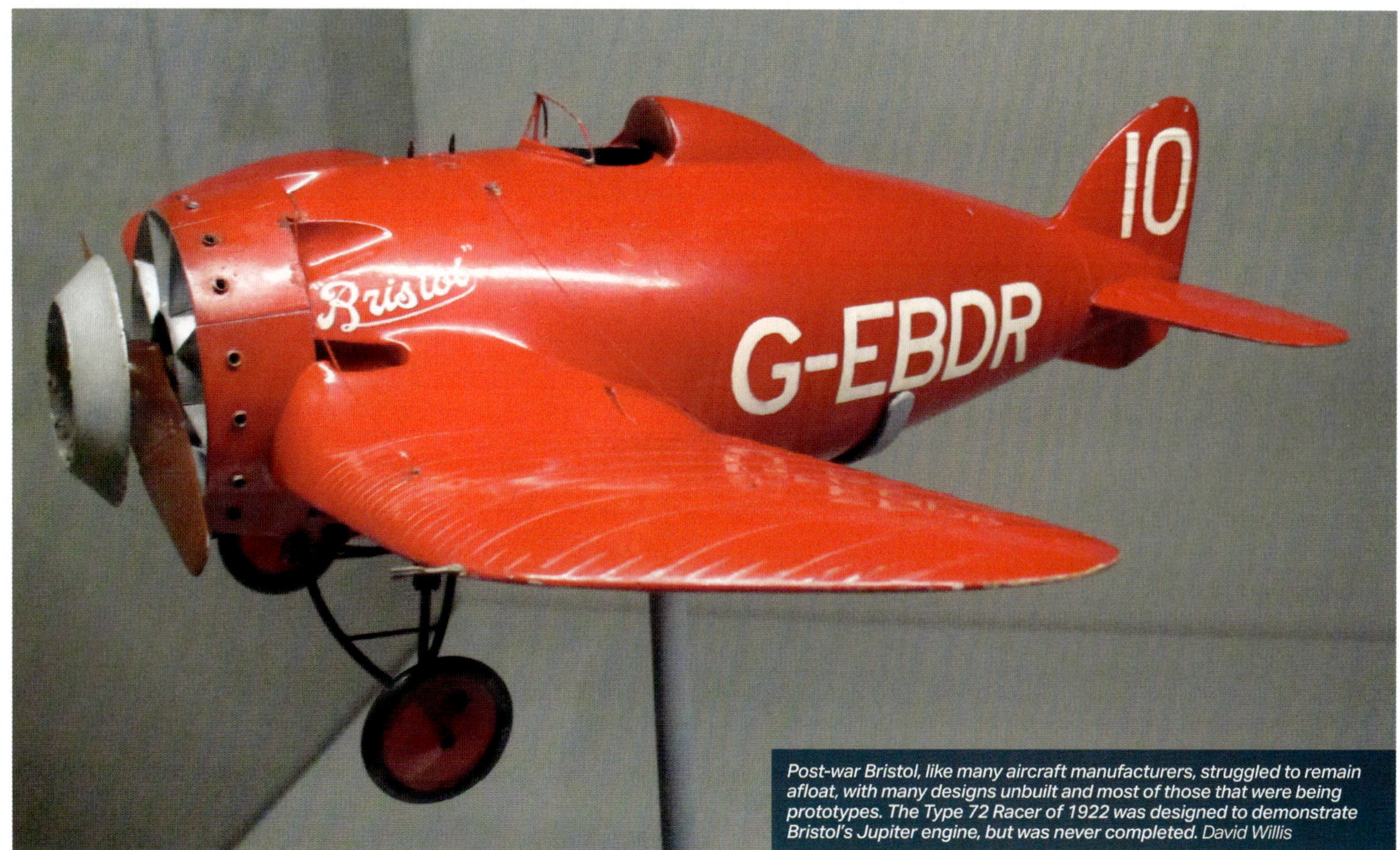

Post-war Bristol, like many aircraft manufacturers, struggled to remain afloat, with many designs unbuilt and most of those that were being prototypes. The Type 72 Racer of 1922 was designed to demonstrate Bristol's Jupiter engine, but was never completed. David Willis

Continued on page 16

Frank Barnwell
Father of the Blenheim

In December 1911, Bristol hired one of its most significant employees, Scottish aviation pioneer Frank Sowter Barnwell, who turned down an offer from de Havilland to go to Filton as a draughtsman. His talent was soon recognised within the company and he became chief designer in the 'X-Department', a secret experimental unit that concentrated on seaplanes. Barnwell's first project was the X.1, an adaptation of the Bristol Gordon England biplane. This, and the subsequent X.2 and X.3, were not successful. A number of aircraft for racing purposes followed, including the Challenger-Dickson and the Type T Racing Biplane.

When his work partner Henri Coandă moved back to Romania in 1915, Barnwell completed a design he had been working on, which emerged as the Baby Tractor biplane and would evolve into the Bristol Scout. Barnwell joined the Royal Flying Corps on the outbreak of war and flew in France with 12 Squadron, which was then operating RAF B.E.2s. In August 1915, the War Department ordered Barnwell back to Bristol, where he would design the M.1 'Bullet', the only monoplane fighter accepted into service by the RFC. Barnwell's most famous early design was the F.2 – better known as the 'Bristol Fighter' – which first saw combat in April 1917. After early setbacks as its crews got to grips with the aircraft, it gained a reputation as probably the best two-seater of the war. Bristol Fighters remained a stalwart of the RAF into the 1930s, notably in the colonial policing role.

After the war, Barnwell designed the one-off Type 32 Bullet racer and the Type 52 Bullfinch. However, the lack of orders for any of his designs resulted in Barnwell quitting Bristol to take a commission as a Squadron Leader, Technical, in the Royal Australian Air Force and he departed England in October 1921. Barnwell's successor, Wilfrid Thomas 'Wilf' Reid also emigrated, going to work for Canadian Vickers; Frank Barnwell returned from Australia in October 1923. The company welcomed him back and appointed him its chief designer.

Among Barnwell's new designs were the Type 84 Bloodhound and Type 93 Boarhound, only built in small numbers. Finally, success returned in 1927-28 when Barnwell designed Bristol's most successful inter-war aircraft, the Type 105 Bulldog fighter. In 1933, he began work on a high-speed, all-metal transport capable of cruising at speeds of 250mph (402kph) or above. This evolved into the Types 142 and 143, which would lead to the Blenheim.

Although he had flown well over 100 types of aircraft, Barnwell had crashed a number of them; in 1937 Bristol reluctantly banned him from flying solo in any of the company's aircraft. That did not stop him experimenting during his own time with a light aircraft he had designed. Captain Frank Sowter Barnwell, OBE, AFC, aged 58, died in the crash of his homebuilt aircraft, the B.S.W Mk 1 G-AFID, at Whitchurch, Bristol, on August 2, 1938. It was not the only tragedy to befall the Barnwell family. Frank's brother Harold had been killed in a crash in 1917, while all three of his sons – David Usher, Richard Anthony and John Sandes – pilots in the RAF, would die in action between June 1940 and October 1941.

Captain Frank Sowter Barnwell, OBE, AFC, November 23, 1880 – August 2, 1938.

Continued from page 14

The Bulldog was Bristol's most successful design of the late 1920s, going on to become the iconic 'silver biplane' for the RAF of the 1930s. Not only did Bristol build the airframe, but it was also responsible for the Jupiter that powered the majority built.

Blenheim Is under construction at Filton in 1938. On the right is the tail of L1164, which was destroyed in a crash on the day Britain declared war on Germany.

THROUGH THE 1920S INTO THE 1930S

The Aerial Derby races of the early 1920s were a showcase for aerial innovation. A Tourer was placed third in the 1921 handicap section and the Type 32 was second overall. In 1922, the M.1D won the handicap section, but despite these successes Bristol's overall record was not spectacular. After the crash of the M.1D in 1923, Bristol withdrew from competition for several years. In October 1921, Frank Barnwell emigrated to Australia to help establish the country's aircraft industry.

Wilfrid Thomas 'Wilf' Reid and Clifford W Tinson, the latter fresh from A V Roe, designed the Type 90 Berkeley to meet a 1923 specification for a multi-purpose bomber. The first flew in March 1925. The second of the Rolls-Royce Condor-powered biplanes was built with an all-wooden structure but the third was all-metal. These were the only examples produced, as the contract was won by Avro with its Aldershot.

Wilf Reid later emigrated to work for Canadian Vickers, but Barnwell had returned from Australia in October 1923; Barnwell said the Royal Australian Air Force had given him little to do beyond designing minor parts. Bristol welcomed him back by appointing him the company's chief designer.

His next aircraft, the Type 91 Brownie was submitted for the 1924 Air Ministry light aeroplane competition. A conventional-looking low-wing monoplane, powered by a 30hp (22kW) Bristol Cherub two-cylinder engine, it was twice considered but eventually rejected as a primary trainer for the RAF. Rebuilt as the Type 91B Brownie II, it took third place in the *Daily Mail* trials at Lympne, Kent, in 1926, before being crashed by Barnwell himself in March 1928. Two more Brownies were built with metal wings and flown as single-seaters.

The Type 92 Laboratory Biplane was an unusual machine with a narrow cylindrical fuselage. Its role was to provide a comparison with wind tunnel tests in the evaluation of the interaction between various engine, cowling and fuselage combinations. It flew

The Type 95 Bagshot – originally named the Bludgeon – was designed to carry a pair of 37mm Coventry Ordnance Works (COW) guns. Just over a decade later, the same weapon was tested in a Blenheim.

The Bombay was a troop transport that could be used as a bomber. The prototype first flew in June 1935, but by July 1937, when the Air Ministry ordered production examples, Bristol's Filton factory was busy assembling Blenheims. The Bombays were built by Short & Harland in Northern Ireland.

in November 1925 with a 3ft (1m) diameter fuselage and later with one of 5ft (1.5m), before being damaged in a landing accident in 1928 and not repaired.

One of the oddest looking of all Bristol aircraft was the Type 95 Bagshot of 1927, a twin-engined, three-seat monoplane fighter. It was to carry two 37mm Coventry Ordnance Works (COW) guns, but these were never fitted. Test flights showed an alarming tendency for the cantilever wing to flex and the ailerons to reverse. Further ground testing revealed the two-spar wing structure was weak and could never support the proposed armament. Rebuilding the Bagshot as a

biplane was considered, but instead it was scrapped in 1931.

The Type 105 Bulldog fighter was the company's great inter-war success, with more than 440 built for the RAF and a number of export customers. Designed to meet Specification F.9/26 and initially flown on May 17, 1927, the first was delivered to the RAF two years later and it went on to form the backbone of the service's fighter squadrons into the early 1930s. The biplane would remain in RAF service long enough to see the formation of Fighter Command, the last being retired by the squadrons in July 1937.

By then the rearmament of the RAF was well under way and contracts from the Air Ministry began to be awarded to the manufacturers at an increasing rate. Another successful design from Bristol that entered service was the Type 130 Bombay, although 49 of the 50 built came off the Short & Harland assembly line in Northern Ireland. Work had also been undertaken on a promising light twin-engined executive transport aircraft, built as the Type 142. Although only one Type 142 would be built, its performance would come to the attention of the Air Ministry. The Type 142 was the ancestor of the Blenheim.

Blenheims, Bolingbrokes and Bisleys

On August 3, 1704, English, Austrian and Dutch forces – united as the Grand Alliance under the command of the Duke of Marlborough – defeated the Franco-Bavarian army on the banks of the River Danube. The fighting took place near the village of Blindheim in Bavaria. It shattered the perception of French invincibility and, to the British, became known as the Battle of Blenheim. For his efforts the Duke was presented with the Palace of Blenheim in Oxfordshire by a grateful nation.

When Bristol was seeking a name for a military version of the Type 142 *Britain First*, it settled on Blenheim. While this was outside the Air Ministry's 1932 naming system for bombers in force when the Blenheim was christened – inland towns of the British Empire or those associated with the RAF were standard – it was adopted.

General purpose and torpedo aircraft received names of British historical individuals. Bolingbroke was the family name of King Henry IV, who reigned between 1399 and 1413. He was born at Bolingbroke Castle and his illegitimate children were given the surname Beaufort.

During the war, the task of naming aircraft became the responsibility of the Ministry of Aircraft Production. Army co-operation aircraft would be named after 'classical words'; how this resulted in Bisley for the close air support version of the Blenheim is

open to speculation. Several Bisley villages existed, but in 1890 the National Rifle Association moved from Wimbledon to Bisley Camp in Woking, Surrey, hosting the shooting events in the 1908 Olympic Games. The Bristol Type 160 became the Bisley, but only for three months into the production run, as on January 8, 1942, it was officially changed to Blenheim V.

While only three main variants of the Blenheim entered production for the RAF, several subtypes adapted for various roles were created. They included the fighter versions of the Mk I and IV, identified by an 'F' suffix, although examples equipped with AI sets received no further marker. Canada retained the name Bolingbroke for those built by Fairchild Aircraft of Longueuil, Quebec, probably because its initial requirement was for a general reconnaissance aircraft. Its interest originally focused on the Bristol aircraft of that name, which spawned the long-nose Blenheim IV.

The differences between the three main variants of Blenheim are visible in these images of Mk I K3074 (top), Mk IV N6212 (middle) and Mk V AZ930 (bottom). Each increased weight and saw a decrease in performance.

Bristol 135

uring 1933, Bristol worked on the Type 135, a light, high-speed six-seat civil transport with a crew of two. Frank Barnwell first sketched out the layout of the design on July 28 that year, the aircraft having a low wing while power was to be provided by a pair of Bristol Aquila engines then under development.

Viscount Rothermere of Hemsted, the proprietor of the *Daily Mail* group of newspapers, was informed about the Bristol 135 by the editor of the *Bristol Evening World*, Robert T Lewis, who was ordered to find out more about the aircraft. The viscount was troubled by the state of British civil aviation and became determined to have the fastest aircraft in Europe. In March 1934, Lewis was informed by Barnwell that the Type 135 with Bristol Mercury engines – which had the advantage of being more powerful and in production – would be capable of at least 240mph (386km/h). Rothermere decided to order such an aircraft, which Bristol designated the Type 142, while the company decided to produce an Aquila-powered version as the Type 143.

Bristol 142

ork on the Type 142 proceeded quickly following Viscount Rothermere's order for the aircraft. It would be powered by a pair of Bristol Mercury VIS 2s, rated at 650hp (485kW), turning four-blade, fixed-pitch, wooden propellers, and featured a solid nose. The Bristol Sequence Number (the company's name for constructor's numbers) 7838 was assigned and the civil registration G-ADCZ allocated on February 25, 1935, although it would never be painted on the aircraft. Instead, the aircraft carried the so-called 'B-class' identity R-12. The aircraft first flew from Filton outside Bristol on April 12, 1935, with the company's chief test pilot, Cyril Uwins, at the controls. Rothermere named the aircraft *Britain First*. A landing lamp was later installed in the tip of the nose, while three-blade Hamilton variable-pitch propellers replaced the original units.

In June 1935, the aircraft was sent to Martlesham Heath, Suffolk, for evaluation by the Air Ministry. It confirmed a maximum speed of 280mph (451km/h) at 16,500ft (5,029m), faster than the prototype Gloster Gladiator prototype. The Air Ministry asked the viscount if it could retain the Type 142, who consented by presenting the aircraft to the nation, and in July it became K7557. Unfortunately, on July 17, it was extensively damaged when the landing gear failed to lock down, going back to Filton for repair. It returned to Martlesham with a new spat over the tailwheel.

Viscount Rothermere still wanted his own aircraft, so tried to order a second improved version of the Type 142 in February 1936. By then, Bristol was busy with orders for the 142M and could not accommodate his request.

The Bristol 142 was transferred to the Royal Aircraft Establishment at Farnborough, Hampshire, in April 1936, and before the end of the year had been flown by 24 and 101 Squadrons for trials by service pilots. It returned to Farnborough in April 1937 and continued to be flown there, primarily testing radio and radar, into 1942, when it was damaged during a Luftwaffe air raid. Withdrawn from flying, it was allocated the 'maintenance' number 2211M and went to 10 School of Technical Training at Kirkham, Lancashire, as a ground instructional airframe. It was scrapped at Cowley, Oxford, in 1944.

Viscount Rothermere presented Britain First *to the nation in July 1935, the aircraft becoming K7557.*

The clean lines of the Bristol 142 gave the aircraft a sparkling performance at the time it first flew. The aircraft is seen wearing the 'B-class' markings R-12 that it wore between April and July 1935.

Bristol 142M Blenheim I
Prototype

I n July 1935, Specification 28/35 was raised by the Air Ministry to satisfy Operational Requirement OR.26 and Bristol was presented with a contract for 150 Type 142Ms as K7033 to K7182. The Type 142M was a medium bomber development of the Type 142.

Power would be provided by a pair of Mercury VIIIs rated at 700hp (522kW), later increased to 840hp (626kW), mounted on a wing raised about 16in (406mm) in comparison to the Type 142, to a mid-body position, allowing bombs to be carried in a bay below the wing spars. A bomb aimer's position and Browning gun would be housed in the nose, and a semi-retractable gun turret on the rear upper fuselage. The horizontal tailplanes were increased in span and raised about 8in (203mm). All passenger fittings, along with the fuselage windows, were removed and structural strength increased. In March 1936, the name Blenheim was adopted for the Type 142M.

Test pilot Cyril Uwins completed the maiden flight of K7033 at Filton on June 25, 1936. The aircraft was unarmed and lacked all the operational equipment specified. It was nearly lost during its second flight, when a faulty flap actuator left the starboard unit up while the port extended. Uwins skilfully landed the aircraft, but it required a new starboard outer wing and propeller, ending plans to display it in the New Types Park at Hendon, north London, that month, although the number '5' had already been painted on the side in anticipation. The aircraft was repaired but the flight test programme was delayed.

Some changes were soon incorporated in the aircraft. Controllable cowl-flaps were added on the engine cowlings, while improved carburettors and air intakes were fitted. The fully retractable tailwheel was locked in the down position. Spinners were tested, but they were rejected as they added to the maintenance burden without any useful gain in speed.

After 22 hours of test flying at Filton, the prototype was sent to Martlesham Heath, Suffolk, for evaluation by the Aeroplane and Armament Experimental Establishment (A&AEE), arriving on October 22, 1936. To compensate for the lack of operational equipment required for a service bomber, representative weights were carried inside the aircraft plus ballast to maintain the centre of gravity. During the evaluation it had a gross weight of 11,776lb (5,342kg). Thus 'equipped', the aircraft was found to have good stability and handling, although it did suffer a vicious wing drop at the stall. The take-off run was 990ft (302m) and a maximum speed of 279mph (449kph) was demonstrated, with a landing speed of 78mph (126kph). The Blenheim could reach 6,500ft (1,981m) in three minutes, 36 seconds, with a rate of climb of 1,890ft (576m) per minute and service ceiling of 31,400ft (9,570m). The A&AEE report on the aircraft was completed in May 1937.

The previous month, the aircraft had been assigned to the Royal Aircraft Establishment at Farnborough, Hampshire, where its landing gear was damaged during a heavy landing on May 28. It spent the rest of its flying career as a testbed, flying from either Farnborough or Filton. In November 1940, K7033 became the ground instructional airframe 2373M.

Spinners were tested on K7033 and also briefly fitted to some of the early aircraft (including K7034), but were found to be an unnecessary complication that was quickly discarded.

Blenheim K7033 served as the prototype for the design, differing from those that followed in subtle ways. The relocation of the wing to the mid-body position made the Type 142M look sleeker than the 142, although the fuselage was the same height.

The Type 142M Blenheim was a militarised version of the Type 142. The most visible difference was the relocation of the wing to run through the middle of the fuselage, rather than the bottom, the deletion of the cabin windows and addition of the turret.

Bristol 142M
Blenheim I

aving missed the opportunity to display the prototype Blenheim K7033 at Hendon in June 1936, the decision was taken to put K7034 on display at that year's Grand Salon Aéronautique in Paris in November. Fitted with spinners, unpainted and devoid of all markings and polished until it gleamed, it caused a stir, mounted on trestles in a flying position, its landing gear (including the tail unit) retracted.

It was one of six pre-production Blenheims, part of the initial contract that would include a batch of 150 Mk Is (K7033 to K7182, c/n 7986 to 8135). Bristol had received additional orders for 434 in July 1936 and then another for 150, to add to the 264 it already held, but the total would continually change, as the Air Ministry refined its plans. Full scale production was authorised in December 1936. Few changes were requested to the airframe of the prototype, although the retractable tail landing gear would quickly be replaced by a fixed unit in production, allowing the retraction mechanism to be deleted.

After making its debut, K7034 was fitted with operational equipment, including a Bristol B.I turret, which was hydraulically-operated by a pump powered by the port engine and armed with a Lewis III gun. It arrived at Martlesham Heath in Suffolk for trials with the Aeroplane and Armament Experimental Establishment there in January 1937.

That April, the unit undertook an operational and armament assessment. Training the Lewis gun on a target was found to be

The second Blenheim I (K7034) was displayed at the Grand Salon Aéronautique in Paris in November 1937. Unmarked and its skin highly polished, it attracted a lot of attention. Bristol took the precaution of sealing its cockpit to keep out unwanted visitors.

Continued on page 24

THE BRISTOL

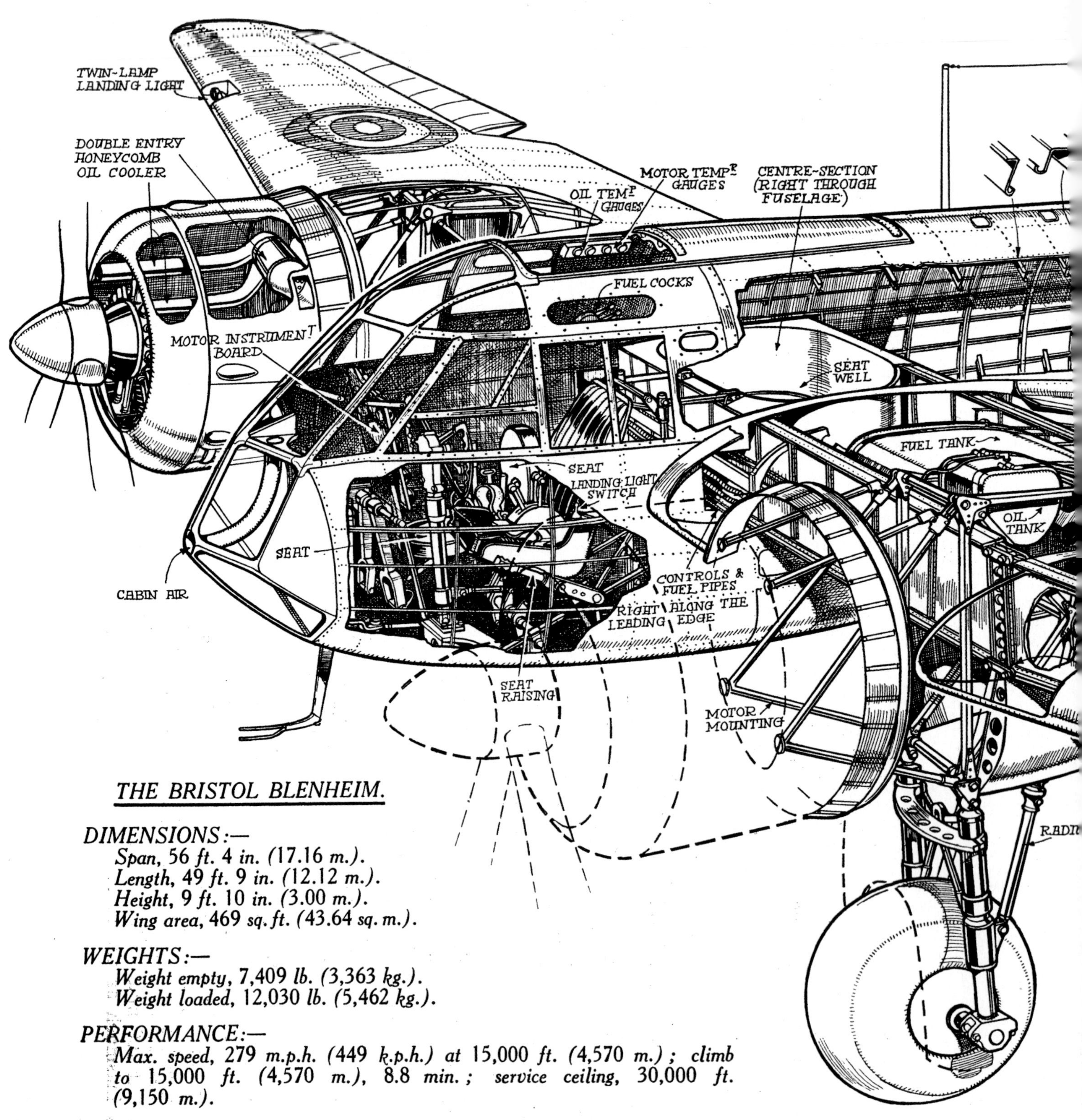

THE BRISTOL BLENHEIM.

DIMENSIONS:—
Span, 56 ft. 4 in. (17.16 m.).
Length, 49 ft. 9 in. (12.12 m.).
Height, 9 ft. 10 in. (3.00 m.).
Wing area, 469 sq. ft. (43.64 sq. m.).

WEIGHTS:—
Weight empty, 7,409 lb. (3,363 kg.).
Weight loaded, 12,030 lb. (5,462 kg.).

PERFORMANCE:—
Max. speed, 279 m.p.h. (449 k.p.h.) at 15,000 ft. (4,570 m.) ; climb to 15,000 ft. (4,570 m.), 8.8 min. ; service ceiling, 30,000 ft. (9,150 m.).

BLENHEIM

HINGED
HATCH COVER
LADDER
RUDDER SERVO LEVER
(ACTUALLY ON
STARBᴰ FACE)
ELEVATOR TRIM
RETRACTING
TAIL-WHEEL
COLLARS
& SLEEVE
UNIV.
JOINT
OPERATING
PLATE & CONNECTION
TO PAIR ON STARBOARD
PORT
WING FLAP
CENTRE-SECTION
PORT FLAP
NG FIXINGS
ROD

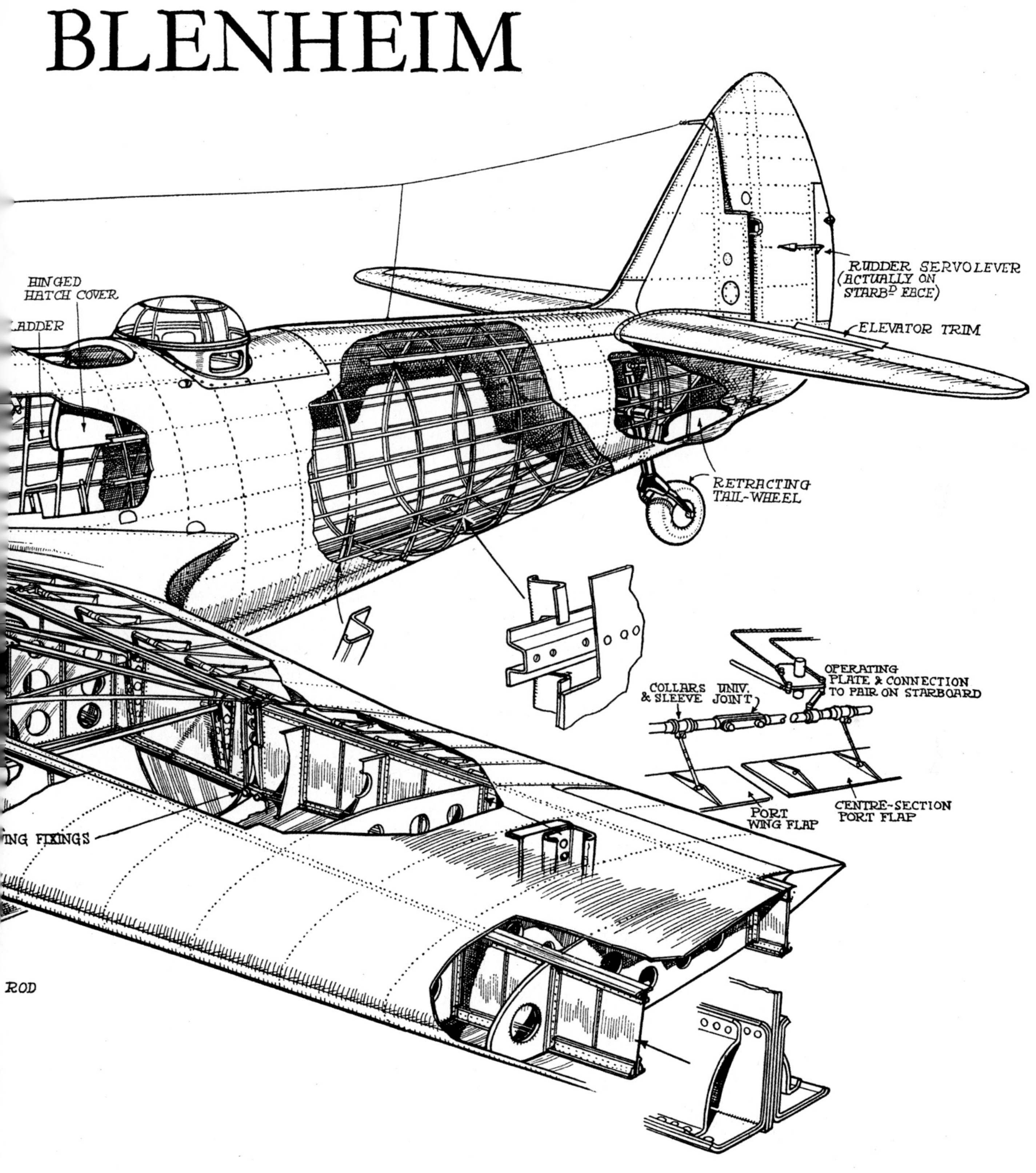

Continued from page 21

Sat outside the factory at Filton in late February/early March 1937, the sixth Blenheim I (K7037) was the first completed to the full production standard. It was delivered to 114 Squadron at Wyton in early March 1937, but was written off there when taking off on May 10, 1938.

difficult, because the movement of the turret was jerky and imprecise. It was replaced in November 1937 by a Bristol B.II, but the gun's trigger mechanism was found to be unacceptable and the turret draughty. A Bristol B.III with a Vickers K gun was fitted in May 1938, but its hydraulic firing mechanism failed during an extended endurance flight. The Vickers K gun in the port wing – where it had been installed rather than in the nose as originally specified – was judged to be difficult to rearm and replaced by a Browning, cutting in half the time taken to reload.

Gross weight of the aircraft was 12,500lb (5,670kg), requiring a take-off run of 1,080ft (329m), while a maximum speed of 253mph (407kph) at 15,000ft (4,572m) was recorded. Climbing to 6,500ft (1,981m) took five minutes, 18 seconds, a full one minute 42 seconds more than the unarmed K7033.

Production aircraft were rolling out of the factory at Filton while the evaluation was under way, beginning at a rate of four a month in January 1937. The early aircraft sat there, waiting for their Bristol B.I turrets to be delivered and installed, but deliveries began without some of the equipment they would need in service installed. Clearance for delivery to the squadrons was received in late February 1937, with dual control-equipped K7035 handed over to 114 Squadron at Wyton, Huntingdonshire, on March 1. The squadron received three more three days later, including K7037, the first completed to the full production standard and fitted with the specified equipment. A further eight had arrived at Wyton by May 7. Compared with the Hawker Audaxes the unit's pilots had previously flown, the monoplane bomber took some getting used to. On March 10,

K7036 was destroyed after landing, the pilot applying the brakes too harshly, tipping the Blenheim over and breaking its back. It was struck-off charge on June 8, the first Blenheim lost.

As production increased, more Bomber Command squadrons converted to the type in 1937, with 90 Squadron following 114 Sqn, then 144 at Hemswell, Lincolnshire; 44 at Waddington, Lincolnshire; and 30 Squadron at Dhibban, Iraq, the first overseas operator. Dhibban was renamed Habbaniyah on May 1, 1938. The production rate had increased to 16 a month by the start of 1938, after 'just' 117 had been delivered in the previous year, down on the Air Ministry's expectation of 300-plus. During 1938, another ten squadrons in Bomber Command converted to the Blenheim I (while four in Fighter Command received Mk IFs), followed by another ten in 1939 (not including three Auxiliary units with Fighter Command), of which six were based overseas in Egypt, Iraq and India. Within Bomber Command, the Blenheim I replaced the Avro Anson, Boulton Paul Overstrand, Hawker Audax, Hind and Hector – all but the first mentioned biplanes – while overseas the Hawker Hardy, Hart and Hind, Vickers Vincent and Wellesley, and Westland Wapiti were supplanted when the squadrons upgraded.

The Blenheim introduced many pilots to an enclosed (if draughty) cockpit, multi-engine handling, a retractable landing gear, radio and adjustable, variable-pitch propellers. Pilots found the aircraft light to control and fully aerobatic, but for many the cost was high, as the Blenheim suffered a high accident rate in its early years. With one engine inoperative it was difficult to handle and, if it occurred at low level, the situation was often fatal. Landing accidents were common, as a generation of pilots taught on a rotary-engine biplane were used to dead-stick landings; the Blenheim needed to be powered on to the ground. As recorded above, slamming on the brakes could overturn the aircraft.

Many Bomber Command squadrons soon re-equipped with the Blenheim IV as soon as it became available, with only four retaining the Mk I by the start of war. At that point the RAF

Blenheim I K7036 of 114 Squadron after its accident on March 10, 1937. It had the distinction of becoming the first Blenheim to be written off.

The first overseas unit to receive Blenheim Is was 30 Squadron at Dhibban in Iraq, which was renamed Habbaniyah on May 1, 1938. With others, K7096 was shipped to Aboukir in Egypt in January 1937, assembled and flown to Iraq to replace the unit's Hawker Hardys.

had 301 Mk Is on strength, including 190 in the Near and Middle East, plus 53 in India. In the next couple of years, several additional squadrons would receive Mk Is, sometimes only briefly, while many second line flying units of various kinds were equipped with the aircraft. Most had been lost or withdrawn by the middle of the war years, but others survived in service into 1945 with some training schools

The original order of 150 Blenheim Is for the RAF were delivered between January 1937 and February 1938. They were followed by 18 aircraft for Finland (c/n 8137 to 8154) as BL-104 to BL-121 and ten for Turkey (c/n 8157 to 8166), which were delivered as G-AFFP to G-AFFZ. The Finnish aircraft were modified in-country to use Swedish-built bombs, while they could also operate on skis.

The second order for the RAF given to Bristol was for 450 aircraft (L1097 to L1546), accepted between February 1938 and March 1939. Two aircraft (G-AFCE and -AFCF, c/n 8814 and 8815) were built alongside them to act as pattern aircraft for the production line in Yugoslavia by Ikarus AD at Zemun. Another order for 118 Blenheim Is was awarded by the Air Ministry as L4817 to L4934, but only 34 (L4817 to L4822 and L4907 to L4934) were completed as the variant, as the order was altered to include 84 Mk IVs instead. Deliveries started in March 1939 and continued into that July. The last Mk Is produced by Bristol were for the second batch for Turkey, comprising 18 aircraft (c/n 9222 to 9239) ferried to the customer as G-AFLA to -AFLS. In total, Bristol produced 684 Blenheim Is.

A total of 250 Blenheim Is were assembled by Rootes Securities at Speke outside Liverpool, Merseyside, under the 'shadow scheme'. The order was placed in October 1936 under Specification 33/36P.

They were allocated the military markings L8362 to L8407, L8433 to L8482, L8500 to L8549, L8597 to L8632, L8652 to L8701 and L8714 to L8731, with most delivered to the RAF between November 1938 and August 1939. The exceptions were L8603 to L8608, L8619, L8620, L8622, L8624 to L8630, L8632, L8652 to L8654, which went to Romania in June 1939.

A V Roe produced a batch of 250 Blenheim Mk Is at its factory at Chadderton, outside Manchester, to Specification 2/37. The aircraft (L6594 to L6843) were delivered from August 1938, with the first aircraft later modified as the sole Blenheim GR.I, while the last was handed over in March 1940. Included among them were examples for Romania (L6696 to L6708 and L6713 to L6718) handed over in June 1939 as well as others for Yugoslavia (L6813, L6814, L6817 to L6834), delivered with the civil registrations YU-BAA to -BAT in February 1940.

Together, the three British producers turned out 1,164 Blenheim I airframes for four customers. Yugoslavia acquired a licence for Ikarus to produce 50 aircraft at Zemun, but establishing the assembly line was delayed, not least because Bristol was occupied delivering as many Blenheims to the RAF as possible as the threat of war increased, and also by a shortage of Mercury engines. The number built by Ikarus is generally accepted as being 18 aircraft, which were delivered, while a further 24 were either ready but lacking engines or in an advanced stage of manufacture before Yugoslavia was overrun by the Axis powers in the spring of 1941. The uncompleted aircraft are understood to have been sabotaged prior to the capture of the factory.

Pre-war Bristol had the opportunity of selling Blenheims to several other countries, had not production been reserved for the RAF. They included South Africa, which received a single Filton-built example (L1431) in early 1939 and wanted at least a squadron's worth. Along with Finland, Lithuania also had an early interest in the aircraft; in 1935 it wanted eight and a licence to build them, but neither a sale nor authority to produce the aircraft was secured.

Blenheim K7147 of 110 Squadron, based at Waddington, Lincolnshire, which became the seventh unit to re-equip with the aircraft, in January 1938. The aircraft was part of the original batch for 150 aircraft built at Filton.

Bristol 142M
Blenheim IF

The Blenheim I had a relatively short career as first line equipment with RAF Bomber Command. Development of the Mk IV saw the Command rush to upgrade to the new variant, making many Mk Is surplus to its requirements. Plenty of uses could be found for the aircraft, including issue to overseas units and re-equipping second-line or training units.

RAF Fighter Command had a desperate need to upgrade its two-seat fighter squadrons, which were flying Hawker Demons, similar to the Harts and Hinds that the Blenheim had supplanted with Bomber Command. The idea of a two-seat, monoplane heavy fighter was appealing, the concept of such an aircraft having reached its zenith in the mid to late-1930s,

notably with the Zerstörer ('destroyer') specification in Germany that spawned the Messerschmitt Bf 110.

Exactly what form a fighter Blenheim should take was the subject of some debate within the RAF. The Air Officer Commanding RAF Fighter Command, Hugh Caswall Tremenheere Dowding, wanted the aircraft to operate as a single-seater, with as much equipment removed as possible to reduce weight and increase performance. If a second crew member had to be carried, Dowding believed he should have a station in the rear of the aircraft, much as was later adopted for the Bristol Beaufighter. No gun would be provided for him, as the main armament would all be concentrated in the nose.

The solution that was eventually adopted was more modest. The power-operated turret and its single Lewis or Vickers K gun

was retained, along with the Browning in the wing. To increase firepower a ventral pack, containing four additional 0.303in (7.7mm) Browning guns, was mounted under the bomb bay. It was designed by the Southern Railway Company at Ashford, Kent, which eventually built 1,375 in their workshops for both Blenheim Is and IVs. A total of 2,000 rounds of ammunition for the guns – 500 each – were contained within the bomb bay, while the pilot was provided with ring-and-bead and GM2 gunsights.

A prototype makeshift pack was mounted on Blenheim LL 1424 in 1938 and tested by the Royal Aircraft Establishment at Farnborough, Hampshire, and the Aeroplane and Armament Experimental Establishment (A&AEE) at Martlesham Heath, Suffolk, but work on the first trial aircraft (L1512) only began in January 1939. Both Blenheims spent time with 25 Squadron, based at Hawkinge, Kent (although the unit participated in trials with the A&AEE, and it is possible they remained at Martlesham and were flown by the squadron's crews).

Around 200 Blenheims were fitted with the gun packs as Mk IFs from early 1939. Unmodified Mk Is had begun reaching Fighter Command squadrons before the Mk IFs became available, from December 1938, re-equipping 23, 29, 64 and 25 Squadrons in that order, followed by 219 Squadron in October 1939. In addition, 600, 601 and 604 Squadrons of the Auxiliary Air Force transitioned to the type, plus squadrons within Coastal Command much later.

Compared with the eight-gun monoplane fighters, the Blenheim IF was lightly armed, while the rifle-calibre of the weapons was not all that effective against all-metal aircraft, especially those with armour in vulnerable places. The gun pack also reduced the speed

Blenheim IF K7159 of 54 Operational Training Unit equipped with AI radar around 1942. The antennas on the wing and nose indicate the aircraft was equipped with AI.Mk III.

of the Blenheim from 280mph (450kph) to 255mph (410kph).

From October 1939, Fighter Command began to re-role all its Blenheim IF squadrons for night-fighting. The aircraft was not ideal for the role, as the extensive cockpit glazing was prone to creating multiple reflections. The development of Airborne Interception (AI) radar offered a way of improving the difficult task of finding enemy aircraft at night, and Blenheims were heavily involved in its development. Blenheims K7033, K7034 and K7044 of the A&AEE's D Flight, formed in August 1938, were among the first aircraft equipped with prototype sets, while at least six others were involved in radar development, calibration and AI trials. Blenheims thus became the world's first radar-equipped night fighters, as the bulk and weight of the original equipment (around 600lb; 272kg), plus the need to accommodate a dedicated operator, precluded using single-seat fighters.

An order was issued to fit AI Mk I sets into Blenheim IFs in July 1939, with most of the installations undertaken at St Athan in Wales. Such aircraft could be distinguished by the single antenna protruding from the nose, while Yagi antennas were mounted under the outer wings, although the antenna configuration changed with the equipment. Six AI-equipped aircraft were assigned to 25 Squadron from the end of August into September 1939 (some of which remained with the Special Duty Flight of the A&AEE, as D Flight had become), followed by three with a flight of 600 Squadron in November 1939 that would go on in early 1940 to become the nucleus of the Fighter Interception Unit (FIU). Others were delivered to 604 Squadron.

The Blenheim IF was equipped with a ventral gun pack under the bomb bay. The inscription on the ladder tends to indicate this example was operated by 600 'City of London' Squadron, which flew the aircraft when war was declared and adopted the night fighting role in May 1940.

Early experience with the sets was poor. They were difficult to use and interpreting the blips on the screen more an art than science. From February 1940 small quantities of AI Mk II were provided to the Blenheim IF squadrons, but the Mk III became standard in the summer of 1940; 140 aircraft had had the equipment installed by that October. Development of tactics and training on the new equipment was organised by the FIU before 54 Operational Training Unit (OTU) formed at Church Fenton, Yorkshire, in November 1940.

The Blenheim IF remained the RAF's principal night fighter until late in 1940, when Bristol Beaufighters began to be delivered to the squadrons in quantity. Towards the end of their use as night fighters in October 1940, many Blenheims had their turrets replaced by a wooden fairing with retractable twin Browning machine guns, while squadrons undertaking intruder missions usually removed the radar to stop it falling into enemy hands should the aircraft be shot down. The Blenheim IF disappeared from frontline squadrons in 1941, but they continued to be flown by OTUs until 1943.

Bristol 142M Blenheim GR.I

Blenheim L6594 was the first of a batch of 250 Mk Is built by A V Roe from August 1938. It was modified to carry a 37mm Coventry Ordnance Works (COW) cannon, a weapon created late in World War One, which was installed between the spars so that it could fire vertically down. The cannon could fire a 1½lb (0.7kg) shell and, in the Blenheim, was intended to be used against surfaced U-boats.

From October 1939, the Blenheim was at Boscombe Down, Wiltshire, where trials of the installation were undertaken by the Aeroplane and Armament Experimental Establishment. The aircraft came to grief in a forced landing in December 1939, curtailing tests of the COW gun. In February 1940, the airframe was allocated the 'maintenance' serial 1805M for use as a ground instructional airframe. The COW cannon was later developed into the 40mm Vickers S gun, which was used by Hawker Hurricanes in the anti-tank role.

Looking for a way of crippling U-boats on the surface, Blenheim L6594 was fitted with a 37mm COW cannon, a weapon envisaged as an anti-aircraft weapon during the inter-war years.

Bristol 142M Blenheim PR.I

The sole Blenheim PR.I became the fastest of all Blenheims, but was considered still not to be quick enough for unescorted reconnaissance missions. The modified nose, reshaped wingtips and Rotol propellers, plus the smooth finish, contributed to its performance.

Frederick Sidney Cotton was a pioneer of aerial reconnaissance. He is best remembered for flying clandestine reconnaissance sorties over Germany prior to the outbreak of war in the suitably modified Lockheed 12A G-AFTL. At the start of the conflict, Cotton was commissioned into the RAF as a squadron leader to develop the service's photo-reconnaissance capabilities.

No.2 Camouflage Flight formed at Heston to the west of London, on November 3, 1939. Its role was photographic reconnaissance – the unit's title was 'camouflage' for its real task; it became the Photographic Development Unit on January 19, 1940. Two Blenheims were assigned to the unit, including Mk I L1348 loaned from 139 Squadron.

Some 250 hours were spent 'cleaning up' the aircraft at Heston and Farnborough in Hampshire, smoothing the airframe and sealing all joints and gaps with tape. It was repainted with Titanine dope and had its undersides painted 'duck-egg blue', the first aircraft to be so. More radically, the lower nose glazing was faired over with metal alloy, all armament and the turret were removed, while the wingtips were reprofiled from the standard rounded planform to shorter, squarer units.

Cotton called the modified aircraft the Blenheim PR.I, although this probably remained an unofficial designation. The aim of all the work was to increase the speed of the aircraft, to make it a more difficult target to intercept, but it only increased maximum speed by around 15mph (24kph), to 278mph (447kph).

The view down and to the rear was improved by replacing the main side windows with Perspex blisters, an innovation later fitted to squadron aircraft. Rotol constant-speed propellers were installed at Staverton, Gloucestershire, and further modifications were undertaken by the Aeroplane and Armament Aircraft Establishment at Boscombe Down in Wiltshire.

These alterations did significantly improve the aircraft's speed; it could now reach 294mph (473kph) at 13,000ft (3,962m). While it made L1348 the fastest Blenheim, it was still not considered to be fast enough to evade Luftwaffe fighters during unescorted reconnaissance missions. At the time, Cotton was pressing hard for Supermarine Spitfires modified for reconnaissance, and as they were handed over interest in the Blenheim PR.I diminished. Nevertheless, Air Chief Marshal Hugh Caswall Tremenheere Dowding, Air Officer Commanding RAF Fighter Command went to Heston to inspect the Blenheim PR.I, keen to see if some of the modifications could be applied to the Mk IF night fighters to improve their performance. Reportedly, he ordered eight further conversions to be completed, but no further information on subsequent work has come to light.

The PR.I later passed to 88 Squadron, which flew Douglas Bostons, along with some Fairey Battles and Blenheim IVs from Sydenham, Northern Ireland. It was struck off charge on June 12, 1941.

The 'solid nose' drastically altered the appearance of the Blenheim PR.I. Cameras would have been installed in the bomb bay, lined up using the transparency under the nose on the starboard.

Bristol 142M Blenheim II

Blenheim II BL-173 was one of five Blenheims that re-entered Finnish Air Force service in the 1950s, although it was the only Mk II and thus the last of its mark operational.

Blenheim L1222 was one of 450 Mk Is delivered between February 1938 and March 1939. It had additional fuel tanks installed in the outer wings, while the landing gear was strengthened to cope with the increased weights of up to 14,000lb (6,350kg) on take-off. Landing at such weights would need a long run, so fuel jettison valves with pipes were installed under the wing to dump fuel. As modified, the Blenheim became the Mk II and first flew in September 1938. The tanks and fuel jettison system were later adopted for the Type 149 Bolingbroke, and would later become standard on the Blenheim IV.

One year later, the aircraft was at the Aeroplane and Armament Experimental Establishment at Boscombe Down, Wiltshire, where it was involved in trials aimed at improving the comfort of Blenheim crews. It was fitted with draught excluders and lagging, and later had four 120-watt electric heaters installed, resulting in the temperature in the cabin increasing by 5°C. The Blenheim later went to the Photographic Development Unit (see under *Bristol 142M Blenheim PR.I*), which formed in January 1940 and lasted until that spring. It was last flown by 604 Squadron at Northolt, northwest London, but was struck off charge on August 31, 1940.

Blenheim II was also allocated by Bristol to the Mk I equivalent aircraft built by Valtion Lentokonetehdas (State Aircraft Factory) at Tampere in Finland. Finnish interest in the Blenheim began around 1935 with military adaptions of the Type 143 (*see next page*), but when the Air Ministry opted for the Type 142M it also altered its preference. A licence to build Blenheims was granted to Finland in April 1938.

Finnish Blenheim Mk IIs differed subtly from British Mk Is. They had revised outer wings, a strengthened landing gear and an enlarged, deeper bomb bay, while a 0.303in (7.7mm) Browning machine gun was fitted into each wing. They could carry 1,764lb (800kg) of munitions in the bomb bay and 379lb (172kg) on racks under the fuselage and on the wings.

Manufacture did not start until after the Moscow Peace Treaty had been signed on March 13, 1940, with the Soviet Union at the end of the Winter War. An initial 15 aircraft were assembled (BL-146 to BL-160) as Sarja II ('series II') – the original batch of 18 Mk Is delivered from England becoming Sarja I – the first flying on June 14, 1941. All were in service by the end of the year. Sarja III and IV were additional Mk IVs and Is, respectively, delivered from RAF stocks, while Sarja V comprised another batch of 30 Finnish-built Mk IIs (BL-161 to BL-190), which were delivered between April and December 1943. A final five Mk IIs (BL-191 to BL-195) were laid down as Sarja VII, but assembly was abandoned following the peace treaty with the Allies on September 19, 1944. Blenheim II BL-173 was revived for further service in the early 1950s and continued to fly until April 1958; it was the penultimate operational Blenheim.

The Blenheim II L1222 carrying an asymmetric bomb load under the wings. Several of the features introduced on the Mk II were incorporated in the Mk IV.

Bristol 143

The success of the original Type 142 reinforced Bristol's desire to build another for its own corporate transport. Rather than building a second example of the aircraft delivered to Viscount Rothermere, some changes were made to the basic configuration, starting with a change of powerplant.

Work on the nine-cylinder, sleeve-valve radial Bristol Aquila, based on the company's Perseus but smaller, began in 1934. It originally developed a modest 365hp (272kW), but this had been raised to 493hp (368kW) for take-off by 1936. Flight testing of the engine was undertaken using the Bristol Bullpup and a Bulldog testbeds.

The airframe itself differed from the Type 142, although around 70% of the components were common to both aircraft. The fuselage was stretched to 43ft 2in (13.16m) to accommodate eight passengers and a crew of two, with a longer, pointed nose tipped by a navigation light. The airframe was constructed before the Type 142 flew and was allocated the civil registration G-ADEK (c/n 7839) on March 22, 1935, although it was never carried on the aircraft, which had the manufacturer's identity R-14 painted on its sides when it was completed at Filton outside Bristol that November. However, it remained on the ground, waiting for its Aquila engines to be granted type approval. These were installed in late 1935 and the maiden flight occurred on January 20, 1936. Bristol used the Type 143 from Filton primarily to support development of the Aquila.

Several other organisations were interested in the Type 143 for their own use. The Ethyl Export Corporation wanted to buy the prototype, after it had been tested by Bristol, as a corporate transport. Interest was also expressed by Imperial Airways. Finland became interested in the Type 143F, which would have had interchangeable nose and rear fuselage sections for different roles, including transport of freight or passengers, or for use as a bomber. Bristol also proposed some versions armed with fixed or dorsally mounted guns.

Investigation of a bomber variant, the Type 143M, highlighted that it would be capable of flying at 262mph (422km/h) at 15,000ft (4,572m). As this was slower than the Type 142M powered by the Bristol Mercury, the Air Ministry proceeded with that aircraft rather than the Type 143M. This data was shared with the Finns, who also elected to abandon the Type 143 for what would become the Blenheim.

Bristol continued to operate the Type 143 prototype until 1938, when interest in the Aquila faded as more powerful alternatives were expected to become available. The aircraft was placed into storage and was eventually scrapped at some point during World War Two.

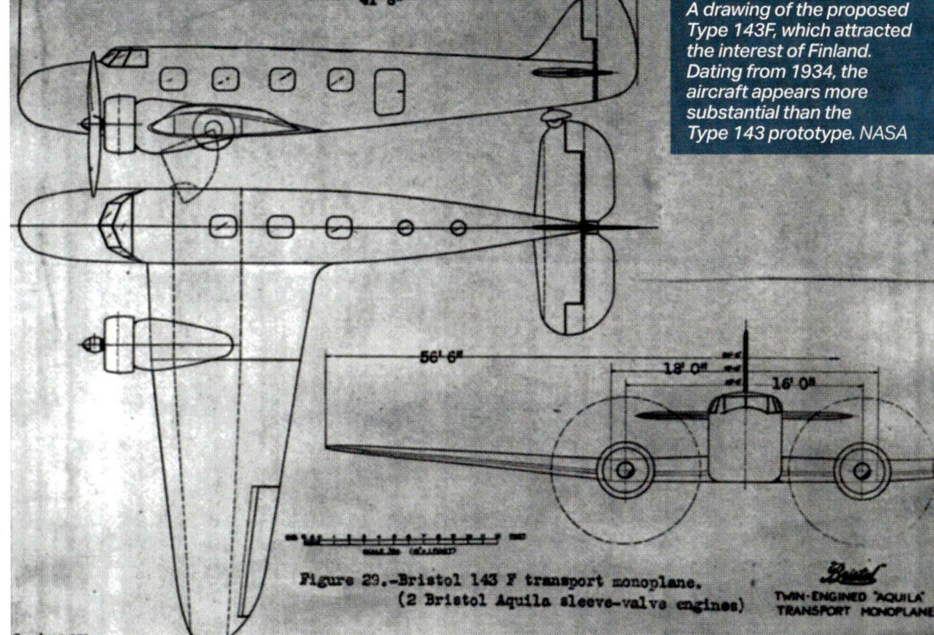

A drawing of the proposed Type 143F, which attracted the interest of Finland. Dating from 1934, the aircraft appears more substantial than the Type 143 prototype. NASA

The Bristol 143 was based on the Type 142, although it was slightly larger and the Mercury engines of the original were replaced by Aquilas. The sole example, which wore R-14 throughout its existence, primarily served as a testbed for the Aquila.

Bristol 149 Bolingbroke I

Bristol investigated adopting the basic Blenheim design to meet two specifications for the RAF released in 1935 and 1936. Operational Requirement OR.25 called for a General-Purpose Reconnaissance Land Plane, which was outlined under Specification G.24/35, as a replacement for the Avro Anson for Coastal Command.

The company's response was the Type 149, which would have a wider fuselage, a new navigator's position, a separate radio operator's station, and a more comfortable and larger turret. Power would be provided by a pair of Bristol Aquila engines, which had the advantage of increasing range over the baseline Blenheim with the same fuel load, although maximum speed would decline to 254mph (409kph). Bristol was not the only manufacturer looking at G.24/35, as Avro, Fairey and Westland also began work on designs to meet the requirement. None progressed to actual hardware, as the requirement was revised and merged with Specification M.15/36, which called for a Shore Based Torpedo Bomber sought under Operational Requirement OR.22. The new combined requirement became Specification 10/36, for which Bristol offered its Type 152 and Blackburn the B-26 that became the Beaufort and Botha, respectively.

The sole Type 149 Bolingbroke had a standard Blenheim airframe from the cockpit aft. When the longer nose was redesigned, it effectively became the prototype of the Blenheim IV.

Bristol retained the Type 149 designation for an Interim General Reconnaissance Aeroplane for Specification 11/36. It was a more conservative alteration of the Blenheim, with the nose extended 3ft (0.9m) to accommodate a navigator/radio operator's position and additional fuel capacity, but it still used the Bristol Mercury VIIIs and was 'all Blenheim' aft of the fuselage. Bomb racks could be fitted under the wings. It was named the Bolingbroke.

Blenheim I K7072 was modified and Cyril Uwins completed its first flight on September 24, 1937. That November, a three-and-a-half-hour assessment of the aircraft was undertaken at Martlesham Heath, Suffolk. It was noted that the pilot's view through the extended nose was not ideal, with unacceptable distortions and reflections, so the decision was taken to redesign it. This involved lowering the level of the nose to create a sloped windscreen for the pilot, while the front upper glazing on the port side was scalloped away to improve his forward view. The modified aircraft flew in December 1937 and returned to Martlesham Heath in July 1938, where the alterations were found to be acceptable. Bolingbroke K7072 was later assessed by 48 Squadron and the Royal Aircraft Establishment.

An initial contract for production Bolingbroke Is had been placed but was later cancelled, as the changes could be introduced on Blenheims already on order. The alteration to the nose contours also saw the end of the Bolingbroke name, at least for British production aircraft, although it would be adopted for those built in Canada. Instead, the aircraft became the Blenheim IV. The sole British Bolingbroke went to Canada in October 1940.

The most obvious change to the Bolingbroke was the longer nose, designed to accommodate the navigator/radio operator and improve the view for the general reconnaissance role. Unfortunately, it did nothing for the pilot's forward view.

Bristol 149 Blenheim III

The Blenheim III was an interim version of the Mk IV without the additional fuel tanks in the wings. It featured the re-profiled, long nose developed for the Bolingbroke. A shortage of the new tanks meant that 68 Blenheims were built with the increased fuel capacity as Mk IIIs, but as the units became available and were installed in them, they became Mk IVs. The unofficial designation Mk IVL was used for such aircraft, but they were no different from production Mk IVs.

Bristol 149 Blenheim IV

The Blenheim IV would become the major production variant of the aircraft. Its main distinguishing feature was the extended redesigned nose first flight tested on the Bolingbroke K7072. It provided the navigator with more space and a dedicated chart table, rather than having to occupy the jump seat besides the pilot with a map on his knees. The Mk IV also introduced the Bristol Mercury XV, which featured an emergency boost capability, adding 30mph (48km/h) at crucial moments.

Like the Bolingbroke, the Mk IV was intended as a long range type for Coastal Command, with additional fuel tanks in the wings to increase range. It was planned that aircraft without the tanks would be known as Blenheim IIIs, but all were delivered as Mk IVs, the little-used suffix L being added to those started as Mk IIIs but upgraded to the full Mk IV standard. However, most Blenheim IVs were delivered to Bomber Command, allowing it to replace its original Mk Is, which found use with Fighter Command and overseas.

The first was delivered in March 1939 and the third (L4845) arrived at Martlesham Heath in Suffolk for the Aeroplane and Armament Experimental Establishment that July. The aircraft had originally been delivered to the army co-operation roled 53 Squadron, the first to receive the Mk IVs. A total of 168 Mk IVs had been taken on charge by the RAF by September 1939 and they were in service with seven Bomber Command squadrons (with another in the process of upgrading from Mk Is) and a pair of units tasked with army co-operation.

The third production batch of Blenheims to be built at Filton were all originally intended to be Mk Is, but emerged as 34 Mk Is and 84 Mk IVs (L4823 to L4906), delivered by July 1939. A further 232 followed in three more batches, comprising 100 (N6140 to N6220 and N6223 to N6242) handed over between April and August 1939; and 70 (P4825 to P4864 and P4898 to P4927) delivered August to October 1939. Nine were earmarked for the Royal Canadian Air Force, equipped with D/F radio, although only four (P4856 to P4859) were completed with it, the other five having the standard RAF fit. All nine were delivered to the RAF. Another batch of 62 (P6885 to P6934 and P9950 to P6961) was built between September 1939 to January 1940. A further 12 were reportedly produced (c/n 9862 to 9873) as replacements for 12 delivered to Greece as G-AFXD to -AFXO.

Rootes Securities built Blenheim IVs at both the Blythe Bridge factory in Staffordshire and at Speke, Merseyside. It would produce nearly two-thirds of the variant. The second batch of Blenheims ordered to be assembled by Rootes Securities included 250 Mk Is and 130 Mk IVs (L8732 to L8761, L8776 to L8800, L8827 to L8876 and L9020 to L9044), built between September and November 1939. The first 80 (L9170 to L9218 and L9237

A late-production Blenheim IV with a Frazer Nash FN.54A turret under the nose and the twin-guns of the Bristol B.IIIA or IV turret. By the time the Blenheim IV had entered service it had become extremely vulnerable to Luftwaffe fighters and the addition of extra guns and armour decreased its performance.

The Bolingbroke prototype after modification, with the redesigned nose, effectively became the prototype of the Blenheim IV.

to L9273) from the third contract were completed as Mk Is and had to be modified before delivery. The batch comprised a total of 220 aircraft (the others being L9294 to L9342, L9375 to L9422 and L9446 to L9482) delivered from November 1939 into March 1940. They were followed by another 250 (R3590 to R3639, R3660 to R3709, R3730 to R3779, R3800 to R3849 and R3870 to R3919), which took deliveries to June 1940.

The complex nose contours of the Blenheim IV were arrived at to give the pilot a good forward view while providing space for the navigator.

Continued on page 36

Bristol 149 Blenheim IV

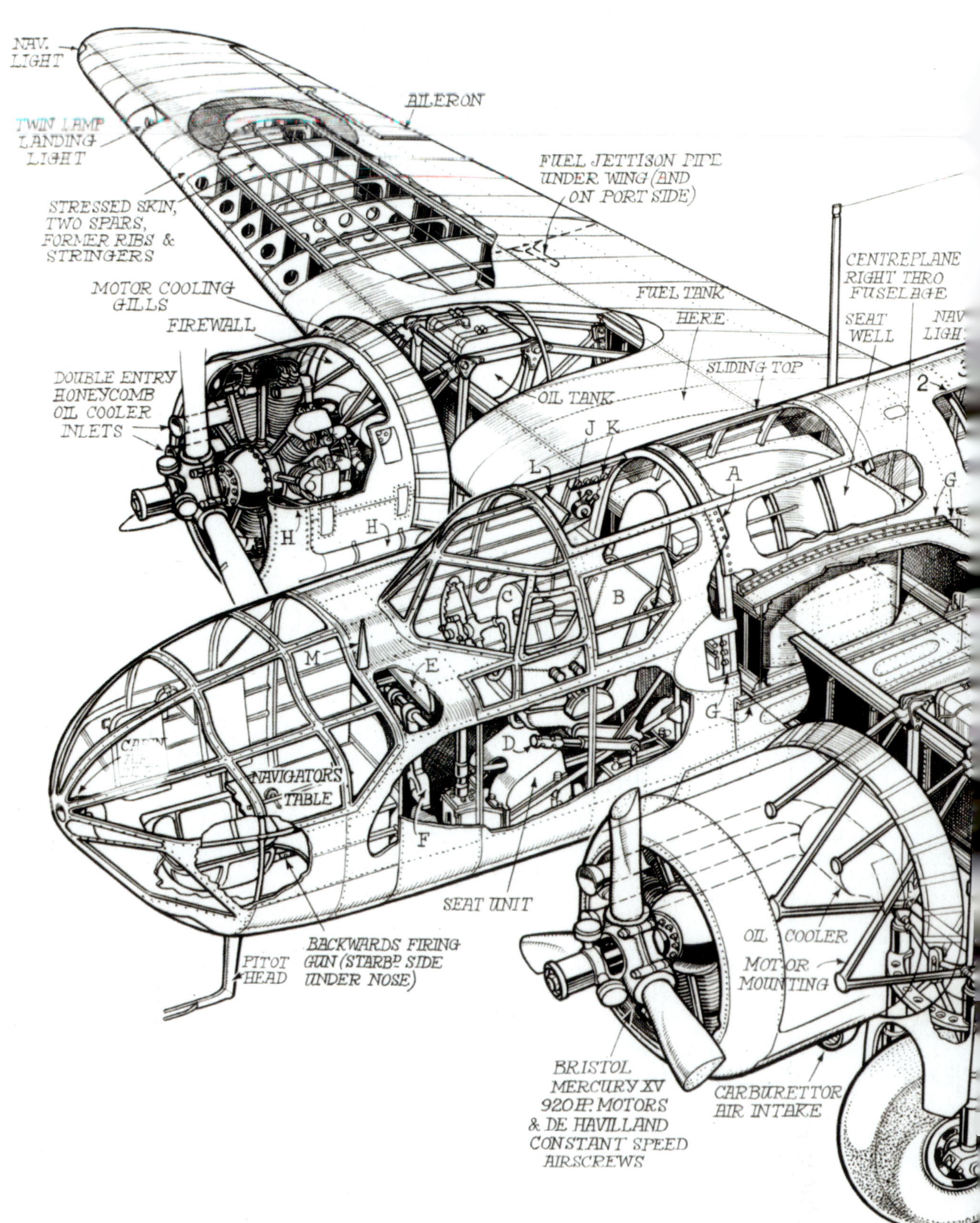

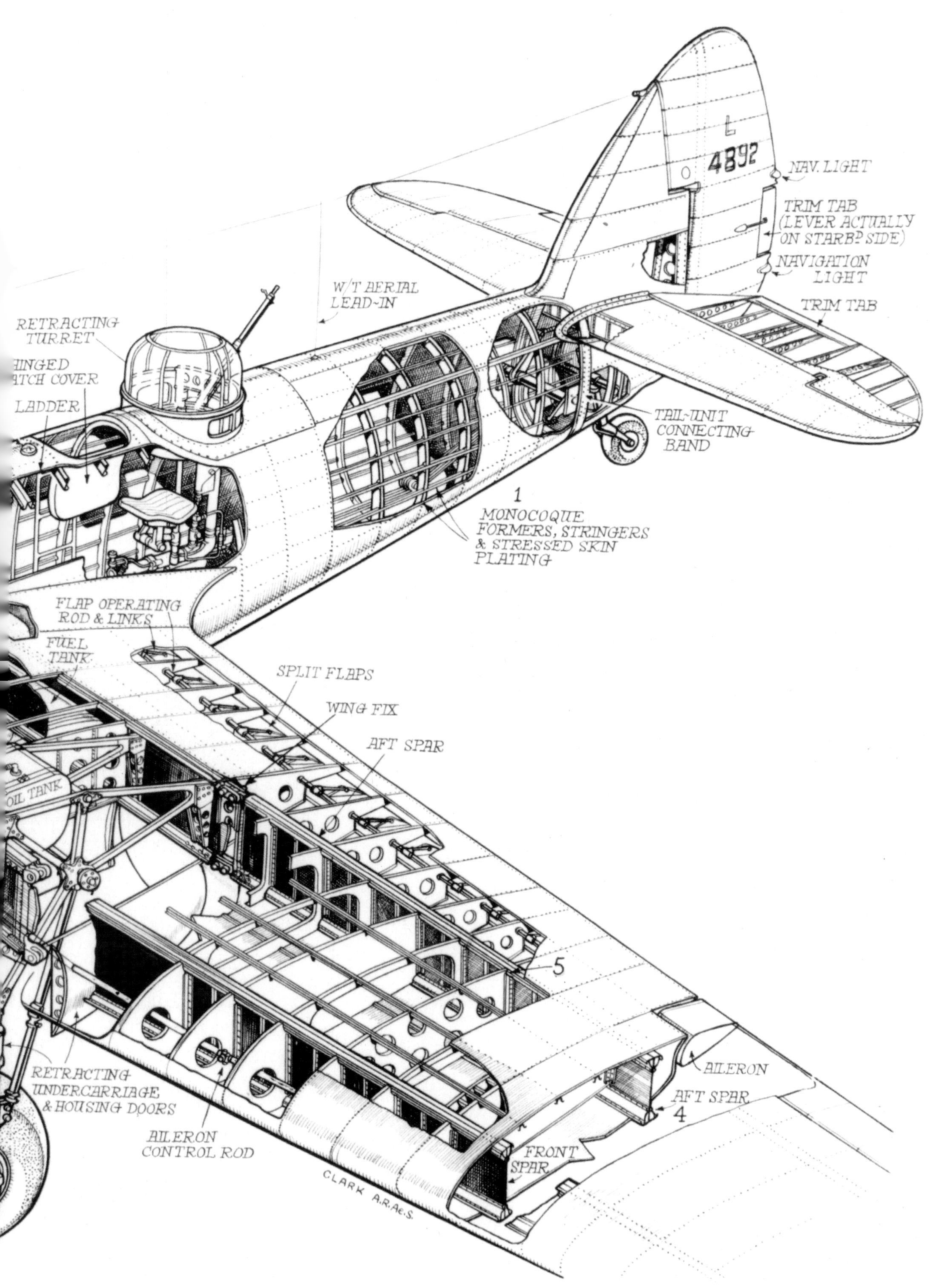
NAV. LIGHT
TRIM TAB
(LEVER ACTUALLY
ON STARBD SIDE)
NAVIGATION
LIGHT
TRIM TAB
4B92
W/T AERIAL
LEAD~IN
RETRACTING
TURRET
HINGED
HATCH COVER
LADDER
TAIL~UNIT
CONNECTING
BAND
1
MONOCOQUE
FORMERS, STRINGERS
& STRESSED SKIN
PLATING
FLAP OPERATING
ROD & LINKS
FUEL
TANK
SPLIT FLAPS
WING FIX
AFT SPAR
OIL TANK
5
AILERON
AFT SPAR
4
RETRACTING
UNDERCARRIAGE
& HOUSING DOORS
AILERON
CONTROL ROD
FRONT
SPAR
CLARK A.R.Ae.S.

Continued from page 33

An early production Filton-built Blenheim IV, without the armament under the nose that later became standard. This aircraft was delivered in mid-1939 to 139 Squadron and was reported missing on May 14, 1940.

Between June and October 1940 another 400 (T1793 to T1832, T1848 to T1897, T1921 to T1960, T1985 to T2004, T2031 to T2080, T2112 to T2141, T2161 to T2190, T2216 to T2255, T2273 to T2292, T2318 to T2357, T2381 to T2400 and T2425 to T2444) were built, followed by a contract for twice that amount (V5370 to V5399, V5420 to V5469, V5490 to V5539, V5560 to V5599, V5620 to V5659, V5680 to V5699, V5720 to V5769, V5790 to V5829, V5850 to V5899, V5920 to V5969, V5990 to V6039, V6060 to V6099, V6120 to V6149, V6170 to V6199, V6220 to V6269, V6290 to V6339, V6360 to V6399, V6420 to V6469 and V6490 to V6529) that was fulfilled by May 1941. The last contract for Rootes Securities covered 600 Mk IVs to be built at Speke, of which 430 (Z7271 to Z7320, Z7340 to Z7374, Z7406 to Z7455, Z7483 to Z7522, Z7577 to Z7596, Z7610 to Z7654, Z7678 to Z7712, Z7754 to Z7803, Z7841 to Z7860, Z7879 to Z7928 and Z7958 to Z7992) were built. They were handed over between May and November 1941. A further 170 (Z7993 to Z8002, Z8050 to Z8099, Z8143 to Z8167, Z8202 to Z8236 and Z8274 to Z8323) were cancelled.

A V Roe at Chadderton, Lancashire, built 750 Blenheim IVs, starting with a batch of 100 (N3522 to N3545, N3551 to N3575, N3578 to N3604 and N3608 to N3631) handed over from March to June 1940. An order for 250 (R2270 to R2805, R2825 to R2864, R2877 to R2926, R2939 to R2963, R2995 to R3040, R3096 to R3123 and R3140 to R3144) was placed, but only 30 (R2270 to R2799) were built with the rest being cancelled, as Rootes Securities would produce them instead. They were delivered in June and July 1941. Avro would go on to build other batches of 420 (Z5721 to Z5770, Z5794 to Z5818, Z5860 to Z5909, Z5947 to Z5991, Z6021 to Z6050, Z6070 to Z6104, Z6144 to Z6193, Z6239 to Z6283, Z6333 to Z6382 and Z6416 to Z6455) and 200 (Z9533 to Z9552, Z9572 to Z9621, Z9647 to Z9681, Z9706 to Z9755 and Z9792 to Z9836), with all 620 delivered between July 1940 and October 1941. It is possible that a further five Blenheims were produced by Avro; AE449 to AE453 were five replacement aircraft, understood to have been delivered directly into store in November 1941. No service record for these aircraft has been discovered. Thus, the total number of Blenheim IVs produced by the three British firms was 3,308 or 3,313.

The Finnish firm Valtion Lentokonetehdas built ten Blenheim IVs (BL-196 to BL-205) at Tampere. These aircraft are understood to have incorporated the components for 15 aircraft built by Ikarus AD at Zemun in Yugoslavia, which were sold by the Germans to Finland after it took over the Balkan nation. Yugoslavia intended to produce the Mk IV as the Ikarus B.4.

The Blenheim IV was subject to several improvements as production progressed.

Soon after war was declared, work parties from Filton were sent to frontline squadrons to add armour plating, self-sealing fuel tanks, IFF (identification friend or foe) and reflector gunsights to their aircraft. The pre-war Bristol B.I and II gun turrets, armed with a single Lewis gun, was replaced by the B.III with a 0.303in (7.7mm) Vickers K gun on new aircraft in production, while a second weapon was added in the B.IIIA or exchanged for Brownings of the same calibre in the B.IV. The additions increased the all-up weight of the Blenheim, which typically reached 14,500lb (6,577kg) by January 1940. These changes made the Mk IV around 12mph (19km/h) slower than the Mk I.

In order to improve defensive armament, some Blenheims deployed to France in 1939-40 had a makeshift arrangement for a gun that could be pointed through the aperture for the tailwheel; although the unit had been fixed in position, the well was not always faired. Some units began adding a single, gimbal-mounted rear-firing gun, under the nose, a modification that quickly gained official sanction and was widely adopted. Later aircraft had a remotely controlled Frazer-Nash FN.54 turret, aimed by a periscope by the navigator, mounted under the nose with a single 0.303in (7.7mm) Browning, later increased to two of the guns in the FN.54A. The unit could be jettisoned in case the crew needed to use the emergency escape hatch.

One of the first batch of Blenheim IVs from the Bristol contract altered from Mk Is to include 84 Mk IVs. L4835 was flown to Boscombe Down, Wiltshire, in September 1939 for evaluation at heavier weights, although these were interrupted when it was damaged in a taxiing accident in March 1940.

The Blenheim IV proved to be a workhorse of the early war years and went on to serve overseas.

Bristol 149 Blenheim IVF

The Blenheim IVF was a similar modification to the Blenheim IF. The aircraft was equipped with the same ventral gun pack designed by the Southern Railway Company of Ashford, Kent, containing four 0.303in (7.7mm) Browning weapons. The Mk IVs fitted with the pack could not carry bombs in the bay, which contained the ammunition for the guns. It also precluded carrying the under-nose weapon.

The additional fuel tanks increased the range of the variant. This was seen as a useful addition for the four 'Trade Protection' squadrons – Nos 235, 236, 248 and 254 – Fighter Command had been forced to establish when it was given the task of protecting shipping off the east coast. In February 1940, the units were transferred to Coastal Command and they began re-equipping with the Mk IVFs, except for 236 Squadron, which hung on to its Mk IFs until July-August 1940. Exactly how many Mk IVs were modified is unknown, but it was a rarer variant than the Mk IF.

Sixteen Blenheim IVFs (P4829 to P4837 and P4844 to P4850) were delivered direct from the factory at Filton to Farnborough, Hampshire, in September and October 1939. There the Royal Aircraft Establishment installed AI radar sets, with four delivered to the Special Duty Flight, three each for 29 and 600 Squadrons, and two each for 23, 25 and 64 Squadrons.

The Special Duty Flight was formed in November 1939 at St Athan in Wales

A Blenheim IVF of 68 Squadron in the black night fighter colours applied to Fighter Command's nocturnal force. The squadron briefly used the aircraft from its formation in January 1941 before receiving Bristol Beaufighters from that May.

(where radar installation work was later undertaken) and had previously been 'D' Flight of Performance Testing, Aeroplane and Armament Experimental Establishment at Martlesham Heath, Suffolk. Its task was the development of radar; 'D' Flight had been controlled from Bawdsey Manor, Suffolk, by Robert Watson-Watt, and had temporarily moved to Perth in Scotland at the start of the war before relocating to the Welsh airfield. It moved to Christchurch, Dorset, in April 1940 to join 22 Group, but was with 70 Group by the end of the year, with an establishment of four Blenheims among a mixed fleet.

On May 12, 1940, Flight Lieutenant Christopher Dermot Salmond Smith and Aircraftman 1st Class Alec William Newton, in radar-equipped P4834 of the Flight, was vectored by Bawdsey Manor off the Hook of Holland, where they intercepted a Heinkel He 111 of I./LG 1 around 1020hrs. Although Smith was wounded and the Blenheim damaged by the bomber's gunners, the Luftwaffe aircraft was shot down. It was the first-ever successful radar-controlled interception of another aircraft.

The Blenheim crash-landed at Martlesham Heath and burned out, while Smith was taken to Colchester Military Hospital, where he recovered from his wounds. Newton's minor injuries were treated in the station sick quarters.

The radar-equipped Blenheim IVFs of the Special Duty Flight that became the first aircraft equipped with an airborne interception set to shoot down another aircraft. The milestone occurred on May 12, 1940, with the Blenheim crash-landing attempting to land back at Martlesham Heath.

The solid nose Type 160CS Bisley (AD657) was the close support variant. By the time production was considered the need for such an aircraft had diminished.

Bristol 160 Bisley

Specification B.6/40 called for a Direct Support Bomber to meet Operational Requirement OR.83, which was to be fulfilled by a variant of the Blenheim IV able to undertake duties in support of the army. 'Direct support' included dive bombing, low-level bombing and attacks against ground targets using front-mounted guns. The aircraft would have a range of approximately 1,150 miles (1,850km) carrying 1,000lb (454kg) of bombs, or 600 miles (965km) with a 500lb (227kg) bombload in the direct support role. Removeable armour for the lower surfaces and frontal quadrant would be installed for the latter role, to protect the crew when diving. The aircraft would also be able to undertake tactical and strategic reconnaissance by day and night.

Defensive armament would comprise a servo-fed rear turret with two 0.303in (7.7mm) Browning guns, able to rotate 360°. A removeable Nash and Thompson FN.54 two-gun, rear-firing mounting would be installed under the nose for the bomber variant. Direct support provision was to be provided for four fixed 0.303in (7.7mm) machine guns, with 600 rounds of ammunition each, while in the bomber role the Blenheim IV's wing-mounted weapons would be installed, each with 400 rounds.

Minimal alterations to the Blenheim airframe were requested, so as not to interrupt production and to speed up entry into service. Power was to be provided by a pair of Bristol Mercury XVs with constant-speed propellers, although the aircraft emerged with the 920hp (686kW) Mk XVI version of the engine. The specification was issued to Bristol on September 12, 1940.

A new nose section was designed to accommodate the four forward firing weapons, which were allocated 1,000 rounds each, while around 600lb (272kg) of armour was added. A Bristol B.X turret was fitted in the upper rear position. Wingspan was reduced slightly, by 3in (76mm), in comparison to the earlier variants.

Two prototypes were ordered by the Air Ministry as the 'close support' Type 160CS (AD657, c/n 9874) and 'high-altitude' Type 160HA (AD661, c/n 9875), both to be known by the name Bisley. (The designations Type 149CS and 149HA are understood to have been used originally.) The solid nose Type 160CS was 43ft 4in (13.21m) long, while the 160HA with a glazed nose and the ventral canoe for the FN.54 was 7in (178mm) longer, making their fuselages 7in (178mm) and 14in (356mm) larger than that of the Blenheim IV.

The nose was later redesigned to accommodate interchangeable gun and high-altitude configurations. However, plans for each aircraft to be able to accept either nose were quickly dropped, as changing them was determined to be too great a task to be performed at squadron level.

The Type 160CS first flew at Filton outside Bristol on February 24, 1941, and arrived for evaluation at Boscombe Down, Wiltshire, that July, where the cockpit layout received praise, although the hydraulics for the turret caused problems. As the threat of a German invasion receded, the need for a direct support aircraft declined so the decision was taken that Bisleys would be completed as level-bombers. Bisley AD657 was struck off charge on July 13, 1942.

Bombing trials with AD661, undertaken at Boscombe Down, saw munitions striking the aircraft's structure on release. Nevertheless, AD661 would become the prototype for the production version. The name Bisley was officially replaced by Blenheim V on January 8, 1942.

Bisley AD661 was later used by 12 (Pilots) Advanced Flying unit at Grantham (renamed Spitalgate in March 1944). It survived until damaged beyond repair during a belly-landing at the airfield's satellite site at Harlaxton, Lincolnshire, on November 23, 1944.

The second prototype Bisley (AD661) was effectively the prototype Blenheim V. The aircraft had an under-nose canoe for the FN.54 gun system.

Bristol 160 Blenheim V

Production of the Type 160 Bisley I was entrusted to the Rootes Securities factory at Blythe Bridge, Meir, Staffordshire. The factory was contracted to build an example of both the Type 160CS close support and Type 160HA high altitude bomber versions. However, interest in the close support version quickly ended and both of the 'pattern aircraft' (DJ702 and DJ707) were completed as Type 160HAs.

This first flew in September 1941 and went to Boscombe Down, Wiltshire, for evaluation of its performance by the Aeroplane and Armament Experimental Establishment (A&AEE) in January 1942. Powered by a pair of Mercury XVs at an all-up weight of 16,300lb (7,393kg), it managed to achieve 243mph (391kph) at 5,900ft (1,798m) and had a service ceiling of 17,800ft (5,425m). The cabin was judged by the A&AEE to be unacceptably cold at altitude.

For production aircraft, power was to be provided by a pair of Bristol Mercury XX or 25s, which were fitted to the early aircraft, although later examples replaced them with the Mk 30. Production aircraft were not fitted with the armour of the original prototypes, but additional radios, provision for an oxygen system for the crew and other operational systems meant the weight of the aircraft was no lower. Empty weight reached 11,000lb (4,990kg), around 1,200lb (544kg) more than the Blenheim IV, requiring the landing gear to be strengthened. The increase meant that the aircraft could not maintain height if one of its engines failed, except at low weights. When operating in the Middle East and North Africa, the weight of an aircraft tended to increase, as it acquired a 'cargo' of sand, which was difficult to keep out of the airframe. The variant was the slowest of all Blenheim variants, even with refinements such as a fully enclosed main landing gear; earlier versions of the Blenheim left part of the wheel exposed to the airflow.

During November 1941, Bristol suggested that the Bisley I name be dropped in favour of Blenheim V. This was officially adopted on January 8, 1942, but Bisley continued to appear in official service records into 1943.

The RAF ordered more than a thousand Bisley Is to be produced at the Rootes Securities facility, comprising two batches covering 880 and 415 aircraft. The first (AZ861 to AZ905, AZ922 to AZ971, AZ984 to AZ999, BA100 to BA172, BA191 to BA215, BA228 to BA262, BA287 to BA336, BA365 to BA409, BA424 to BA458, BA471

The first Blenheim V 'pattern aircraft', DJ702, in February 1942 during its evaluation by the Aeroplane and Armament Experimental Establishment. The aircraft is armed with a Bristol B.X turret with two guns and has flame dampers under the engines.

Blenheim V AZ930, seen at Boscombe Down, Wiltshire, in January 1942, was fitted with Mercury 25s, while Mk XVs powered the prototypes. This aircraft later went to 42 Operational Training Unit and served with other second-line units until being struck off charge in September 1944.

to BA505, BA522 to BA546, BA575 to BA624, BA647 to BA691, BA708 to BA757, BA780 to BA829, BA844 to BA888, BA907 to BA951, BA978 to BA999, BB100 to BB102 and BB135 to BB184) were delivered from November 1941. Only 160 of the second batch were built (EH310 to EH335, EH371 to EH420, EH438 to EH474, EH491 to EH517), which were handed over to the RAF between December 1942 and June 1943, while the other 255 on order (EH518 to EH533, EH550 to EH581, EH599 to EH634, EH651 to EH700, EH718 to EH749, EH763 to EH796, EH802 to EH831, EH848 to EH872) were cancelled. Including the two pattern aircraft, Rootes built 942 Blenheim Vs.

Several different subvariants were created. By the time the Blenheim V was available Bomber Command had other, better alternatives to equip its light bomber

squadrons. Most of the aircraft were dispatched overseas, with many being ferried to units in North Africa. The Type 160D Blenheim VD was a tropicalised version, fitted with a Vokes filter to protect the Mercury engines from ingesting sand and dust. It was the most numerous of the subtypes. The Type 160HA was the Blenheim VA, the standard 'bomber' without the filter, while the Type 160T Blenheim VC was a dual control trainer. The turret and under-nose ventral gondola were often removed from the Mk VCs in service. The Mk VB was reserved for the Type 160CS close support variant, but none of them were completed as such.

Blenheim Vs briefly served with 139 Squadron flying from airfields in England between June and September 1942, while a few were operated by 515 Squadron in Scotland. The variant also served with eight

operational training units at home – usually alongside other types – as well as others based in Egypt, India and Kenya. RAF squadrons in Aden (No.8), Egypt (No.162), India (Nos 34, 42 and 113) Northwest Africa (Nos 13, 18, 114 and 614), Sharjah (No.244) and the Western Desert (No.203) all flew the aircraft, many on patrols off the coast looking for enemy shipping and U-boats. Others were supplied to units of the Australian, Free French, Hellenic and South African air forces, while a handful were briefly used by the US Army Air Forces in Northwest Africa.

The surplus of Blenheim Vs meant that it could be supplied to other countries without impacting the RAF. Examples were sold to Turkey, while others that had to divert to Portugal on their way from England to North Africa were eventually turned over to that country.

Typical of many late-production Blenheim Vs, Mk VD EH495 served with a second-line unit through its service career, in this case the 1578 Calibration Flight at Blida in Algeria.

Fairchild Aircraft
Bolingbroke I

n the late 1930s Canada began to look to upgrade its armed forces. By early 1937, the Royal Canadian Air Force (RCAF) had a requirement for a new general reconnaissance aircraft with longer range and better navigational facilities than those already flown by its operational squadrons. Canada wished to build the new aircraft under licence, guaranteeing that they would be available if overseas supplies ended.

Types under consideration were the Blackburn Botha, Bristol's Type 142M Blenheim, 149 Bolingbroke and 152 Beaufort. Both the Beaufort and Botha were still in development and would not be available in time, while the Blenheim was ruled out because of poor visibility from its cockpit, making it unsuitable for general reconnaissance. This left the Type 149 Bolingbroke, although by then the British had decided to redesign the nose section of the aircraft to create the Blenheim IV. This proved to be acceptable to Canada, although it was decided to retain the Bolingbroke name for their aircraft. In service this was usually shortened by the Canadians to 'Bolly'.

A contract for 18 as Bolingbroke Is was signed with Fairchild Aircraft of Longueuil, Québec, in November 1937. Fairchild Aircraft received the Blenheim IV 'prototype', K7072, which had originally been the British Bolingbroke. It was

The first of the Bolingbrokes built in Canada was Mk I 702. In most respects, the variant was equivalent to the Blenheim IV.

dispatched to Longueuil in October 1940 to act as a pattern aircraft for Canadian production, along with a full set of jigs, tools and drawings for production. The company's factory was expanded for the project.

The Bolingbroke Is used components and sub-assemblies imported from Britain. They were powered by Bristol Mercury VIIIs of 840hp (627kW), as used by Blenheim Is. The RCAF serials 702 to 719 were allocated (701 presumably going to K7072). Two aircraft, 705 and 717, became the Bolingbrokes II and

III (*see next page*). The initial Canadian-built Bolingbroke I first flew on September 14, 1939, in the hands of James Harold 'Red' Lymburner. It was taken on charge by the RCAF on November 15 and nine days later was with the Test and Development Establishment at RCAF Station Rockcliffe, Ontario, for evaluation. A least 703 and 707 were fitted with dual controls.

Many Bolingbroke Is were later equipped with the four 0.303in (7.7mm) gun pack under the centre fuselage as fighters. The aircraft were envisaged as good enough to intercept Japanese bombers or reconnaissance aircraft operating off the western coast, although it was recognised that they did not have the performance to engage fighters. They notably served with 115 (F) Squadron from RCAF Station Patricia Bay, British Colombia.

Towards the end of their flying careers, Mk Is were increasingly issued to Bombing and Gunnery Schools, although several had been withdrawn by mid-1943. At least three were modified as target-tugs in May 1943. Another three became instructional airframes; 707 in September 1942 as A184, 709 as A406 in June 1944, with 704 becoming A431 in October 1944. The last Bolingbroke I in squadron service (702) belonged to 147 (BR) Squadron, which disbanded at RCAF Station Tofino, British Colombia, on March 15, 1944. The final operational example is understood to have been 718, which had been on loan to the Test and Development Establishment for pilot training at Rockcliffe, on October 2, 1944. The unit had finished with the Bolingbroke I by mid-January 1945.

The Bolingbroke Is had relatively long careers with the RCAF. Aircraft 702 went to Rockcliffe in Ottawa, Ontario (as seen here), was with 119 (BR) Squadron from August 1940, and then with 147 (BR) Squadron from July 1942 until March 1944.

Fairchild Aircraft **Bolingbroke II**

Bolingbroke I 705 suffered Category C damage on March 31, 1940, at RCAF Station Uplands, Ottawa, while undergoing acceptance tests with the Test and Development Establishment. The aircraft overran the runway and came to rest in deep snow. It was repaired by Fairchild Aircraft and on June 27, 1940, was assigned to 119 (BR) Squadron, based at Royal Canadian Air Force (RCAF) Station Yarmouth, Nova Scotia. However, on August 25 it crashed again departing Fairchild's airfield at Longueuil, Quebec, and so went back to the factory for repairs.

The opportunity was taken to incorporate some features of the Bolingbroke IV in the airframe for testing. This included installation of American instrumentation and equipment, after which it became the sole Bolingbroke II. The work was completed on November 18, 1940, the same day it was assigned to Eastern Air Command. It is understood to have been evaluated by the Test and Development Establishment.

On October 8, 1941, it was transferred to Western Air Command, but on November 22 passed to 1 Training Command (TC) for issue at 1 Bombing and Gunnery School at RCAF Station Jarvis, Ontario. The Bolingbroke II was placed into storage within 1 TC in April 1943 and, one year later, was allocated to 6 Repair Depot at RCAF Station Trenton, Ontario, for scrapping. It was struck off charge on June 21, 1944.

Fairchild Aircraft **Bolingbroke III**

The Bolingbroke III on the Ottawa River in its original guise, without the ventral fin later added to improve longitudinal stability.

Canadian authorities always envisaged that the Bolingbroke should be developed as a seaplane for coastal reconnaissance. Nearly all the Bolingbroke Is were equipped with the fittings that would have allowed them to be converted as seaplanes, in which form they would have been designated Mk IFs.

Wind-tunnel tests of a Bolingbroke floatplane model were undertaken by the National Research Council in Ottawa. The choice of floats came down to designs from Short Brothers and the Edo Corporation of New York. The Northern Ireland floats were rejected as having too narrow a track. Fairchild Aircraft ordered 24 sets of Edo 37-15.750 floats from MacDonald Bros Aircraft of Winnipeg, Manitoba, with the provision that one pair would be produced and delivered, with the others dependent on the successful outcome of testing.

During November 1939, the RCAF concluded that the Bristol Mercury VIIIs of the Bolingbroke I would not be powerful enough to lift the aircraft off water, and replacement by Mercury XVs of 825hp (615kW) would be required. Other changes needed included local strengthening of the wing and fuselage structures. These changes resulted in the change of designation of the floatplane to Bolingbroke III.

After making its first flight as a land plane from the airfield at Longueuil, Quebec, on July 25, 1940, Bolingbroke 717 was delivered to RCAF Station Rockcliffe, Ontario, for the Test and Development Establishment on August 8. There it was fitted with Edo floats and on August 28 Fairchild's test pilot James Harold Lymburner flew it off the Ottawa River. Three flights were completed that day, with the aircraft reaching 175mph (282kph) with reduced power at 2,500ft (762m) and 2,200rpm; at the same settings the Bolingbroke I could fly at 220mph (354kph).

Initial flights demonstrated that the aircraft had poor longitudinal stability, resulting in a large ventral fin being added that cured the problem. Although the aircraft was found to handle well on water, Lymburner suggested introducing a hydraulic mechanism to raise and lower the heavy water rudders to improve steering.

Operational trials were undertaken by 5 (BR) Squadron, based at RCAF Station Dartmouth, Nova Scotia, from November 5, 1940, alongside the unit's Supermarine Stranraers. This continued into February 1941, after which the floats were removed and the aircraft became a land plane again. During its time with the squadron, it was found that the magnesium alloy components used in its airframe had been badly affected by salt water. From September 26, 1941, the Bolingbroke was repaired by Clark-Ruse Aircraft, which had its main facility at Dartmouth and specialised in overhaul and maintenance work. It remained with the company until January 6, 1942, after which it was placed into temporary store at Yarmouth, Nova Scotia, quickly moving to 4 Repair Depot at Relief Landing Field Scoudouc, New Brunswick, in late February 1942. The following month it was issued to 1 Training Command (TC) for one of its flying schools.

In May and June 1943, the Bolingbroke was with 6 Repair Depot at RCAF Station Trenton, Ontario, but was placed into storage by 1 TC the following month. In April 1944, the airframe was assigned to 6 Repair Depot at Trenton for disposal and struck off charge on June 21.

Canada has the world's longest coastline, with many bays from which coastal reconnaissance aircraft could operate. The Bolingbroke III was not adopted for widespread service because its payload with full fuel was just 500lb (227kg).

Fairchild Aircraft
Bolingbroke IV

Production of the Bolingbroke II was undertaken as the Mk IV, using the American instrumentation and equipment tested in the earlier aircraft. They were powered by Bristol Mercury XV or XXs. At least the first 25 built had the structural provisions to be equipped with floats, although these were not fitted. They also could use interchangeable skid landing gear.

A total of 201 Bolingbroke IVs were ordered with the Canadian serials 9001 to 9201. The last 50 (9152 to 9201) were later cancelled, although the airframes were later ordered as Mk IV-Ts (9152 to 9201). Of the 151 completed, 15 were fitted with Pratt & Whitey Twin Wasps as Mk IV-Ws, while a single aircraft was tested as the Mk IV-C and others modified for target-towing.

Deliveries to the Royal Canadian Air Force (RCAF) began in January 1941 and the variant went on to equip home-based squadrons of the service, including the bomber-reconnaissance (BR) units, which were primarily used on coastal patrols. For the role the aircraft were equipped with emergency dinghies for the crew, while de-icing boots were fitted to the leading edges of the main planes and the horizontal tailplane. Operational Bolingbroke IVs served with eight RCAF squadrons, starting with 119 (BR) Squadron in July 1940. Some examples were equipped with a locally made ventral gun pack containing four 0.303in (7.7mm) weapons, in a similar modification that created the RAF's Blenheim IVFs, serving with 115 (F) Squadron.

Acceptance of the last Bolingbroke IV built (9151) was delayed when its landing gear collapsed at RCAF Station Fingal, Ontario, during its delivery flight on February 26, 1942. It was taken on charge after the damage was repaired.

A Bolingbroke IV of 115 (BR) Squadron on Annette Island in Alaska in February 1943. The squadron previously used the aircraft as a fighter, but it became a bomber-reconnaissance unit in mid-1942. Canada Department of Defence

Fairchild Aircraft Bolingbroke IV-C

A shortage of 100-octane fuel in Canada resulted in a search for alternative powerplants for the Bolingbroke IV. Wright GR-1820-G3Bs Cyclones, each rated at 850hp (634kW), with constant speed Hamilton propellers, were fitted in larger nacelles to Mk IV airframe 9074, which became the Bolingbroke IV-C. The aircraft completed its maiden flight at Longueuil, Quebec, on April 23, 1942.

After testing by Fairchild Aircraft, the Bolingbroke IV-C was taken on strength by 3 Training Command on June 29, 1942, before being evaluated by the Test and Development Establishment at RCAF Station Rockcliffe, Ontario. Although the Cyclones burning 93-octane fuel gave the aircraft a better performance than Bolingbrokes powered by the Bristol Mercury XV, the decision had been taken to make the Mercury XX the standard powerplant for Mk IVs. It offered a similar performance without the need to modify the airframe. The larger nacelle required by the Cyclone also restricted the view each side of the cockpit. On May 1, 1944, Bolingbroke 9074 was assigned to 9 Repair Depot at RCAF Station St Jean, Quebec. There it was struck off charge on June 8.

The Bolingbroke IV-C followed the earlier Mk IV-W as a testbed for alternative engines for the aircraft. The Cyclone provided similar performance to the Mercury XX, which powered later Mk IVs, but would have required changes on the production line.

From the front, the size of the revised nacelles of the Bolingbroke IV-C are apparent.

Fairchild Aircraft Bolingbroke IV-T

Arguably the most important version of the Bolingbroke was the Mk IV-T, a navigation and gunnery trainer that played a crucial role in the British Commonwealth Air Training Plan. It equipped 11 Bombing and Gunnery Schools (B&GSs).

The Bolingbroke IV-T was also the most numerous of the Canadian-built Blenheims, with 457 produced. A contract for 350 Mk IV-Ts (9850 to 10199) was placed, the aircraft delivered between March 1942 and May 1943, followed by another for 57 (10200 to 10256), while during 1942 a cancelled contract for 50 Mk IVs was reinstalled for the same number of Mk IV-Ts, retaining the originally allocated serials (9152 to 9201). In addition, a further 51 airframes without serials were produced and not taken on charge by the RCAF; they are understood to have been used as spares.

The first Bolingbroke IV-T (9850) fitted with long-range fuel tanks, was allocated to the Test and Development Establishment at RCAF Station Rockcliffe, Ontario, on March 28, 1942, where it was involved in cabin heating experiments. Bolingbroke IV-Ts were fitted with a Boulton Paul Type C turret, although they did not always contain weapons. From at least 10192, the 810hp (600kW) Bristol Mercury XX engine was installed in new production examples at the factory. The last (9201) was taken on charge on November 26, 1943.

The service career of the variant was tied to the British Commonwealth Air Training Plan (BCATP). Eight B&GSs continued to operate into 1945, but five of them closed that February and all but one had gone by the end of June. Large numbers of Bolingbrokes were placed into store and were sold for scrap. All had been struck off charge by mid-1947.

Fairchild Aircraft Bolingbroke IV-TT

The Bolingbroke IV-TT was a target-towing conversion of Mk IVs and IV-Ts, although the designation may have been unofficial. At least 39 Bolingbroke IVs and 128 Mk IV-Ts could tow targets, with some of the latter fitted with the equipment from delivery. The aircraft were widely used within the units of the British Commonwealth Air Training Plan, as well as home-based Royal Canadian Air Force units, such as 121 and 122 (Composite) Squadrons at RCAF Stations Dartmouth in Nova Scotia and Patricia Bay, British Columbia.

Tests of the aircraft as a target-tug were undertaken at the Test and Development Establishment (T&DE) at RCAF Station Rockcliffe, Ontario, in the second half of 1942. A Type C5 target-towing winch was installed in a Bolingbroke IV in place of the radio operator's table. The lower rear emergency door was replaced by a transparent sliding hatch, from which the cable for the banner was deployed. The target banner was released from the bomb bay and towed until released at the end of the training. An additional generator was installed to provide power for the winch used to reel in the banner. A series of guard wires mounted around the aircraft's tailplane protected it from damage from errant banners.

The aircraft modified as a testbed is identified as 9075 in an official report, although an image (dated October 10, 1942) clearly shows it as 9035. Bolingbroke 9075 was with the T&DE from January 12, 1942, but which unit 9035 was assigned to that October has not come to light.

Built as a Bolingbroke IV-T, 9932 became a Mk IV-TT target-tug at 6 Repair Depot at RCAF Station Trenton, Ontario, in June 1944.

Twelve of the 15 Bolingbroke IV-Ws lined up at the Fairchild Aircraft facility at Longueuil outside Montreal, Quebec. Designed to secure production in case supplies of Mercury engines became unavailable, the variant was found to be underpowered.

Fairchild Bolingbroke IV-W

Supplies of Bristol Mercury XV engines for Fairchild's Bolingbroke production line had to travel across the Atlantic to Canada. With merchant shipping at risk from predation by German U-boats, threatening to interrupt deliveries, it became prudent to seek an alternative for the Bolingbroke, resulting in the selection of the 750hp (559kW) Pratt & Whitney Twin Wasp Junior SB4G as a possible alternative. They required a nacelle with a revised profile, while the two-position propellers used by other Bolingbroke versions were replaced by constant-speed Hamilton units.

Bolingbroke IV 9005 was converted to have the Twin Wasp Juniors on the production line at Longueuil, Quebec, becoming the prototype of the Mk IV-W. It completed its first flight on February 10, 1941, and was used by Fairchild Aircraft to evaluate the new engines for the airframe. It was taken-on charge by the Eastern Air Command of the Royal Canadian Air Force (RCAF) on July 4, originally going to 8 (BR) Squadron at RCAF Station Sydney, Nova Scotia.

Production of Bolingbroke IV-Ws started with 9010 and continued up to 9023, with all taken-on strength by the RCAF between July and August 1941. The first was delivered to the Test and Development Establishment at RCAF Station Rockcliffe, Ontario, by the start of November 1941. It was reportedly fitted with special 'AI equipment' – presumably radar – at the end of June 1942, which it retained when flown by 121 (Composite) Squadron at RCAF Station Dartmouth, Nova Scotia. The equipment was removed at Rockcliffe in April 1943.

Most production Bolingbroke IV-Ws initially went to 8 (BR) or 115 (F) Squadrons, the later at RCAF Station Yarmouth, Nova Scotia. In service it was found that the variant was incapable of maintaining altitude on one engine, the standard bomb load having to be reduced to 500lb (227kg) to compensate for the lower power of the engines. Faced with these deficiencies, the squadrons quickly replaced their Mk IV-Ws, with most of the aircraft passing to 1 Training Command (TC) by the end of 1941, although some were used by 115 (F) Squadron. No.1 TC began to place the Bolingbroke IV-Ws into storage from July 1943 and most were allocated to 6 Repair Depot at RCAF Station Trenton, Ontario, for scrapping in April 1944.

Bolingbroke IV-W 9021 was taken-on strength by the RCAF on August 13, 1941, going to 119 (BR) Squadron at RCAF Station Yarmouth, Nova Scotia. It was transferred to 1 Training Command in January 1942 and stored from July 1943.

Britain First

The Royal Air Force was the first and largest operator of the Blenheim. Around 5,250 Mk Is, IVs and Vs were delivered to the RAF, although many were supplied to Allied air forces and other operators from its stocks. Others were diverted to overseas customers from RAF contracts during production, often to augment aircraft previously delivered direct from Bristol.

It is widely stated that the aircraft flew with every command of the service, although this is not strictly correct; RAF Balloon Command never had Blenheims, for obvious reasons. The primary operator of frontline Blenheim squadrons was RAF Bomber Command's 2 (Bombing) Group, which controlled three wings, each with two squadrons, plus an independent squadron, at the end of September 1939. RAF Fighter Command started the war with seven Blenheim fighter squadrons, but also controlled army-co-operation squadrons until RAF Army Co-operation Command was established in December 1940. RAF Coastal

Blenheim I L1295 of 107 Squadron in 1938. The squadron re-equipped with Mk IVs in May 1939. It took part in the first raid on German warships at Wilhelmshaven on September 4, 1939, in strikes against the invasion force heading for Norway in April 1940 and in raids during the Battle for France. In early 1941, it was transferred from Bomber to Coastal Command for two months, before being returned and sent to Malta in late August 1941. It disbanded on January 12, 1942.

Command received its initial four Blenheim squadrons in February 1940, when they were transferred from Fighter Command.

Other commands had a more peripheral association with the Blenheim; support for the type in the British Isles was provided by RAF Maintenance Command, while RAF Ferry Command flew them where they were needed, becoming part of RAF Transport Command in March 1943. RAF Training Command split into Flying Training and Technical Training Commands in May 1940, with the former receiving many Blenheims after they had been replaced in the frontline squadrons, while the latter used them as instructional airframes.

What is true is that the Blenheim fought in all the theatres of war that the RAF was engaged in during the first half of World War Two. Apart from operations from Britain, it was particularly active around the Mediterranean, during the campaigns launched from Egypt into the Western Desert; in the Anglo-American operation to capture Northwest Africa; flying sorties from Malta; and fighting in Greece. Blenheims supported the Allied occupations of Syria and Iran, and flew missions during the brief Iraqi revolt. They participated in operations in East Africa against the Italians, in Abyssinia, Eritrea and Sudan. In the Far East, Blenheims fought the Japanese when they invaded Malaya, Singapore and the Dutch East Indies, supported operations in Burma and helped defend Ceylon from possible invasion.

Blenheims saw a lot of active service around the Mediterranean. Mk I L8529, either of 223 Squadron or 70 Operational Training Unit, is seen on approach to an unidentified airfield in Egypt or Libya in late 1941 or early 1942.

RAF Blenheim
Squadrons and Units

A total of 87 RAF squadrons flew Blenheims at various times between March 1937 and May 1945. Release for the Blenheim I to enter squadron service with the RAF was granted in late February 1937 and deliveries began on March 1. On that date, K7035 equipped with dual controls was handed over to 114 Squadron at Wyton in Huntingdonshire to allow it to begin the process of replacing its Hawker Audax biplanes. Three more aircraft arrived for the squadron three days later and another eight had been handed over by May 7.

After 114 Squadron, Blenheims were sent to 90 Squadron in May and June 1937 to replace its Hawker Hinds, then 139 Squadron. By August 1939 another 15 bomber squadrons (144, 44, 110, 61, 62, 82, 57, 104, 101, 34, 107, 21, 53, 59 and 18 Squadrons, in that order), four Fighter Command units (23, 29, 64 and 25), three Auxiliary Air Force (600, 601 and 604) and overseas squadrons (30, 84, 55, 211, 60, 45 and 39) had received Blenheim Is. Deliveries of Blenheim IVs began in March 1939, with 53 Squadron, an army co-operation unit, becoming the first to receive the aircraft. As the variant built in the largest numbers, the Blenheim IVs served with the most RAF squadrons of all the versions produced.

By 1942, the days of the Blenheim within frontline squadrons were drawing to a close, but many other squadrons overseas received the aircraft. Most of the Blenheim Vs were issued to units that served outside the home commands. Blenheims were also flown by second line units in Britain, some of which were established as squadrons. It was with 526 and 527 Squadrons, at Inverness by the Moray Firth in Scotland and Digby, Lincolnshire, respectively, that the Blenheim last served in squadron colours. Both were

radar calibration units (*see below*). With the end of the war in Europe, the need for their services disappeared and they disbanded in May 1945, ending the career of the Blenheim with the RAF squadrons.

Blenheims did not survive long after the end of the war. By then it was truly obsolete, and with more aircraft that it could possibly need, even for second line duties, the RAF quickly disposed of those still active. They were soon consigned to the melting pot; today not a single former RAF example exists intact.

No. 62 Squadron was reformed from 'B' Flight of 40 Squadron at Abingdon, Oxfordshire, initially with Hawker Hinds, before receiving Blenheim Is in the spring of 1938. It departed for the Far East just before the war started and was wiped out in February 1942 fighting the Japanese. The nearest aircraft (L1131) was posted as missing in April 1940.

The first RAF unit to re-equip with the Blenheim IV was 53 Squadron, an army co-operation unit. Mk IV L4852 was one of the first batch of 84 of the variant built at Filton. It was lost on August 5, 1940.

Blenheim I K7059 of 90 Squadron with its post-Munich 'TW' code. The squadron began receiving Mk IVs in March 1939 and operated as a training unit for 6 Group, Bomber Command, before merging with 35 Squadron in April 1940 to create 17 Operational Training Unit.

RAF BLENHEIM SQUADRONS

Unit	Version	Code	Base(s)	Dates
6 Sqn	Blenheim IV	JV	Kufra, Libya	11/41-01/42
8 Sqn	Blenheim I		Khormaksar, Aden	04/39-01/44
	Blenheim IV			08/41-04/43
	Blenheim V			09/42-01/44
11 Sqn	Blenheim I	(OY)	Risalpur, India	07/39-08/39
			Tengah, Singapore	08/39-04/40
			Lahore, India	04/40-05/40
			Ismailia, Egypt	05/40-06/40
			Sheikh Othman, Aden	06/40-12/40
	Blenheim IV		Helwan, Egypt	12/40-01/41
			Eleusis, Greece	01/41-01/41
			Larissa, Greece	01/41-02/41
			Paramythia, Greece	02/41-02/41
			Larissa, Greece	02/41-03/41
			Almyros, Greece	03/41-04/41
			Menidi, Greece	04/41-04/41
			Heliopolis, Egypt	04/41-05/41
			Ramleh, Palestine	05/41-08/41
			Habbaniya, Iraq	08/41-09/41
			LG09, N Africa	09/41-10/41
			LG104, N Africa	10/41-10/41
			LG116, N Africa	10/41-12/41
			Bu Amud, Libya	12/41-01/42
			LG116, N Africa	01/42-02/42
			Helwan, Egypt	02/42-02/42
			Ratmalana, Ceylon	02/42-03/42
			Colombo Racecourse, Ceylon	04/42-01/43
			Baigachi, India	01/43-02/43
			Feni, India	02/43-08/43
			Ranchi, India	08/43-09/43
13 Sqn	Blenheim IV	OO	Odiham	07/41-08/42
			Macmerry	08/42-09/42
	Blenheim V		Macmerry	09/42-11/42
			Gibraltar	11/42-11/42
			Blida, Algeria	11/42-12/42
			Canrobert, Algeria	12/42-02/43
			Oulmene, Algeria	02/43-05/43
			Blida, Algeria	05/43-09/43
			Protville II, Tunisia	09/43-10/43
			Sidi Ahmed, Tunisia	10/43-10/43
			Sidi Amor, Tunisia	10/43-12/43
14 Sqn	Blenheim IV		Port Sudan, Sudan	09/40-04/41
			Heliopolis, Egypt	04/41-05/41
			LG21, N Africa	05/41-07/41
			Petah Tiqwa, Palestine	07/41-08/41
			Habbaniya, Iraq	08/41-08/41
			Qayara, Iraq	08/41-10/41
			Habbaniya, Iraq	10/41-10/41
			Lydda, Palestine	10/41-11/41
			LG15, Egypt	11/41-11/41
			LG75, N Africa	11/41-12/41
			Gambut, Libya	12/41-01/42
			Bu Amud, Libya	01/42-02/42
			LG116, N Africa	02/42-05/42
			El Firdan, Egypt	05/42-06/42

RAF BLENHEIM SQUADRONS

Unit	Version	Code	Base(s)	Dates
			LG116, N Africa	06/42-06/42
			Qassassin, Egypt	06/42-08/42
			LG224, N Africa	08/42-09/42
15 Sqn	Blenheim V	LS	Wyton	12/39-04/40
			Alconbury	04/40-11/40
18 Sqn	Blenheim I	GU	Upper Heyford	05/39-09/39
		WV	Beauvraignes, France	09/39-10/39
			Méharicourt, France	10/39-02/40
	Blenheim IV		Méharicourt, France	02/40-05/40
			Poix, France	05/40-05/40
			Crecy & Abbeville, France	05/40-05/40
			Watton	05/40-05/40
			Gatwick	05/40-06/40
			West Raynham	06/40-09/40
			Great Massingham	09/40-04/41
			Oulton	04/41-07/41
			Horsham St Faith	07/41-08/41
			Manston	08/41-08/41
			Horsham St Faith	08/41-10/41
			Malta	10/41-01/42
			Helwan, Egypt	01/42-02/42
			LG05, N Africa	02/42-02/42
			Fuka, Egypt	02/42-03/42
			Dundonald	05/42-05/42
			Ayr	05/42-05/42
			Wattisham	05/42-08/42
			West Raynham	08/42-09/42
	Blenheim V		West Raynham	09/42-11/42
			Blida, Algeria	11/42-11/42
			Canrobert, Algeria	11/42-12/42
			Setif, Algeria	12/42-12/42
			Canrobert, Algeria	12/42-03/43
			Oulmene, Algeria	03/43-04/43
21 Sqn	Blenheim I	JP	Eastchurch	08/38-03/39
			Watton	03/39-09/39
	Blenheim IV	YH	Watton	09/39-06/40
			Lossiemouth	06/40-10/40
			Watton & Bodney	10/40-05/41
			Lossiemouth	05/41-06/41
			Watton	06/41-07/41
			Manston	07/41-07/41
			Watton	07/41-09/41
			Lossiemouth	09/41-09/41
			Watton	09/41-12/41
			Luqa	12/41-03/42
			Bodney	03/42-07/42
23 Sqn	Blenheim IF	MS/YP	Wittering	12/38-05/40
			Collyweston	05/40-09/40
			Ford	09/40-04/41
25 Sqn	Blenheim IF	RX	Hawkridge	12/38-08/39
	Blenheim IF, IVF		Northolt	08/39-09/39
		ZK	Filton	09/39-10/39
			Northolt	10/39-11/39
	Blenheim IF		North Weald	01/40-06/40
			Martlesham Heath	06/40-09/40
			North Weald	09/40-10/40
			Debden	10/40-11/40
			Wittering	11/40-01/41
27 Sqn	Blenheim IF		Risalpur, India	11/40-02/41
		EG ?	Kallang, Singapore	02/41-05/41
			Butterworth, Malaya	05/41-08/41

RAF BLENHEIM SQUADRONS

Unit	Version	Code	Base(s)	Dates
			Sungei Patani	08/41-12/41
			Butterworth, Malaya	12/41-12/41
			Kallang, Singapore	12/41-01/42
			Palembang, Sumatra	01/42-02/42
29 Sqn	Blenheim IF	YB/RO	Debden	12/38-04/40
			Drem	04/40-06/40
			Digby	06/40-07/40
			Wellingore	07/40-02/41
30 Sqn	Blenheim I, IF	(DP)	Habbaniya, Iraq	01/38-09/38
			Heliopolis, Egypt	09/38-10/38
			Habbaniya, Iraq	10/38-08/39
		VT	Ismailia, Egypt	08/39-07/40
			Ikingi Maryut, Egypt	07/40-11/40
			Eleusis, Greece	11/40-04/41
			Malerne, Greece	04/41-05/41
34 Sqn	Blenheim I	LB	Upper Heyford	07/38-03/39
			Watton	03/39-08/39
		EG ?	Tengah, Singapore	09/39-11/41
	Blenheim IV		Tengah, Singapore	11/41-01/42
			Palembang, Sumatra	01/42-02/42
			Lahat	02/42-02/42
			Batavia	02/42-02/42
			Chakrata, India	04/42-04/42
			Allahabad, India	04/42-06/42
	Blenheim V		Ondal, India	06/42-01/43
			Jessore, India	01/43-03/43
			Silchar, India	03/43-03/43
			Kumbhirgram, India	03/43-04/43
35 Sqn	Blenheim IV	XZ	Cranfield	11/39-12/39
			Bassingbourn	12/39-02/40
			Upwood	02/40-04/40
39 Sqn	Blenheim I		Tengah, Singapore	08/39-09/39
			Kallang, Singapore	09/39-04/40
			Lahore, India	04/40-05/40
			Heliopolis, Egypt	05/40-05/40
			Sheikh Othman, Aden	05/40-12/40
	Blenheim I, IV		Helwan, Egypt	12/40-01/41
40 Sqn	Blenheim IV	BL	Wyton	12/39-11/40
42 Sqn	Blenheim V	AW	Yelahanka, India	02/43-03/43
			Rajyeswarpur, India	03/43-05/43
			Kumbhirgram, India	05/43-10/43
44 Sqn	Blenheim I	JW	Waddington	12/37-02/39
45 Sqn	Blenheim I	DD	Ismailia, Egypt	06/39-08/39
		OB	Fuka, Egypt	08/39-06/40
			Helwan, Egypt	06/40-07/40
	Det		Erkoweit, Sudan	07/40-08/40
			Wadi Gazouza, Sudan	09/40-12/40
			Helwan, Egypt	12/40-12/40
			Qotafiya, Egypt	12/40-12/40
			Menastir, Egypt	12/40-02/41
			Helwan, Egypt	02/41-03/41
	Blenheim IV		Helwan, Egypt	03/41-04/41
			Gambut, Libya	04/41-04/41
			Fuka, Egypt	04/41-06/41
			Wadi Natrum, Egypt	06/41-06/41
			Aqir, Palestine	06/41-08/41
			Habbaniya, Iraq	08/41-09/41
			LG16, Egypt	09/41-11/41
			LG75, N Africa	11/41-12/41
			Gambut, Libya	12/41-01/42
			Helwan, Egypt	01/42-02/42
			Magwe, Burma	02/42-03/42
			Lashio, Burma	03/42-05/42
			Asansol, India	05/42-08/42
52 Sqn	Blenheim IV		Mosul, Iraq	10/42-02/43
			Kasfareet, Egypt	02/43-02/43
53 Sqn	Blenheim IV	TE	Odiham	01/39-09/39
		PZ	Plivot, France	09/39-10/39
			Poix, France	10/39-05/40
			Crecy, France	05/40-05/40
			Andover	05/40-06/40
			Eastchurch	06/40-06/40
			Gatwick	06/40-07/40
			Detling	07/40-11/40
			Thorney Island	11/40-02/41
			Bircham Newton	02/41-02/41
			St Eval	02/41-07/41
55 Sqn	Blenheim I	(GM)	Habbaniya, Iraq	03/39-08/39
			Ismailia, Egypt	08/39-06/40
			Fuka, Egypt	06/40-12/40
	Blenheim IV		Fuka, Egypt	12/40-01/41
			LG79, Egypt	01/41-01/41
			Amseat, Libya	01/41-02/41
			Bu Amud, Libya	02/41-02/41
			Heliopolis, Egypt	02/41-04/41
			Maraua, Libya	04/41-04/41
			Derna, Libya	04/41-04/41
			Great Gambut, Libya	04/41-04/41
			Maaten Bagush, Egypt	04/41-05/41
			LG95, Egypt	05/41-06/41
			Helwan, Egypt	06/41-07/41
			Wadi Natrun, Egypt	07/41-08/41
			Aqir, Palestine	08/41-09/41
			Fuka, Egypt	09/41-01/42
			Bu Amud, Libya	01/42-01/42
			Benina, Libya	01/42-01/42
			Berka Main, Libya	01/42-01/42
			El Gubba, Libya	01/42-01/42
			Gambut, Libya	01/42-02/42
			Fuka, Egypt	02/42-03/42
			Helwan, Egypt	03/42-04/42
			Luxor, Egypt	04/42-04/42
57 Sqn	Blenheim I	BQ	Upper Heyford	03/38-
		DX	Roye/Amy, France	09/39-10/39
			Rosières-en-Santerre, France	10/39-05/40
	Blenheim IV		Poix, France	05/40-05/40
			Crécy-en-Ponthieu, France	05/40-05/40
			Wyton	05/40-05/40
			Gatwick	05/40-06/40
			Lossiemouth	06/40-08/40
			Elgin	08/40-11/40
59 Sqn	Blenheim IV	PJ	Andover	05/39-10/39
		TR	Poix, France	10/39-05/40
			Crécy-en-Ponthieu, France	05/40-05/40

RAF BLENHEIM SQUADRONS

Unit	Version	Code	Base(s)	Dates
			Andover	05/40-06/40
			Odiham	06/40-07/40
			Thorney Island	07/40-02/41
			Manston	02/41-03/41
Det			Bircham Newton	03/41-06/41
			Thorney Island	03/41-06/41
			Detling	06/41-07/41
			Thorney Island	07/41-09/41
60 Sqn	Blenheim I	MU	Ambala, India	06/39-09/40
Det			Dum Dum, India	08/39-
Det			St Thomas Mount, India	09/39-
Det			Juhu, India	10/39-
Det			Drigh Road, India	11/39-
			Lahore, India	09/40-02/41
			Mingaladon, Burma	02/41-02/42
Det			Kuantan, Malaya	11/41-
Det			Tengah, Singapore	11/41-
	Blenheim IV		Asansol, India	03/42-12/42
			Jessore, India	12/42-01/43
			Dohazari, India	01/43-07/43
			Yelahanka, India	07/43-07/43
			St Thomas Mount, India	07/43-07/43
			Yelahanka, India	07/43-08/43
61 Sqn	Blenheim I	LS	Hemswell	01/38-03/39
62 Sqn	Blenheim I	JO	Cranfield	02/38-08/39
		FX/PT	Tengah, Singapore	09/39-02/41
			Alor Star, Malaya	02/41-12/41
			Butterworth, Malaya	12/41-12/41
			Tengah, Singapore	12/41-01/42
64 Sqn	Blenheim IF	ZQ/SH	Church Fenton	12/38-04/40
Det			Evanton	12/39-01/40
68 Sqn	Blenheim IF	WM	Catterick	01/41-04/41
			High Ercall	04/41-05/41
82 Sqn	Blenheim I	OZ	Cranfield	03/38-08/39
	Blenheim IV	UX	Watton	08/39-10/40
			Bodney	10/40-04/41
			Lossiemouth	04/41-05/41
			Bodney	05/41-03/42
Det			Malta	06/41
84 Sqn	Blenheim I	VA	Shaibah, Iraq	02/39-09/40
			Heliopolis, Egypt	09/40-11/40
			Menidi, Greece	11/40-04/41
	Blenheim IV		Heraklion, Greece	04/41-04/41
			Aqir, Palestine	04/41-05/41
			Habbaniya, Iraq	05/41-06/41
			Mosul, Iraq	06/41-09/41
			Habbaniya, Iraq	09/41-10/41
			Amriya, Egypt	10/41-11/41
			LG116, Egypt	11/41-11/41
			LG75, Egypt	11/41-12/41
			Gambut, Libya	12/41-01/42
			Heliopolis, Egypt	01/42-01/42
			Drigh Road, India	04/42-06/42
86 Sqn	Blenheim IV	BX	Gosport	12/40-02/41
			Leuchars	02/41-03/41
			Wattisham	03/41-05/41
			North Coates	05/41-07/41
88 Sqn	Blenheim IV	RH	Sydenham	02/41-07/41
			Swanton Morley	07/41-08/41
			Attlebridge	08/41-12/41
90 Sqn	Blenheim I	TW	Bicester	05/37-03/39
	Blenheim I, IV		Bicester	03/39-05/39
			West Raynham	05/39-09/39
			Weston-on-the-Green	09/39-09/39
			Upwood	09/39-04/40
	Blenheim IV		Polebrook	10/41-02/42
92 Sqn	Blenheim IF	GR	Tangmere	11/39-12/39
			Croydon	12/39-03/40
101 Sqn	Blenheim I	LU	Bicester	06/38-04/39
	Blenheim IV		Bicester	04/39-05/39
		SR	West Raynham	05/39-05/41
104 Sqn	Blenheim I	PO	Bassingbourn	05/38-09/39
		EP	Bicester	09/39-10/39
	Blenheim I, IV		Bicester	10/39-04/40
105 Sqn	Blenheim IV	GB	Honington	06/40-07/40
			Watton	07/40-10/40
			Swanton Morley	10/40-07/41
			Luqa, Malta	07/41-09/41
107 Sqn	Blenheim I	BZ	Scampton	08/38-08/38
			Harwell	08/38-05/39
	Blenheim IV	OM	Wattisham	05/39-03/41
			Leuchars	03/41-05/41
			Great Massington	05/41-08/41
			Luqa, Malta	08/41-01/42
108 Sqn	Blenheim I	MF	Bassingbourn	06/38-09/38
			Bicester	09/38-10/39
	Blenheim I, IV	LD	Bicester	10/39-04/40
110 Sqn	Blenheim I	AY	Waddington	01/38-05/39
			Wattisham	05/39-06/39
	Blenheim IV	VE	Wattisham	06/39-03/42
Det			Lossiemouth	04/40-05/40
Det			Horsham St Faith	02/41-03/41
Det			Manston	05/41-06/41
Det			Luqa, Malta	07/41-07/41
Det			Lindholme	09/41-09/41
Det			Lossiemouth	12/41-12/41
113 Sqn	Blenheim I	BT	Heliopolis, Egypt	06/39-03/40
	Blenheim IV		Heliopolis, Egypt	03/40-06/40
			Maaten Bagush, Egypt	06/40-01/41
			Sidi Barrani, Egypt	01/41-02/41
			Gambut, Libya	02/41-02/41
			Kabrit, Egypt	02/41-03/41
			Menidi, Greece	03/41-03/41
			Larissa, Greece	03/41-04/41
			Niamata, Greece	04/41-04/41
			Menidi, Greece	04/41-04/41
	Blenheim I, IV		Maaten Bagush, Egypt	06/41-11/41
			Giarabub, Libya	11/41-11/41
			LG116, Egypt	11/41-12/41
			Helwan, Egypt	12/41-01/42
	Blenheim IV		Mingaladon, Burma	01/42-01/42
			Toungoo, Burma	01/42-02/42
			Magwe, Burma	02/42-03/42
			Dum Dum, India	03/42-04/42
			Fyzabad, India	04/42-04/42
			Asansol, India	04/42-10/42
	Blenheim V		Asansol, India	10/42-12/42
			Jessore, India	12/42-01/43
			Feni, India	01/43-02/43
			Chandina, India	02/43-05/43
			Comilla Main, India	05/43-06/43
			Feni, India	06/43-08/43

RAF BLENHEIM SQUADRONS

Unit	Version	Code	Base(s)	Dates
			Kharagpur, India	08/43-09/43
			Yelahanka, India	09/43-09/43
114 Sqn	Blenheim I	FD	Wyton	03/37-04/39
	Blenheim I, IV	RT	Wyton	04/39-05/39
	Blenheim IV		Wyton	05/39-12/39
			Condé-Vraux, France	12/39-05/40
			Nantes/Chateau Bougon, France	05/40-05/40
			Wattisham	05/40-06/40
			Horsham St Faith	06/40-08/40
			Oulton	08/40-03/41
			Thornaby	03/41-05/41
			Leuchars	05/41-07/41
			West Raynham	07/41-09/42
	Blenheim V		West Raynham	09/42-11/42
			Blida, Algeria	11/42-12/42
			Setif, Algeria	12/42-02/43
			Canrobert, Algeria	02/43-04/43
139 Sqn	Blenheim I	XD	Wyton	07/37-09/39
	Blenheim IV		Wyton	09/39-11/39
			Alconbury	11/39-11/39
			Wyton	11/39-12/39
			Bétheniville, France	12/39-02/40
			Plivot, France	02/40-05/40
			West Raynham	05/40-06/40
			Horsham St Faith	06/40-05/41
Det			Luqa, Malta	05/41-06/41
			Oulton	07/41-08/41
Det			Manston	08/41-09/41
			Horsham St Faith	10/41-12/41
			Oulton	12/41-12/41
	Blenheim V		Horsham St Faith	06/42-
			Oulton	06/42
			Horsham St Faith	06/42-
			Marham	09/42-10/42
140 Sqn	Blenheim IV	ZW	Benson	09/41-10/41
			Weston Zoyland	10/41-05/42
			Mount Farm	05/42-08/43
141 Sqn	Blenheim IF	TW	Grangemouth	11/39-04/40
			Turnhouse	04/40-05/40
143 Sqn	Blenheim IVF	HO	Aldergrove	06/41-04/42
			Limavady	04/42-06/42
			Thorney Island	06/42-07/42
			Docking	07/42-09/42
144 Sqn	Blenheim I	NV	Hemswell	08/37-04/38
			North Coates	04/38-03/39
145 Sqn	Blenheim IF	SO	Croydon	11/39-04/40
162 Sqn	Blenheim IV		Shallufa, Egypt	03/42-04/42
			Bilberis	04/42-07/42
	Blenheim V		Bilberis	07/42-04/43
			Benina	04/43-08/43
			LG91	08/43-03/44
173 Sqn[1]	Blenheim IV		Heliopolis, Egypt	07/42-02/44
203 Sqn	Blenheim I, IV		Sheikh Othman, Aden	03/40-05/40
			Khormaksar, Aden	05/40-04/41
			Kabrit, Egypt	04/41-04/41
			Heraklion, Greece	04/41-04/41
			Kabrit, Egypt	04/41-06/41
			LG101, N Africa	06/41-11/42
211 Sqn	Blenheim I	(LJ)	Ismailia	05/39-08/39
		UQ	El Daba	08/39-06/40

RAF BLENHEIM SQUADRONS

Unit	Version	Code	Base(s)	Dates
			Qotafiya	06/40-11/40
			Ismailia	11/40-11/40
			Menidi, Greece	11/40-02/41
			Paramythia, Greece	02/41-04/41
			Agrinion, Greece	04/41-04/41
			Menidi, Greece	04/41-04/41
			Heraklion, Greece	04/41-04/41
			Heliopolis, Egypt	04/41-04/41
			Ramleh, Palestine	04/41-04/41
			Lydda, Palestine	04/41-05/41
			Aqir, Palestine	05/41-06/41
	Blenheim IV		Heliopolis, Egypt	06/41-06/41
			Wadi Gazouza, Sudan	06/41-12/41
			Palembang, Sumatra	01/42-02/42
			Kalidjati, West Java	02/42-02/42
212 Sqn	Blenheim IV		Heston	02/40-06/40
218 Sqn	Blenheim IV	HA	Oakington	07/40-11/40
219 Sqn	Blenheim IF	FK	Catterick	10/39-10/40
			Redhill	10/40-12/40
222 Sqn	Blenheim IF	ZD	Duxford	11/39-03/40
223 Sqn	Blenheim I		Shandur, Egypt	05/41-01/42
Det			Fuka, Egypt	10/41-12/41
Det			El Gubbi, Libya	12/41-01/42
226 Sqn	Blenheim IV	MQ	Sydenham	02/41-05/41
			Wattisham	05/41-11/41
229 Sqn	Blenheim IF	RE	Digby	11/39-03/40
234 Sqn	Blenheim IF		Leconfield	11/39-03/40
235 Sqn	Blenheim IF, IVF	LA	North Coates	02/40-04/40
			Bircham Newton	04/40-05/40
	Blenheim IVF		Detling	05/40-06/40
			Bircham Newton	06/40-06/41
			Dyce	06/41-12/41
236 Sqn	Blenheim IF	FA	Martlesham Heath	12/39-02/40
			North Coates	02/40-04/40
			Speke	04/40-05/40
			Filton	05/40-06/40
	Blenheim IF, IVF		Middle Wallop	06/40-07/40
	Blenheim IVF		Thorney Island	07/40-08/40
			St Eval	08/40-03/41
			Carew Cheriton	03/41-02/42
			Wattisham	02/42-03/42
242 Sqn	Blenheim IF	(LE)	Church Fenton	12/39-12/39
244 Sqn	Blenheim IV		Shaibah, Iraq	04/42-01/43
Det			Sharjah	04/42-05/42
	Blenheim V		Shaibah, Iraq	10/42-03/44
			Masirah, Muscat	03/44-04/44
245 Sqn	Blenheim IF	DX	Leconfield	11/39-03/40
248 Sqn	Blenheim IF	WR	Hendon	12/39-02/40
	Blenheim IVF		North Coates	02/40-04/40
			Thorney Island	04/40-04/40
			Gosport	04/40-05/40
			Dyce	05/40-07/40
			Sumburgh	07/40-01/41
			Dyce	01/41-06/41
			Bircham Newton	06/41-07/41
252 Sqn[3]	Blenheim IF, IVF	PN	Chivenor	12/40-04/41
254 Sqn	Blenheim IF		Stradishall	11/39-12/39
			Sutton Bridge	12/39-01/40
			Bircham Newton	01/40-03/40
	Blenheim IVF	QY	Bircham Newton	03/40-04/40

RAF BLENHEIM SQUADRONS

Unit	Version	Code	Base(s)	Dates
			Hatston	04/40-05/40
			Sumburgh	05/40-07/40
			Dyce	07/40-01/41
			Sumburgh	01/41-05/41
			Aldergrove	05/41-12/41
			Dyce	12/41-02/42
			Carew Cheriton	02/42-07/42
267 Sqn[1]	Blenheim I, IV	KW	Heliopolis, Egypt	08/40-08/42
			Bilbeis	08/42-01/43
			Marble Arch	01/43-01/43
			Cairo West, Egypt	01/43-11/43
			Bari, Italy	11/43-02/45
272 Sqn	Blenheim IVF	XK	Aldergrove	11/40-04/41
285 Sqn	Blenheim I	VG	Wrexham	12/41-03/42
287 Sqn	Blenheim IV	KZ	Croydon	11/41-03/42
288 Sqn	Blenheim IV	RP	Digby	11/41-12/41
289 Sqn	Blenheim IV	YE	Kirknewton	11/41-01/42
500 Sqn	Blenheim IV	MK	Detling	04/41-05/41
			Bircham Newton	05/41-11/41
516 Sqn	Blenheim IV		Dundonald	05/43-12/44
521 Sqn	Blenheim IV		Bircham Newton	08/42-03/43
526 Sqn	Blenheim IV	MD	Inverness	06/43-05/45
527 Sqn	Blenheim IV	WN	Castle Camps	06/43-02/44
			Snailwell	02/44-04/44
			Digby	04/44-05/45
528 Sqn	Blenheim IV		Filton	06/43-05/44
			Digby	05/44-09/44
600 Sqn	Blenheim IF	MV	Hendon	01/39-08/39
		BQ	Northolt	08/39-10/39
			Hornchurch	10/39-10/39
			Rochford	10/39-10/39
			Hornchurch	10/39-11/39
	Blenheim IF, IVF		Hornchurch	11/39-12/39
			Manston	12/39-03/40
	Blenheim IF		Manston	04/40-05/40
			Northolt	05/40-06/40
			Manston	06/40-08/40
			Hornchurch	08/40-09/40
			Redhill	09/40-10/40
			Catterick	10/40-02/41
601 Sqn	Blenheim IF	YN	Hendon	1/39-09/39
		UF	Biggin Hill	09/39-12/39
			Tangmere	12/39-03/40
604 Sqn	Blenheim IF	WQ	Hendon	01/39-09/39
		NG	North Weald	09/39-01/40
			Northolt	01/40-05/40
			Manston	05/40-07/40
			Gravesend	07/40-07/40
			Middle Wallop	07/40-01/41
608 Sqn	Blenheim IV	UL	Thornaby	03/41-07/41
614 Sqn	Blenheim IV	LJ	Macmerry	07/41-09/41
			Odiham	09/41-10/41
			Macmerry	10/41-08/42
	Blenheim V		Odiham	08/42-11/42
			Blida, Algeria	11/42-12/42
			Canrobert, Algeria	12/42-02/43
			Oulmere, Algeria	02/43-05/43
			Tafaraoui, Algeria	05/43-08/43
			Borizzo, Sicily	08/43-02/44

Notes: [1] Communications squadrons, with small numbers of Blenheims used among a large variety of other types; [2] Night reconnaissance unit, primarily flying Supermarine Spitfire IVs and XIs; [3] Equipped with Bristol Beaufighters from December 1940, although part of unit retained Blenheims

OPERATIONAL TRAINING UNITS

The role of Operational Training Units (OTU) was to train aircrews with the skills they would require to joining a frontline squadron. The expansion of the RAF in the late 1930s and the role the Blenheim played in it meant that the aircraft was extensively used by such units, as fresh personnel arrived from the schools they had learnt their trade at to form crews. In most cases, the OTU would operate the type they were destined to fly in the squadrons.

Individual OTUs operated the largest fleets of Blenheims of any RAF units. No.13 OTU was created in 6 Group, from the 2 Group Pool of 104 and 108 Squadrons, to train Blenheim light day bomber crews. It had an establishment of 24 (plus eight reserve) Blenheim IVs, and 12 plus four dual-control Mk Is in May 1940. By August 1941, this had increased to 48 Blenheims. By the time the last Blenheims left the unit in April 1944, around 265 of the aircraft had passed through the OTU.

Most OTUs – especially early in the war – operated aircraft handed down from the frontline squadrons, some of which had already seen considerable use. Flown by pilots who had little if any experience flying Blenheims, the accident rate was high.

In addition to the units listed in the table, which were primarily equipped with Blenheims, the aircraft was also flown in smaller numbers by 12 OTU at Benson; 15 OTU Harwell; 18 OTU Hucknall and Bramcote; 20 OTU Lossiemouth; 52 OTU Debden and Aston Down; 55 OTU Ashton Down; 56 OTU Sutton Bridge; 63 OTU Honiley; 71 OTU Ismailia, Egypt; 73 OTU Sheik Othman, Aden; 108 OTU Wymeswold; and 152 (Bomber) OTU at Peshawar in India.

A line-up of well-used Blenheim Is of 9 (Pilots) Advanced Flying School at Spitalgate (Grantham until 1942). Pre-war vintage L1158 '10' was originally delivered to 61 Squadron and later served with 144 Squadron, 5 Bombing and Gunnery School and the Air Transport Auxiliary before joining the unit. It was struck off charge in October 1943.

No. 8 Squadron was among the early overseas operators of the Blenheim I, receiving its initial examples at Khormaksar in Aden in April 1939. Aden was an important stop-over for shipping heading to the Far East. The squadron received Blenheim IVs in August 1941 and Mk Vs in September 1942, which it flew alongside its Mk Is until the start of 1944. Avro-built Blenheim I L6655 later went to 211 Squadron.

Typical of the many Blenheim Vs sent to North Africa, EH403 was assigned to 301 Ferry Training Unit and prepared for delivery by 1 Overseas Aircraft Despatch Unit at Portreath, Cornwall.

OPERATIONAL TRAINING UNITS WITH BLENHEIMS

Unit	Base(s)	Dates	Notes/Command
1 (Coastal) OTU	Silloth	04/40-08/40	CC
	Prestwick	08/40-11/40	'D' Flight
2 (Coastal) OTU	Catfoss	10/40-?/42	CC
3 (Coastal) OTU	Chivenor	11/40-?/?	CC
5 OTU	Aston Down	03/40-11/40	FC
6 (Coastal) OTU	Andover	06/41-07/41	CC
13 OTU	Bicester[1]	04/40-04/44	BC
17 OTU	Upwood	04/40-04/43	BC
42 OTU	Andover[2]	07/41-10/42	AAC
51 OTU	Debden	07/41-08/41	FC
	Cranfield	08/41-?/43	
54 OTU	Church Fenton	11/40-05/42	FC
	Charterhill	05/42-?/43	
60 OTU	Leconfield	04/41-06/41	FC
	East Fortune	10/41-11/42	
70 OTU	Ismailia, Egypt	12/40-07/41	'A' Flight, ME
	Nakuru, Kenya	07/41-05/43	
72 OTU	Wadi Gazouza, Sudan	11/41-04/42	ME
	Nanyuki, Kenya	04/42-05/43	
75 OTU	Gianaclis, Egypt	03/43-06/45	ME
79 OTU	Nicosia, Cyprus	04/44-07/45	ME
132 (Coastal) OTU	East Fortune	11/42-07/43	CC

Notes: [1] Finmere and Hinton-in-the-Hedges used as satellites; [2] Thruxton used as satellite July 1941 to October 1942. **Code:** AAC = Army Co-operation Command, BC = Bomber Command, CC = Coastal Command, FC = Fighter Command and ME = Middle East

TARGET PROVISION

As the Blenheim became surplus to the home-based front line squadrons, some aircraft were handed over to Anti-Aircraft Co-operation Units (AACU). The role of AACUs was to provide target facilities for ground-based defences and the Blenheim served alongside other types in them. Blenheims also acted as targets for Fighter Command's single seaters within Anti-Aircraft Co-operation Flights assigned to 9, 10, 11, 12 and 13 Groups. Four of the units, those of 9, 11, 12 and 13 Groups, became 285, 287, 288 and 289 Squadrons in November/December 1941, flying Airspeed Oxfords, Boulton Paul Defiants, Hawker Hurricanes, Lockheed Hudsons and Westland Lysanders, as well as Blenheims.

ANTI-AIRCRAFT CO-OPERATION UNITS WITH BLENHEIMS

Unit	Base(s)	Notes
1 Anti-Aircraft Co-operation Unit	Farnborough	various flights
6 Anti-Aircraft Co-operation Unit	Ringway	various dets
7 Anti-Aircraft Co-operation Unit	Castle Bromwich	various dets
8 Anti-Aircraft Co-operation Unit	Filton, Old Sarum, Cardiff	various dets
22 Anti-Aircraft Co-operation Unit	Drigh Road, India	to Indian AF 03/43
1 Coastal Artillery Co-operation Flt	Thorney Island, Detling	Unit 06/37-05/40

COMMUNICATIONS

Many communication (comms) flights assigned to various command organisations included examples of the Blenheim within their varied fleets. Most Blenheims with such units operated around the Mediterranean, where examples of the aircraft were readily available.

GETTING TO THE FRONT

As production got under way, Blenheims needed to be ferried from the factories to the squadrons, a task assigned to the Air Transport Auxiliary. As World War Two progressed and other regions of the world became theatres of war, a much larger organisation was established to deliver replacement aircraft to the squadrons. In the case of the Blenheim, this was primarily to North Africa and the Middle East. Units were established to prepare both the aircraft and train crews for the task, while the actual delivery flights were aided by Ferry Control units, which supported the various sites along which aircraft travelled. Most ferry units did not operate Blenheims; instead, the aircraft passed through them on their way to end users.

WEATHER REPORTS

Blenheims served with several Meteorological Flights from bases in the British Isles, Ceylon and India, and from Ikeja in West Africa (Nigeria). In all cases the aircraft served alongside other types. No.1401 (Meteorological) Flight became 521 Squadron in August 1942, flying Blenheim IVs (until March 1943) as well as de Havilland Mosquito IVs, Gloster Gladiator IIs, Lockheed Hudson IIIs and Supermarine Spitfire Vs.

A line-up of 21 Squadron Blenheim Is, including L1345, L1350 and L1363, at Eastchurch, Kent, where it received the aircraft in August 1938. The squadron moved to Watton, Norfolk, in March 1939, while L1345 was supplied to Finland in February 1940.

Blenheim IVs with the code 'LW' are understood to have served with the calibration flights of 74, 75 and 76 (Signals) Wings. The wings were formed within 60 Group in February 1941 out of Radio Servicing Sections, usually with an establishment of four Blenheims and a Hornet Moth.

METEOROLOGICAL FLIGHTS WITH BLENHEIMS

Unit	Base(s)	Notes
401/1401 Met Flight	Bircham Newton	
	Manston, Docking	to 521 Sqn
402/1402 Met Flight	Aldergrove	
4003/1403 Met Flight	Bircham Newton	
4004/1404 Met Flight	St Eval	
4005/1405 Met Flight	Aldergrove	
1300 Meteorological Flight	Alipore, India	
	Baigachi, Alipore	
1301 Meteorological Flight	Delhi and Nagpur, India	
1302 Meteorological Flight	Yelahanka & St Thomas Mount	
1303 Meteorological Flight	Ratmalana, Ceylon	
1561 Meteorological Flight	Ikeja, West Africa	

RECONNAISSANCE

Blenheims were used for long-range photographic reconnaissance from Britain by several squadrons and independent units, although by 1940 its performance was not conducive to surviving deep penetrations of enemy-occupied airspace. Overseas, 1434 Flight did perform reconnaissance missions, flying over Turkish border positions from the Middle East in the second quarter of 1942 in case of a possible German advance through the country. A survey of the Levant, Syria and Iran was undertaken by 1438 Flight.

RECONNAISSANCE UNITS WITH BLENHEIMS

Unit	Base(s)	Notes
2 Camouflage Unit	Heston	to PDU
431 Flight	Luqa, Malta	to 69 Sqn
1416 (Reconnaissance) Flight	Hendon, Benson	to 140 Sqn
1434 (Photographic Survey) Flt	Habbaniyah, Rayak, Tehran, Aleppo	
1438 (Strategic Reconnaissance) Flt	Hadera, Alpeep, Tehran, Mosul	
1439 (Strategic Reconnaissance) Flt	Helwan, Egypt	
Photographic Development Unit (PRU)	Heston	ex 2 CU
1 PRU	Benson	
3 PRU	Oakington, Benson	

CALIBRATING THE RADARS

One of the Blenheim's least known roles was the calibration of radars. Highly simplified, it helped make sure that the 'blips' on the screens of the operators on the ground accurately indicated the height, speed and direction of the target. Blenheims were used for this role alongside a mixed bag of other, largely obsolete types.

Each Signals Wing in Britain initially had its own calibration flight, but in June 1943 they were amalgamated into numbered squadrons, which flew a diverse group of aircraft (from Hawker Hurricanes to de Havilland Hornet Moths). Overseas, ad hoc units were formalised as flights.

RADAR CALIBRATION UNITS WITH BLENHEIMS

Unit	Base(s)	Notes
Bengal Calibration Flight	Amarda Road, Salbani, Alipore	to 1583 Flt
1 Calibration Flight	Speke	
1578 Calibration Flight	Blida, Reghaia	
1579 Calibration Flight	Ratmalana, Ceylon	
1580 Calibration Flight	Yelahanka, Cholavrium	
1581 Calibration Flight	Alipore, India	
1582 Calibration Flight	Kumbhirgram, Tuihal, SilcharWest, Kumbhirgram, Imphal, Kalemyo, Monywa, Meiktila, Mingaladon, Ramree, Alipore, Dalbhumgarh	

RADAR CALIBRATION UNITS WITH BLENHEIMS

Unit	Base(s)	Notes
1583 Calibration Flight	Chittagong, Diohazari, Chittagong, Maubyn, Akyab West, Sambre, Trichinopoly	
Radar Direction Finding Calibration Flight	Blida, Tunisia	
70 (Signals) Wing	Inverness	to 526 Sqn
71 (Signals) Wing	Dyce	to 526 Sqn
72 (Signals) Wing	Turnhouse	to 526 Sqn
73 (Signals) Wing	Church Fenton	to 1 Cal Flt
74 (Signals) Wing	Duxford	to 527 Sqn
75 (Signals) Wing	Biggin Hill	to 527 Sqn
76 (Signals) Wing	Filton	to 528 Sqn
77 (Signals) Wing	Speke	to 1 Cal Flt
78 (Signals) Wing	Exeter	to 528 Sqn
79 (Signals) Wing	Long Kesh	to 1 Cal Flt

TRAINING

As the Blenheim was replaced in frontline squadrons, many were issued to training units in Britain, India and the Middle East. In addition to the operational training units (*see above*), the aircraft was operated by several of the main flying training units for the instruction of pilots, observers (navigators) and gunners, while numerous small units used the aircraft for check flights or conversion training overseas. At least four Beam Approach Training Flights had Blenheims, alongside other types, to train bomber pilots how to use landing aids.

Blenheims were also operated as support aircraft (ie, not the primary equipment) of many units, including: 2 Air Gunners School at Dalcross; 3 Air Observers School at Bobbington (Halfpenny Green); 2 (Observers) Advanced Flying Unit at Millom; 2 and 7 Bombing and Gunnery Schools (B&GS) at Millom and Stormy Down, respectively; Central Flying School at Upavon, Boscombe Down and Hullavington, which became the Empire Central Flying School at the last airfield mentioned; 1 Electrical & Wireless School at Cranwell; 9 Flying Training School; Mosquito Training Unit and 1655 (Mosquito) Conversion/Training Unit at Horsham St Faith (and the latter later at Marham); RAF College at Cranwell; RAF College Refresher Flight at Wellingore; 2, 4 and 6 Radio Schools; School of Flying Control; and 1 and 3 Schools of General Reconnaissance.

TRAINING UNITS WITH BLENHEIMS

Unit	Base(s)	Notes
Aden Command Training Flight	Sheikh Othman, Khormaksar, Aden	
1 Air Armament School	Manby	
Air Firing Training Unit	Amarda Road, India	
Aircrew Transit Pool	Poona, India	ex 3 RFU
1 Air Gunners School	Pembrey	
1 Air Gunnery School (India)	Bairagah, India	
Air Landing School (India)	Willingdon, India	
Air Navigation School	Willingdon, India	
1 Air Observers School	Wigtown	
5 Air Observers School	Jurby	
9 Air Observers School	Penrhos	to 9 (O)AFU
9 (Observers) Advanced Flying Unit	Penrhos	ex 9 AOS
12 (Pilots) Advanced Flying Unit	Grantham/Spitalgate	
ATA (Training) Ferry Pool	White Waltham, Hawarden	to ATA School
1506 Beam Approach Training Flt (BATF)	Waddington, Fulbeck	ex 6 BATF
1507 BATF	Finningley, Cottesmore	ex 7 BATF
1508 BATF	Watton, Horsham St Faith, Swanton Morley	ex 8 BATF

TRAINING UNITS WITH BLENHEIMS

Unit	Base(s)	Notes
1526 BATF	Andover, Thruxton	ex 26 BATF
Blenheim Conversion Flight	Hendon	
Blenheim Flight	Thruxton, Odiham	
Blenheim Refresher Unit	Peshawar and Poona	
5 B&GS	Jurby	
9 B&GS	Penrhos	
10 B&GS	Warmwell, Dumfries	
Central Gunnery School	Warmwell, Chelveston, Sutton Bridge	
Check & Conversion Flt	Mauripur, India	
1672 (Mosquito) Conversion Unit	Yelahanka, India	
Fighter Pilots Practice Flight	Setif, Algeria	
10 Flying Training School	Ternhill	
General Reconnaissance and Anti-Radar Flight	Takoradi	
Greek Training Flight	Aqir, Palestine	
1572 Ground Gunnery (GG) Flight	St Thomas Mount, India	
1573 GG Flight	Amarda Road, India	
2 Group Training Flight		
2 Group Target Towing Flight	West Raynham	to 1482 (TT&G) Flt
1483 (TT & Gunnery Co-op) Flt	Newmarket	1483 (B) Gunnery Flt
I (Middle East) Check & Conversion Flt	Bilbeis, Egypt	
1 Middle East Training School (METS)	El Ballah, Egypt	to (ME) Central Gunnery School
3 METS	Amman, Transjordan	
5 METS	Shallufa, Egypt	
Pilot Training Unit & Reinforcement Pool	Abu Sueir, Egypt	to R&RP
3 Radio School	Prestwick	ex AI/ASV School
3 RDF School	Carew Cheriton	
3 Refresher Flying Unit	Poona, Bairagarh	ex Aircrew Transit Pool
Reinforcement and Reserve Pool	Ismailia, Egypt	ex PTU&RP, to TU&RP
17 Service Flying Training School	Cranwell, Spitalgate	
School of Army Co-operation (SoAC)	Old Sarum	1 SoAC
2 SoAC	Andover	
3 Signals School (India)	Hakimpet, India	
Training Unit & Reserve Pool	Ismailia, Egypt	ex R&RP

FLEET AIR ARM

It is often overlooked that the Fleet Air Arm (FAA) of the Royal Navy operated a significant number of Blenheims during the war. The Blenheim joined the Navy because it was suitable for the tasks required, was readily available and was not required for any more pressing roles.

At least 16 Mk Is and 72 Mk IVs were transferred from RAF stocks. Initial examples were received in early 1941, with the first, L1210, delivered that January. No. 771 Squadron was the initial FAA squadron to fly Blenheim Is, with Mk IVs starting to be used during 1943. All served in second line units in a number of roles, although they can be divided into fleet requirements units, trials and testing units and training squadrons. Blenheims were never the sole equipment of any FAA squadron and in nearly all cases only small numbers – possibly just one in some – served with each unit.

Six Fleet Requirements Units (FRU) operated Blenheims. Their task was to support the Royal Navy's warships, with the provision of targets for air defence gunnery practise a primary role, although communications was also provided. Blenheims were used by FRUs alongside a wide mix of other aircraft, including the Boulton Paul Defiant and Miles Martinet TT.1s target-tugs, Grumman Martlet/Wildcat and Hawker Hurricane single-seat fighters, and Avro Anson and Airspeed Oxford communication aircraft. In most cases, only small numbers of Blenheims were flown by the units.

No. 787 Squadron was the Naval Air Fighting Development Unit (NAFDU), attached to the RAF's Air Fighting Development Unit at Duxford, Cambridgeshire. As such, it tested FAA fighters, including against examples of captured Axis aircraft. A handful of Blenheims were operated, including Mk I L6674 and Mk IV R3888.

Although Blenheims served with several FAA training units, in most cases it was in small numbers and the aircraft was never the primary equipment of a squadron. No. 748 Squadron had become 10 Naval Operational Training Unit (OTU) by May 1943, with Hawker Sea and 'land' Hurricanes, Grumman Martlets and Supermarine Spitfires. In April 1943, 759 Squadron became the Advanced Flying School component of 1 Naval Air Fighter School (NAFS), primarily equipped with Sea Hurricanes, Fairey Fulmars and Miles Masters, gaining Supermarine Seafires from August 1943. A Conversion Course Unit (CCU), one of 780 Squadron's tasks was to convert pilots trained on biplanes to the Fairey Barracuda, until moving from Lee-on-Solent in Hampshire to Charlton Horethorne, Somerset, when it became a Pilot Training Squadron. No. 798 Squadron ran the Advanced Conversion Course (ACC), equipped with Fulmars and Barracudas, Bristol Beaufighters and Beauforts, as well as Blenheims, plus Masters, de Havilland Tiger Moths and Airspeed Oxfords. Part of the squadron was detached to form the core of 762 Squadron at Yeovilton, Somerset, on March 15, 1944, as the Two Engine Conversion Unit, moving at the end of the month to Dale in Haverfordwest.

The Blenheim continued to serve within the Fleet Air Arm until the end of the war. Within the training units it was replaced by more modern twins, typically de Havilland Mosquitoes, but continued to fly with some of the FRUs until the end of hostilities. All of the aircraft had been withdrawn by the end of 1945.

FAA BLENHEIM SQUADRONS WITH BLENHEIMS

Unit	Aircraft	Base	Date	Role
748 Squadron	Blenheim IV	Chivenor[1]	11/43-02/44	10 NOTU
		Henstridge	02/44-03/44	
759 Squadron	Blenheim IV	Yeovilton[2]	07/43-09/44	1 NAFS
762 Squadron	Blenheim IV	Yeovilton	03/44-03/44	
		Dale	03/44-?/45	
770 Squadron	Blenheim I	Crail	03/42-06/42	FRU
	Blenheim IV	Dunino	03/44-07/44	
		Drem	07/44-06/45	
771 Squadron	Blenheim I	Donibristle	04/41-07/42	FRU
		Twatt	07/42-06/43	
	Blenheim IV	Twatt	04/44-05/45	
772 Squadron	Blenheim IV	Ayr	03/44-01/45	FRU
		Ronaldsway[3]	01/45-04/45	
775 Squadron	Blenheim IV	North Front	03/45-08/45	FRU
		Dhekelia, Cyprus	08/45	
776 Squadron	Blenheim IV	Speke[4]	01/44-04/45	FRU
	Blenheim I, IV	Speke	04/44	
780 Squadron	Blenheim I	Lee-on-Solent	06/43-10/43	CCU
		Charlton Horethorne	10/43-12/43	
787 Squadron	Blenheim I	Duxford	10/42-03/43	NAFDU
	Blenheim I, IV	Wittering	03/43-02/44	
	Blenheim IV	Wittering	02/44-01/45	
		Tangmere	01/45-05/45	
788 Squadron	Blenheim IV	Mombasa, Kenya	06/42-?/42	FRU
798 Squadron	Blenheim IV	Lee-on-Solent	10/43-03/44	ACS

Notes: [1] B Flight at Yeovilton, Somerset, September 1943 to February 1944; [2] Detachment (as the Naval Air Firing Unit) at Angle, Pembrokeshire, July to November 1943; [3] B Flight of 772 Squadron; [4] detachments at Millom and Walney Island. See main text for role decode

Blenheims of Fighter Command

Jon Lake outlines Fighter Command's use of the Blenheim by day and night.

Conversion of Blenheim I bombers into fighters offered a chance to convert Hawker Demon squadrons to a modern, faster monoplane fighter. In November 1938, the decision was taken to re-equip 23, 29, 64 and 25 Squadrons (in that order) with 19 Blenheims each. Almost immediately, it was also decided that 600, 601 and 604 Squadrons would also re-equip with Blenheims. Other squadrons received

the aircraft as interim equipment, pending receipt of Hawker Hurricanes or Supermarine Spitfires.

The fighter Blenheim was also well-suited to long-range intruder missions, although its poor performance in comparison to single-seat fighters meant missions usually had to be undertaken in the dark. However, in the early months of the war, Blenheim intruders operated successfully by both day and night.

Standard, unconverted Mk Is in the maintenance units began to be allocated to fighter squadrons in December 1938

and deliveries began later the same month. Although a hastily-modified fighter conversion was already flying at Martlesham Heath in Suffolk, a full trial conversion using L1512 was not started until January 26, 1939. The original 150 gun packs for Fighter Command's Blenheims were fitted at Aircraft Storage Units and frontline stations by service personnel and contractors' working parties.

Many more Blenheim gun packs were produced under subsequent production contracts, but most of these were fitted to Blenheim IVs as Mk IVFs, mainly for Coastal Command. A handful of Mk VIFs were

A flight of four Blenheim IFs of 601 Squadron wearing the 'YN' codes that were replaced by 'UF' when war was declared. The four gun ventral pack of the variant is clearly visible under the bomb bay.

No. 600 Squadron was one of three Auxiliary Air Force units that was re-equipped with Blenheim IFs and assigned to Fighter Command.

operated by Fighter Command, most notably by 68 Squadron. But even within Fighter Command, Blenheim fighters were used as much for shipping protection, convoy escort and intruder duties as for air defence.

RADAR

Although the Mk IF was fully equipped for night flying, the type was not initially seen as a dedicated night fighter, as reflections in the heavily glazed nose made it difficult to fly in the dark. When an aircraft was needed to train airborne radar operators from Bawdsey, Suffolk, a Blenheim was detached to Martlesham Heath and it proved sufficiently capacious to carry the bulky new AI radar equipment.

The success of this first radar-equipped Blenheim led to the conversion of others. Experimental airborne radar sets were first flown in 1937 and by the end of 1938 contracts had been placed for production examples. It became increasingly clear that an AI-equipped fighter should have two engines and a crew of two. In the absence of alternatives, the choice came down to the Blenheim IF. On July 17, 1939, a secret minute called for 12 Mk IFs to be fitted with radar, so equipment was rushed to the Royal Aircraft Establishment (RAE) at Farnborough, Hampshire, from the Pye and Metrovick factories. The radar was installed there allowing deliveries of AI-equipped Blenheims to 52 Squadron to begin at the end of July. Around 15 AI-equipped aircraft were on charge by the time war was declared.

In November 1939, 600 Squadron received three AI-equipped Blenheim IFs, and these equipped a detached flight at Manston, Kent, commanded by Squadron Leader (later Air Marshal) Walter Pretty, who had previously commanded one of the first Chain Home Low radar stations. This unit in turn formed the basis for the Fighter Interception Unit (FIU) at Tangmere, West Sussex, which operated Blenheims carrying a succession of AI radar versions and helped pioneer radar night-fighting tactics and techniques, while other units began to re-equip.

LONG-RANGE SORTIES

Despite these developments, Fighter Command's Mk IFs remained primarily dedicated to convoy protection and long-range fighter-bomber duties. On the day that war began, 29 and 604 Squadrons both despatched six Blenheim IFs over the North Sea to search for inbound German raiders, but found none. On November 28, six Mk IFs of 25 and 601 Squadrons flew 250 miles (402km) across the North Sea and strafed the Luftwaffe seaplane base at Borkum. All returned safely.

The first radar-directed kill by a Blenheim was not made by a squadron aircraft. Instead, an aircraft assigned to calibrate the Chain Home radar station at Bawdsey and later fitted with an experimental radar installation, was vectored on to a Heinkel He 111 by Wing Commander W R Farnes at Bawdsey on the morning of February 5, 1940. Flight Lieutenant Christopher D S 'Blood Orange' Smith attacked the enemy aircraft, guided by Farnes and his own radar man, Aircraftman 1st Class A W Newton, but made the mistake of following it down to confirm the kill. Before the He 111 hit the sea its gunner opened fire, hitting Smith in the chest and upper arm. He managed to make a forced landing at Martlesham Heath and subsequently recovered from his injuries, but Blenheim IVF P4834 burned out on the airfield. Radar – and especially AI radar – was still in its infancy, and it would be some time before frontline radar-equipped aircraft were able to score kills.

BATTLE FOR FRANCE

The start of the Blitzkrieg in the West saw Fighter Command Blenheims committed once again. On May 10, Squadron Leader Anderson of 600 Squadron engaged several He 111s at 0340hrs, returning to crash-land at Manston. Later that morning, six 600 Squadron Blenheim IFs were sent to attack German transport aircraft as they unloaded at Waalhaven. Five were shot down by Messerschmitt Bf 110s, but one flown by Flying Officer Norman Hayes returned to base after destroying a Junkers Ju 52 on the ground and another in the air, despite having received damage from the Bf 110s. He also attacked the Messerschmitts, breaking up their formation. Hayes and his gunner, Corporal G H Holmes, were awarded a DFC and a DFM, respectively, for their actions. Another crew member survived a forced landing, while the gunner and observer in the lead aircraft also escaped with their lives.

Less than two hours later, XV Squadron with Blenheim bombers also attacked Waalhaven, causing further damage. After lunch 600 Squadron sent out four more Blenheims, damaging a He 111 before returning to base, having been relieved on patrol by 25 Squadron. No. 604 Squadron was also operational on the 10th, escorting Wattisham Wing Blenheims as they bombed Ju 52s unloading at Waalhaven and on beaches north of the Hague. Its

A Blenheim IF of 25 Squadron. The unit was based at Hawkridge, Kent, until August 1939 when it moved Northolt near London and then Filton outside Bristol at the start of the war. Between January and June 1940, it was based at North Weald, Essex.

crews claimed four Ju 52s destroyed and three damaged, but lost an aircraft, with the crew walking 'home' after setting fire to their Blenheim.

On May 12, three Blenheim fighters of 235 Squadron were engaged by Bf 109s and Bf 110s while covering the evacuation of the Dutch Queen by Royal Navy destroyers and British Royal Marines. Two Blenheims were shot down, but they downed a Bf 109 and a Bf 110.

Blenheims of 235, 248 and 254 Squadrons – still Fighter Command units, although they were soon to transfer to Coastal Command – were in action the next day. No. 600 Squadron returned to Hendon in north London on May 15, after suffering heavy losses, and was replaced at Manston by 604 Squadron. It soon became clear that the Blenheim IF was too vulnerable for ground strafing by day, so the squadrons began switching to night intruder operations and night-fighter patrols. Before France fell, Blenheim night-fighter operations accounted for a He 111, claimed as a probable by Flying Officer Hunter of 604 Squadron, on May 18.

NIGHT OPERATIONS

When the Luftwaffe switched to night attacks during the Battle of Britain, the Blenheim fighter was one of the only countermeasures available to Fighter Command. Even before radar had been fitted to many aircraft, Blenheims began their night-time vigil, relying on the Mk 1 eyeball and search-lights, with generally frustrating results, although there were some successes.

On the night of June 18/19, for example, seven 23 Squadron Blenheims (and one from 29) found a 70-strong raid by He 111s. As soon as they fired, the Blenheims gave away their own position, making them vulnerable to heavy counter-fire, but three scored victories. Unfortunately, the 29 Squadron Blenheim was

forced to ditch after being hit by fire from its victim, its pilot drowning, while another was also shot down.

On July 19, Fight Lieutenant David Clackson of 600 Squadron found an enemy aircraft 'blip' on his radar set, but was unable to engage. The same squadron's Pilot Officer 'Archie' McNeil Boyd engaged Heinkel 59s on July 20 and 25, albeit without success. Finally, on the night of July 22/23, the FIU scored its first kill using radar, the honour falling to Flying Officer G Ashfield, his gunner Pilot Officer G Moris and radar operator Sergeant R H Leyland, flying a Blenheim with AI.IV. Their victim was an inbound Dornier Do 17Z of 2./KG 3, which fell into the Channel. This marked the beginning of a brief spell of success for radar-equipped Blenheims. They also continued to operate by day, too.

AUGUST AND SEPTEMBER 1940

On August 1, two Blenheims of 604 Squadron, escorted by three 152 Squadron Spitfires, attacked ships and an He 59 on the sea 30 miles (48km) off the French coast; they all fought their way back, despite the intervention of six Bf 109s. On September 1, the squadron flew a similar sortie, during which a Do 18 under tow by E-boats was attacked.

In the wake of a daylight raid against Driffield and Scarborough on August 15, 12 Blenheims of 219 Squadron engaged enemy bombers without success. One pilot, Sergeant Dube, was wounded, but was assisted making a wheels-up landing at Driffield by his gunner, Sergeant Bannister. Both men were awarded the DFM.

By August 1940, Manston was home to the FIU and 600 Squadron. The airfield

Most Fighter Command Blenheim IFs were painted black for the night-fighting role, although many were not equipped with AI sets and the crews had to rely on searchlights and their own vision to find enemy aircraft.

Although closely associated with the night-fighter role and the introduction of airborne radar, Fighter Command's Blenheim IFs primarily operated during the day in the early years of the war, until its vulnerability to enemy fighters became clear.

was heavily bombed and strafed on the 12th, 14th, 16th and 20th of the month. The last raid (by ten Bf 109s) was opposed by three 600 Squadron Blenheim IFs, although their efforts were frustrated by wild firing from the airfield's anti-aircraft Bofors guns.

KG 35 lost a He 111 to Pilot Officer R A Rhodes and Sergeant Gregory of 29 Squadron on the night of August 17/18. They picked up the intruder near Chester and followed it to Spurn Head, where they engaged the bomber and sent it spinning into the sea off Cromer. On August 20/21, Flight Lieutenant J Adam and Pilot Officer Watson of 29 Sqn downed another raider off the Isle of Wight, catching the aircraft only when it circled to get its bearings. Three days later, 29 Squadron's Flight Lieutenant 'Bob' Braham (who was to become the RAF's leading night-fighter ace) found a He 111P of III./KG 5 in Hull's searchlights while flying Blenheim IF L1463. The two aircraft exchanged fire and searchlight crews later reported seeing the German aircraft burning on the sea.

On September 4, Pilot Officer Rofe of 25 Squadron attacked three night raiders, but his aircraft was damaged by friendly anti-aircraft fire before he could conclude the engagement successfully. His squadron-mate, Pilot Officer M Herrick, had more success early the next morning, despatching a 1./KG 1 He 111 near Bentwaters and claiming one more as a possible. Herrick downed another He 111 near Sheering on September 14, making him the most successful Blenheim fighter pilot with two kills and a possible. No. 600 Sqn downed a Ju 88 off Bexhill on September 15/16, which was credited to its most successful Blenheim pilot, Flight Lieutenant C Pritchard.

At the end of the Battle of Britain, the RAF had six Blenheim units (23, 25, 29, 219, 600 and 604), two Boulton Paul Defiant squadrons and one Hurricane unit to counter the Luftwaffe's night blitz. Expansion of the night-fighter force was completed using Hurricanes as interim equipment, but the Blenheims (relatively few of which had radar) were earmarked for replacement by AI-equipped Beaufighters that had entered

service with the FIU in August 1940, and with 23, 25, 29, 600 and 604 Squadrons in September. The Beaufighters trickled to the squadrons in ones and twos and operated alongside Blenheims for some time, with 25 and 604 Sqns becoming the first to fully re-equip. They withdrew their Blenheims from operations in January 1941.

When the Luftwaffe attacked Coventry on the night of November 14/15, Blenheims flew 35 sorties, Beaufighters 12, Defiants 30 and Hurricanes 43. Thereafter, Beaufighters began to replace Blenheims at an accelerating rate. From December 12 Blenheim night fighters began flying intruder missions against Luftwaffe bomber bases. Blenheims began Operation Intruder when six Mk IFs of 32 Squadron attacked bomber airfields in Normandy. While conversion to the Beaufighter was under way, on January 7, 1941, a new Blenheim night-fighter squadron (68) was formed at Catterick, Yorkshire, under the leadership of Hurricane ace Wing Commander the Honourable Max Aitken. The squadron moved to High Ercall, Shropshire, in April 1941.

A radar-equipped Blenheim IF (although the wartime censor has 'removed' the antenna on the port wing) serving with an operational training unit. The Blenheim was quickly replaced as a night fighter within Fighter Command as Beaufighters equipped with AI sets became available.

Blenheim IVFs of 254 Squadron in May 1941, shortly after the unit moved from Sumburgh in the Shetlands to Aldergrove in Northern Ireland. The unit was first of the Fighter Command squadrons transferred to Coastal Command.

Coastal Command
Blenheims Over the Seas

Jim Winchester provides an overview of the role played by the Blenheim with RAF Coastal Command.

Although often forgotten, Coastal Command's Blenheims flew alongside those of Fighter and Bomber Commands in the early years of the war. Some of Coastal's fighter Blenheims were converted to bombers and some bomber variants flew long-range fighter sweeps, as well as attacks on ports and airfields when required.

At the outbreak of war, two squadrons of Vickers Vildebeests were the only strike aircraft in the Coastal Command inventory. These were joined by types such as the Avro Anson for coastal patrol and the Lockheed Hudson for long-range patrol, but the Command required a fast bomber for anti-shipping missions.

Following the evaluation by 217 Squadron of a Blenheim IV from March to August 1939, Coastal Command began introducing the type into operational service in February 1940, when four squadrons (235, 236, 248 and 254) were transferred from Fighter Command and designated 'Trade Protection' units. In operations over Norway, the first of these to be declared operational, 254 Squadron, equipped with Mk IVs and a few Mk Is at Leuchars south of Edinburgh, Scotland, flew a number of notable missions. A strafing attack on Stavanger Airfield on April 5 destroyed two Junkers Ju 52s and a Heinkel He 59, while a Junkers Ju 88 was shot down on the 25th and a Dornier Do 18 on June 4. Unfortunately, an escort mission for a strike on the battleship *Scharnhorst* at Trondheim by Fleet Air Arm Blackburn Skuas saw the Blenheims arrive too late to prevent the loss of seven of 15 of the naval aircraft.

The other Coastal Command Blenheim squadrons (236, 246 and 248) were awarded Battle of Britain honours, having passed back and forth with Fighter Command during the course of the fighting. No 235 Squadron at Manston, Kent, was transferred to Coastal Command control on February 27, 1940, for fighter-reconnaissance duties. The squadron flew patrols over Holland in May 1940 and during the Battle of Britain performed convoy protection and reconnaissance missions over the North Sea. No 246 Squadron moved from Thorney Island, Sussex, to North Coates, Norfolk, at the end of February 1940 to join Coastal Command, but reverted

A 'pure' bomber Blenheim IV of 59 Squadron. Coastal Command primarily operated the fighter variants of the aircraft.

A 'gaggle' of Blenheim IVFs of 235 Squadron on the ground at Manston, Kent, in 1940. The squadron was transferred to Coastal Command control in February 1940.

to Fighter Command control in April after relocating to Speke in Merseyside. During May and June, the squadron flew defensive patrols over shipping in the English Channel and on July 4 rejoined Coastal Command for fighter and reconnaissance duties. Likewise, 248 Squadron with Blenheim IVFs joined Coastal Command at the end of February 1940. It then moved to North Coates and later to Thorney Island and Gosport, Hampshire. On May 22 the squadron returned to Fighter Command at Dyce, with a detachment at Montrose in Scotland. One month later it went back to Coastal for reconnaissance flights off the Norwegian coast and attacks on enemy shipping.

Thereafter it moved or sent detachments to the Shetlands, Dyce and Wick in Scotland. The far north and south of Norway were out of range of UK-based Blenheims. Some sources say that 248 had 'special armoured' Blenheim IVFs.

Even as the Battle of Britain raged, Bomber Command was taking offensive action over the continent. The RAF's policy was for constant aerial offensive and the Blenheim was the only bomber not committed to night operations. Blenheims of Bomber and Coastal Commands raided ports where barges were being gathered for Operation Sealion, the proposed German invasion of Britain. In the period June 23 to July 3 at least 14 Coastal Command Blenheims were shot down over France and the Netherlands. From August 1 to September 30, another 27 failed to return from operational sorties. Luftwaffe bomber attacks on Detling and Manston destroyed eight and damaged others.

Many of Coastal Command's Blenheims were the Mk IVF fighter variant, which lacked a bomb bay, but could be converted to bombing duties by the addition of external light bomb carriers. This allowed them to retain the four-gun ventral pack of the 'F' variants. Some were fitted with twin-gun dorsal turrets. In mid-1940, only 53 and 59 Squadrons had pure bomber Blenheims, which were actually faster than the IVFs because of the drag from the gun-packs.

Under the code-names 'Circus' and 'Roadstead', offensive daylight sweeps with heavy fighter escort were flown with the aim of forcing Luftwaffe fighters to launch and wear them down by attrition. The Blenheims of 2 Group, Bomber Command, operated

A Blenheim IVF of 235 Squadron armed with light bombs on the racks under the centre fuselage, departing from Bircham Newton, Norfolk. The gun pack carried by the variant prevented such weapons being carried in the bomb bay.

Blenheim 'TR-J' of 59 Squadron in August 1940, one month after the unit had been transferred to Coastal Command. The aircraft has several bullets holes on the rear fuselage, although it was repaired and continued to be operated by the squadron until written-off in December 1940.

its Blenheims onto overseas commands from November. Coastal Command carried on – in December they began raids against coastal targets in Norway. On December 27, 1941, 404 Squadron's Mk IVFs provided fighter cover for the commando raid on South Vågsøy and also strafed Herdla airfield. Some aircraft conducted diversionary anti-shipping operations during the raid.

During the course of 1942 the squadron, part of 18 Group and based at Wick in northern Scotland, lost nine aircraft, six of them to causes other than enemy action, such as bad weather.

Blenheims were withdrawn from Roadstead missions in October 1941. The RAF had made great claims for the success of these operations, but post-war analysis showed that results had been exaggerated by a factor of three, with only 27 ships sunk and 21 others seriously damaged. Further south, 16 Group comprising 53, 59, 320 and 407 Squadrons were allocated the area between the

alongside Coastal Command, sharing the burden and losses on these risky missions.

After the Blackburn Botha proved a disappointment in its intended role as a torpedo bomber, the Blenheim squadrons were ordered to send detachments to cover the Western Approaches. In late 1940 234 and 235 Squadrons sent IVFs to Aldergrove in Northern Ireland and 86 and 252 Squadrons were re-formed, at Gosport, Hampshire and Bircham Newton, Norfolk, respectively, the latter soon moving to Chivenor in Devon. A further 25 Coastal Blenheims failed to return between the beginning of October and the end of December 1940, with many others damaged beyond repair.

In January 1941 Coastal Command expanded to four operational groups, 15, 16, 18 and 19, plus one training group, 17. In May, 500 Squadron replaced its Ansons with Blenheims and began operations from Bircham Newton, and 143 re-formed at Aldergrove in June, while 608 exchanged its Bothas for Blenheim Is in February.

From March, following a directive from Prime Minister Winston Churchill, the major RAF commands were ordered, as their top priority, to counter German U-boats and surface raiders, which were taking an increasing toll on merchant shipping, while at the same time blockade the enemy's own ports and disrupt its seaborne trade. In March 53, 59, 107 and 114 Squadrons were loaned to Coastal Command from Bomber Command.

Exercise 'Channel Stop', intended to close the Channel to enemy shipping, began in April 1941. Such sorties often involved only small formations of Blenheims, as few as a flight of three, with escort provided by several squadrons of Supermarine Spitfires and Hawker Hurricanes, usually based at forward airfields such as Manston, Kent. Nonetheless, losses to fighters and Flak were very high and some squadrons were withdrawn after just two or three weeks to rebuild their strength in aircraft and personnel. During the period between April and June, 2 Group lost 36 aircraft in the course of 297 attacks on shipping, while the Coastal squadrons made 143 attacks for the loss of 52 aircraft. In the course of 1941 a total of 698 ships were attacked, resulting in 41 being claimed sunk. This came at the cost of a total of 123 aircraft. Bomber Command realised this was not a sustainable proposition and passed

In addition to its operational squadrons, Coastal Command controlled several operational training units that flew Blenheims. These aircraft, seen in April 1941, served with such a unit.

No 143 Squadron reformed on June 15, 1941, at Aldergrove, Northern Ireland, as a coastal strike unit with personnel from 252 Squadron, which had departed overseas. 'HO-C' is Blenheim IVF Z6034, which was eventually transferred to the Admiralty.

meteorological flights at Birch Newton, St Eval in Cornwall, and Aldergrove.

The majority of the Blenheim squadrons in Coastal Command re-equipped with Beaufighters during 1942. Conversion of 143 and 254 Squadrons began in July, but some Blenheims were still in use in September. The last frontline operator was 404 Squadron, the Royal Canadian Air Force unit starting to transition to the 'Beau' in September, although it still operated Blenheims on detachments at Dyce and Sumburgh as late as January 1943.

One notable mission in July 1942 was to escort Beauforts on a strike against the German heavy cruiser *Prinz Eugen* off Norway. The 404 Squadron crews were tasked with providing fighter cover and making dummy torpedo attacks to confuse the enemy's Flak defences. No Blenheims were lost, but eight Beauforts were shot down without inflicting damage on the Hipper-class heavy cruiser.

Despite the wind-down of Blenheim operations in 1942, Coastal Command continued to suffer operational losses, 14 of them between February 14 and July 26, including a 236 Squadron aircraft that failed to return from a weather reconnaissance sortie over Norway. This was not quite the end of the Coastal Command Blenheim story, however, as the PRU (later 140 Squadron), which was under its control, operated Mk IVs on coastal reconnaissance duties over the Channel Coast until August 1943. The meteorological flights became squadrons in the 500 series from July 1942, retaining some Blenheims, and the CACU and radar calibration flights kept the Blenheim in service with the Command until December 1944.

Although the Blenheim's record as a maritime attack aircraft can be described as only partially successful, it paved the way for the establishment of the Strike Wings, which would wreak havoc on enemy shipping with the Beaufighter and later the de Havilland Mosquito in the latter part of the war.

Elbe estuary and the Hook of Holland for anti-shipping patrols.

Channel escort missions proved particularly dangerous. As well as the many Luftwaffe fighters within range of the English Channel, enemy convoys were well protected by Flak ships, bristling with guns of 88mm, 40mm, 37mm and 20mm calibre. Blenheims also fell victim to the masts of ships and the blast of the bombs they released at low level. Normally bombs with an 11-second delay were used, allowing the aircraft to escape. The low-level nature of these operations meant that few aircrews survived being shot down, as the aircraft were usually going too fast to ditch successfully and not high enough to allow the crew to bail out.

By April 1941 Blenheims were being phased out in favour of other types:

53 converted to Hudsons, 86 to Bristol Beauforts and 248 and 272 to Bristol Beaufighters. A number of units are not mentioned in most histories of Coastal Command or the Blenheim, probably due to the short duration of their association with the type. These include 407 (RCAF) Squadron at Thorney Island, which operated Mk IVFs for two months from May 1941 before converting to Hudsons at North Coates. In January 1942 489(NZ) Squadron received Blenheim Mk IVFs at Leuchars, and although the unit converted them to bombers, it did not fly any operational missions with the type and exchanged them for Handley Page Hampdens in April. Other lesser-known Coastal Command users included 1 Coast Artillery Co-Operation Unit (CACU); B Flight of 1 Photo Reconnaissance Unit (PRU); 2 Operational Training Unit; and

Coastal Command was also responsible for photo reconnaissance, with 140 Squadron, which was formed in September 1941 with Spitfires and Blenheim IVs.

A Blenheim IV of 40 Squadron in July 1940, at the time the unit was based at Wyton in Huntingdonshire. The crew of R3612 was lost when it went missing on a raid against invasion barges at Ostend in Belgium on the night of September 8-9, 1940.

Bomber Command
Blenheims at War

Jon Lake details Blenheim operations in France and those of Bomber Command's 2 Group during the early years of World War Two.

The Blenheim performed the first RAF sortie of the war when Flying Officer Andrew McPherson flew Mk VI N6215 of 139 Squadron from Wyton to Wilhelmshaven. There, his observer, Commander Thompson, photographed enemy naval units as they left the harbour from 22,000ft (6,706m). The crew had been on standby for two days, but had not been given the order to launch. On September 3 it was received, but the aircraft arrived home too late for its photos to be used to allow a bombing raid to be launched that afternoon. Accordingly, a second reconnaissance was mounted the following day by McPherson. These first sorties (and subsequent missions) won McPherson the DFC.

RESTRICTED TARGETS

Bomber Command was restricted to attacks of peripheral importance during the first months of the war. The Air Ministry stated that the intentional bombing of civilians was 'illegal', that identification and distinguishing a target was a prerequisite and that "bombardment must be carried out in such a way that there is a reasonable expectation that damage will be confined to the objective". Bomber Command's activities were restricted to dropping propaganda leaflets, plus operations against German coastal areas, primarily aimed at dispersing fighters between Germany and the Czech and French fronts.

On September 4, 15 Blenheims were among 29 aircraft tasked to attack German warships at Wilhelmshaven. No.139 Squadron's five aircraft turned back before reaching the target, because of poor weather. The first wave of 110 Squadron attacked successfully, losing only one aircraft. Four Blenheims from 107 Squadron in the second wave were shot down, with one crashing into the forecastle of the destroyer *Emden*. Two, possibly more, 500lb (227kg) bombs hit *Admiral Scheer*, but none exploded. Solo reconnaissance missions by Blenheims of the German navy and the northern coast had a loss rate approaching 20%; they were eventually abandoned in late November. Anti-shipping searches and strikes had little more success, most returning without finding the enemy. When enemy aircraft were encountered, things tended to go badly. On January 10, 1940, for example, four Messerschmitt Bf 110s of 2./ZG 76 tangled with nine 110 Squadron Blenheims, shooting down one, while two had to be written off after landing.

INCREASING LOSSES

When the war started, the RAF had eight frontline Blenheim IV bomber squadrons (21, 82, 90, 101, 107, 110, 114 and 139), with two more operating in the army co-operation role. Two more bomber units (81 and 75 Squadrons) flew Mk Is, but soon transferred from 1 to 6 (Training) Group. They later went to the Air Component of the British Expeditionary Force (BEF) in France and re-equipped with Mk IVs, principally operating in the strategic reconnaissance role.

The Air Component sent to France on the outbreak of war had four Blenheim squadrons – 18, 53, 57 and 59 – as well as Westland Lysander and Hawker Hurricane units by the time the Germans invaded. The BEF was supported by an Advanced Air Striking Force (AASF) with ten squadrons of Fairey Battles, which reported to Bomber Command. In December 1939, two AASF Battle squadrons (15 and 40) rotated home to re-equip with Blenheims, and were immediately replaced by the Blenheim-equipped 14 and 139 Squadrons. The Air Component and AASF effectively merged when all RAF assets in France were brought under the British Air Forces in France (BAFF).

The six BAFF Blenheim squadrons took over the brunt of reconnaissance missions when it became clear how vulnerable the Battle was, but large numbers were lost in accidents. Even before war broke out, it was apparent the Blenheim could not survive in the face of fighter opposition. No. 2 Group continued to mount daylight missions and lose Blenheims, even when the rest of Bomber Command switched to night bombing.

On April 6, 1940, Basil Embry led 107 Squadron in an attack against the *Scharnhorst*, the *Gneisenau* and a convoy heading north for the invasion of Norway. *Scharnhorst* was hit, but the bombs failed to penetrate its armour. Even after Norway fell, bombing attacks continued, with 2 Group Blenheim squadrons rotating detachments to Lossiemouth in Scotland for operations off Norway almost immediately.

BLITZKRIEG

The Wehrmacht began its Blitzkrieg in the West on May 10, 1940, smashing through the Netherlands and Belgium and

For many targets, the bomb load and the size of the munitions carried by the Blenheim was totally inadequate. Early in the war, Blenheim crews found that dropping the ordnance at low level did not allow the bombs time to arm. These 125lb (57kg) bombs had a low ratio of explosive to weight.

into France. British Prime Minister Neville Chamberlain was forced to step down, replaced by Winston Churchill. Although the scramble to halt the German drive through France saw RAF bombers used wastefully against tactical targets, there was a new enthusiasm for attacks on targets in Germany itself. The bombing of Rotterdam by the Luftwaffe on May 14 convinced Churchill that the informal ban on bombing civilians was over.

The German advance into northern France saw the RAF thrown into the fray to stop advancing armour and to destroy bridges across rivers and canals. The only hope for the Allies was to bomb them, but the German tanks led by General Heinz Guderian brought up flak units, so they were soon heavily defended. Blenheims and Battles fell in large numbers, but achieved little, even when those based in France were augmented by units from 2 Group. On May 10, nine XV Squadron Blenheims attacked Waalhaven aerodrome with some success and 12 from 40 Squadron hit Ypenburg, two falling to Bf 110s. Finally, 12 Blenheims from 110 Squadron struck Waalhaven, claiming the destruction of Ju 52s. One 2 Group Blenheim was lost on a reconnaissance mission that day, along with

four Air Component Blenheims and five Fighter Command Mk IFs.

On May 1, almost all of 114 Squadron's Blenheims were destroyed on the ground at Condé-Vraux by Dornier Do 172s of II./KG 2. Four more Air Component Blenheims were also lost, along with two from 110 Squadron. The latter had managed to severely damage the bridge that had been its target, plus claim a fighter destroyed. No. 21 Squadron returned from a 12-aircraft raid on German armour with all its Blenheims, although eight were subsequently declared unserviceable. Remarkably, no further attacks were made, such was the need to conserve aircraft and crews.

On May 12, seven of nine 139 Squadron Blenheims were shot down by Bf 109s of JG 27 while attacking armoured columns and bridges near Maastricht, having pressed on despite the non-appearance of a fighter escort. Around 15 aircrew were killed. Later that day, 107 Squadron lost four crews trying to bomb the Maas bridges, with XV losing six more an hour later. Only two of the surviving aircraft could be repaired to fly again.

Out of 11, two of 110 Squadron Blenheims were shot down on a similar mission, and one 12 Squadron aircraft was downed during an

Bomber Command's Blenheim units had re-equipped with the Mk IV by the start of the war, although the army co-operation roled 53 Squadron at Odiham, Hampshire, was the first to receive the long-nose variant. No. 53 Squadron operated in the strategic reconnaissance role with the Air Component of the British Expeditionary Force in France. These aircraft, lined up in January 1939, are headed by L4841 (coded 'TE-N'), which failed to return from a sortie on May 19, 1940.

evening sortie, although 82 Squadron was luckier, escaping losses during its mission. Another seven BAFF Blenheims were destroyed that day.

WORST DAY

Despite an official stand-down, four more Blenheims were recorded missing in action on May 13. The next day was the worst yet for the RAF in France. Heinkel He 111s of KG 54 took out the heart of Rotterdam, prompting the Netherlands to surrender. A maximum effort against German bridges across the Meuse at Sedan saw 44 of 71 attacking aircraft lost, including five of eight Blenheims of 139 and 14 Squadrons.

Six 107 Squadron Blenheims attacked the advancing Germans without loss, but 110 Squadron lost five of 12 aircraft despatched despite fighter protection, although they did claim a Bf 109 shot down. No. 12 Squadron lost one aircraft, but shot down at least two Bf 109s. It was the RAF's highest losses of the war to date.

Seven Blenheims fell the next day, two to RAF Hurricanes – victims of misidentification. Two more were lost from 40 Squadron, which mounted a combined raid with nine of its aircraft accompanied by three XV Squadron Blenheims. The remaining casualties included one of four 139 Squadron Blenheims that

attacked Monthermé. The withdrawal of the Air Component and AASF squadrons began on May 15.

A further pair of Blenheims was brought down by Hurricanes on May 16, along with two on reconnaissance missions, although two Henschel Hs 126s were downed by a gunner, while 14 and 139 Squadrons received orders to return to England. On the following day, 82 Squadron was all but destroyed, losing 11 Blenheims, ten to Bf 109s. On May 18 it was the turn of XV Squadron, which lost three of six aircraft despatched, with two more badly damaged. Seven aircraft sent out by 40 Squadron fared better, beating off attacks by Bf 109s without loss.

No. 110 Squadron converted to the Blenheim I from the Hawker Hind in January 1938 at Waddington, Lincolnshire, and moved to Wattisham in East Anglia on May 11, 1939, where it quickly re-equipped with Blenheim IVs.

DUNKIRK

Over the next two days, nearly all surviving Blenheims returned to England, although 2 Group squadrons continued to fly missions over France. As the Germans advanced, plans for evacuation of the BEF were hastily made, while Blenheims could operate within range of escorting fighters. During the last days of the campaign, Blenheim losses declined dramatically.

The situation on May 28 looked very bleak. Belgium capitulated, while all available fighters were committed to covering the Dunkirk evacuation. No. 2 Group's units mounted several missions, with XV, 40, 82, 107 and 110 Squadrons recording no losses, although 21 and 59 Squadron lost a single aircraft each. Nos 114 and 139 Squadrons finally returned to England on May 29, and raids by XV, 21, 40, 82, 107 and 110 recorded no losses on that day, or the next four.

Operation Dynamo officially concluded on June 4, but for the Blenheims of 2 Group sorties continued. On June 6, Flight Lieutenant Robert Bat of 40 Squadron flew an eventful solo recce mission during which his observer claimed an enemy fighter as a possible; he was awarded the DFC, and both gunner and observer received

DFMs. On the same day, his squadron lost five aircraft during a 12 Blenheim mission. No. 107 Squadron lost a Blenheim on June 7 and three two days later, but the operational tempo began to slow afterwards, although Blenheims covered the evacuation from French Atlantic ports on June 18. No. 82 Squadron flew what could be regarded as the last Blenheim operation of the Battle of France that day. Five days later, France surrendered. The Battle of France cost the RAF 200 Blenheims; 37 from the Advanced Air Striking Force (AASF), 41 from the Air Component and 97 of Bomber Command, with the others from Fighter and Coastal Commands.

CIRCUSES

The heavy losses suffered by the Blenheim during the Battle of France continued after France fell in late June 1940, with 2 Group mounting attacks for little gain. Squadrons decimated in France were reformed. Airfield attacks were occasionally successful. On August 7, just two of 29 Blenheims hit their targets, but one stick of bombs that fell on Haamstede destroyed two Bf 109s and damaged four more, killing five airmen and injuring another 17.

Five Blenheim IVs of 101 Squadron. The aircraft leading the formation was shot down by flak off Boulogne on May 3, 1941.

A line-up of 82 Squadron Blenheim IVs at Watton in Norfolk in July 1940, after the unit was re-equipped after effectively being wiped out during a raid on Gembloux on May 17. Eleven of its 12 Blenheims were shot down. The tragedy was repeated on August 13 during a raid on Aalborg in Denmark. The squadron crossed the Danish coast early, exposing it to flak and Luftwaffe fighters, which again claimed 11 of the 12 Blenheims, the survivor having returned home before reaching the target.

As the threat of invasion grew, Bomber Command was thrown into operations against channel shipping and invasion barges in channel ports. They reduced the 3,000-strong fleet by about 12%, helping convince Hitler that invasion was too dangerous. The Führer turned his attention eastwards, while U-boats intensified their campaign to starve Britain into submission. Blenheims then played their part against the U-boat, principally by attacking submarine pens, shipping and ports.

During early 1941, Bomber Command participated in 190 'Circuses' – heavily escorted raids to draw fighters up to do battle with RAF fighters. Some of these were made against land targets, others against shipping. All were very costly. Following the invasion of the Soviet Union on June 22, 1941, they assumed greater importance, since they presented a way of drawing German forces from the East. Between mid-June and the end of 1941, RAF fighter pilots claimed 731 aircraft destroyed, most on 'Circus' operations, although actual Luftwaffe losses were only 103. The RAF lost 123 fighter pilots in six weeks on 'Circus' operations alone and they were equally costly for the Blenheims. Whole squadrons would attack a heavily defended target and often most would fail to return.

From June 5, 1940, Bomber Command had directed 2 Group's Blenheims to perform hit-and-run raids to force Luftwaffe fighters to be spread over a wide area. A reluctant concession was that such attacks would be carried out only when there was sufficient (7/10ths) cloud cover to avoid enemy fighters. Fine summer weather in 1940 had ensured such attacks were rare and there was little change that winter.

Bomber Command raids on the Kriegsmarine's capital ships in Brest harbour, including those by Blenheims, eventually provoked the 'Channel Dash'. While the RAF failed to sink the ships as they sailed for home, *Gneisenau* was so badly damaged by mines and subsequent air raids on Kiel that she spent the rest of the war in dry dock, while *Prinz Eugen* was repaired too late to play an active

No. 40 Squadron flew Blenheim IVs between December 1939 and November 1940 from Wyton. The squadron re-equipped with Vickers Wellingtons two months later, one of several 2 Group units to do so around the same time.

part in the war. *Scharnhorst* was forced into a nomadic existence avoiding bombers and warships, until her luck ran out in the North Sea. None of these ships could break out into the Atlantic to attack Allied convoys.

From June 15, 1940, 2 Group Blenheims had begun to raid German airfields in France, escorted by Hurricanes when they were within range. These continued throughout the Blenheim's operational career and usually had a low loss rate. An exception involved 21 and 57 Squadrons, which lost six aircraft attacking Stavanger/Sola on July 9, while 107 lost five of six attacking Amiens the next day. Worse was to befall 82 Squadron during an attack on Aalborg on August 13, when it crossed the Danish coast too early.

Eleven of its 12 Blenheims were shot down by Bf 109s or flak.

Nos XV, 40, 57, 101 and 218 Squadrons re-equipped with Vickers Wellingtons in November 1940, reducing the number of Blenheims available for the daylight offensive. Despite this, Blenheims played a role in Bomber Command's early large-scale night raids, with nine aircraft participating in its first mass raid, against Manheim, on December 16-17, 1940. Blenheims also played a significant role in the attack on Wilhelmshaven town on January 15, 1941, then the RAF's largest raid.

Much of the Blenheim's work with 2 Group was against Axis shipping, augmenting those of Coastal Command. A directive from Churchill on March 6, 1941, saw 18, 21,

107 and 139 Squadrons specifically tasked with halting enemy convoys by day, while other units also played a part in the campaign. The coast of occupied Europe, from Bergen to Oslo and from northern Denmark to Bordeaux, was divided into 19 'beats', patrolled by Blenheims looking for ships.

Anti-shipping operations were extremely costly. Such operations were collectively known as 'Roadsteads' and became more common from March 1941, when Churchill promulgated them as a 'top priority'. Between mid-March and mid-April 1941, nine Blenheims were lost on 'Roadsteads' and 36 more fell from mid-April to mid-June (12% of aircraft despatched). During this period, 2 Group mounted 297 anti-ship attacks,

Losses among Bomber Command's Blenheim crews were extremely heavy. The tasks the squadrons were required to undertake took a heavy toll, with the chances of completing a tour nearly impossible in the war's early years.

losing 63 aircraft, while Coastal Command despatched 143 aircraft, losing 25. August saw the loss rate soar to 30%, with 23 of 77 aircraft failing to return. Only 31 Blenheims engaged in other daylight operations were lost in the same month. From March 31, 1941, aircraft involved in the anti-shipping campaign began mounting so-called 'fringe attacks', penetrating to attack land targets on a 'hit-and-run' basis.

Usually, a Blenheim squadron was maintained on detachment at Manston for 'Channel Stop' operations from April 1941, with the aim of closing the English Channel to enemy shipping. Typically, three aircraft were heavily escorted by Spitfires and Hurricanes, but losses were heavy and many units had to be withdrawn after only a couple of weeks. Blenheims flew at low level over the water, attacking at mast height, which sometimes prevented flak ships from firing for fear of hitting ships behind the aircraft.

At a conference of 2 Group station commanders on November 3, 1941, Air Vice-Marshal (AVM) Donald F Stevenson finally announced the end of the anti-shipping campaign, although it continued (albeit at a less intense pace) until his replacement (AVM Alan Lees) took command of the Group. Stevenson had been ordered to conserve his crews on August 30. Blenheims and their crews were urgently needed elsewhere, most notably Malta and in the Mediterranean. Thus, Bomber Command's 2 Group was released from anti-ship operations officially on November 25, although Coastal Command's fought on. However, Blenheims of 2 Group would occasionally be called on to attack shipping in the months to come.

It was officially estimated that between March and October 1941, 2 Group had successfully attacked 590 ships (1,303,000 tons), resulting in the sinking of, or serious damage to, 107 vessels (355,000 tons). Post-war research suggests the true figure was lower, with 29 (29,836 tons) sunk and another 12 (43,715) damaged. These losses were negligible, but cost 2 Group the lives of its most experienced crews, none of whom managed to complete 50 operations or 200 hours. The virtual impossibility of

Blenheim IV R3600 of 110 Squadron being serviced at Wattisham, Suffolk, with armourers preparing 250lb (113kg) GP bombs and incendiaries in Small Bomb Containers. The Blenheim was with the unit in July 1940 having come from the Photographic Development Unit. It was lost in an attack on a convoy on May 6, 1941.

completing a tour destroyed morale. A total of 170 Blenheims were lost during the same period, excluding aircraft destroyed during detachments to Malta or on 'Circus' raids against land targets.

PENETRATION RAIDS

On August 12, 1941, a force of 54 Blenheims from 18, 21, 82, 107, 114, 139 and 226 Squadrons, escorted part of the way by hundreds of fighters, attacked power stations in the towns of Knapsack and Quadrath in North Rhine-Westphalia. The attacks were made at very low altitude and caused significant damage, but the towns were well defended with anti-aircraft artillery (AAA) and the Blenheims had to contend with fighters on the way home. The attacks were the deepest penetrations of Germany to date; 12 aircraft failed to return.

On July 16, 1941, 18, 21, 105, 139 and 226 Squadrons, with cover from two more

of Spitfires, launched 73 aircraft against Rotterdam docks. The first wave consisted of 12 aircraft from 21 Squadron and six from 226, led by Wing Commander Peter Webster, who won the DSO for his part in the raid. The second wave included eight aircraft from 18 Squadron, four from 93 and seven of 105. Three Blenheims were lost, but 17 ships were claimed destroyed or damaged, and considerable damage was inflicted on the docks' infrastructure. A follow-up mission by 17 Blenheims on August 28 resulted in the loss of seven aircraft.

A rather different sortie occurred on August 19, 1941, when R3843 of 18 Squadron flew to its target via the German fighter aerodrome at St Omer, where it dropped a case containing a spare leg for the recently captured pilot Douglas Bader, shot down ten days earlier.

On December 27, 1941, 13 Blenheims from 114 Squadron and six from 110 Squadron mounted an attack against the Luftwaffe airfield at Herdla in Norway, to prevent

A line-up of Blenheim IVs of 40 Squadron at Wyton in 1940. The aircraft code 'BL-U' (L9402) was built by Rootes Securities and sent to the unit, later serving with 139 Squadron until being struck off charge on March 14, 1940.

interference in a commando raid against Vågsøy. The Blenheims hit the wooden runways within one minute of noon, after a 300-mile (483km) over-water low-level flight. A Bf 109 starting its take-off run during the attack fell into a bomb crater. Five aircraft were lost, but the mission was a success. Blenheims from 404 Squadron provided fighter cover and mounted a diversionary attack.

FADE AWAY

The Blenheim faded from the scene in Western Europe quickly during 1942, with 2 Group's squadrons re-equipping with Douglas Bostons, North American Mitchells and Lockheed Venturas. The eight long-term Blenheim squadrons declined to three by the end of February 1942. Blenheims continued to be used, with for example 14 Squadron – the RAF's only home-based night intruder unit until 18 Squadron completed night-intruder training in April. On the night of May 30/31, Blenheims from both squadrons, plus those of Army Co-operation Command's 13 and 614 Squadrons, were among the aircraft despatched on Bomber Command's first 1,000 bomber raid against Köln, although the Blenheims attacked night fighter bases and other targets, rather than the city.

Blenheims completed their last sorties over Germany on August 17-18, 1942, when 18 Squadron sent its Mk IV night intruders against several German fighter airfields. Blenheims also participated in the Dieppe Raid on August 19, laying smoke as cover for the landings. The type then disappeared from 2 Group.

The Blenheim V did not offer sufficient advantages over the Mk IV to be considered suitable for operations over occupied Europe, although the last four Blenheim units, 18 and 14 Squadrons in 2 Group and 13 and 614 Squadrons in Army Co-operation Command, re-equipped with the aircraft. They were quickly transferred to the Mediterranean. No. 139 Squadron also briefly flew Mk Vs while transitioning to de Havilland Mosquitoes.

Although the Blenheim was increasingly obsolete, it remained in use with Bomber Command into 1942 in diminishing numbers. After leaving the squadrons, the aircraft was used by operational training units to train crews for the medium bomber force.

A 614 Squadron Blenheim V, which 'upgraded' to the variant from the Mk IV at Odiham, Hampshire, in August 1942. The aircraft was judged unsuitable for operations over western Europe and the unit departed for Northwest Africa in November 1942 to support Operation Torch.

Blenheims Around the
Mediterranean

The first Blenheims in the Middle East were delivered to 30 Squadron at Dhibban in Iraq, replacing its Hawker Hardies in January 1938. The airfield was renamed Habbaniyah in late March. When Italy entered the war on July 10, 1940, 30 Squadron had been replaced by 84 Squadron in Iraq, while other Blenheim operators in the region included 8, 11 and 39 in Aden and 30, 45, 55, 113 and 211 Squadrons in Egypt. The next day 45, 55 and 113 Squadron sent 26 Blenheims to bomb El Adem in Libya, two of which were shot down by flak and another crashed heading back to base.

When Italy invaded Greece through Albania, 30 Squadron was detached to Eleusis on November 1, 1940, where it was joined by one flight from 84 Squadron, which moved to Menidi with the rest of the unit, alongside 211 Squadron. No.11 Squadron moved to Larissa in mid-January 1941, and 113 Squadron to Menidi in March. Losses began to mount when the Germans intervened on April 6; 113 Squadron lost all its Blenheims on April 15 and the remaining aircraft from most of the others were withdrawn to Egypt at the end of month, with the newly arrived 203 Squadron joining them there in May.

In April 1941 Blenheims helped put down a German supported coup in Iraq. Habbaniyah was besieged by Iraqi ground forces and came under air attack from German aircraft.

Tropicalised Blenheim IV Z7910 was destroyed when it stalled landing at Luqa, Malta, on December 5, 1941. Bomber Command Blenheim squadrons were deployed to the island, while Blenheims transiting it were 'acquired' as reinforcements.

Blenheim IVs of 203 Squadron began operations from H4 in Jordan, aimed at denying the use of Iraqi airfields at Ar-Rutbah and H3 to the Luftwaffe. The pro-British Iraqi regime was reinstalled on June 1.

Vichy-controlled Syria supported German operations over Iraq. Blenheims of 114 Squadron began attacking Luftwaffe transports as they unloaded at Syrian airfields on May 14, which were later also hit by 84 and 203 Squadron aircraft. Blenheims conducted most of the bombing and reconnaissance sorties in support of the allied invasion of Syria, with aircraft drawn from 11, 45 and

84 Squadrons. At least eight were shot down during the fighting.

An integral part of the campaign for North Africa was waged from the island of Malta in the mid-Mediterranean. The deployment of Blenheims there began on April 26, 1941, with a detachment of six crews from 21 Squadron. No. 2 Group of Bomber Command then began a regular rotation of Blenheim units, each between five and six weeks each. The first was undertaken by 82 Squadron in June 1941. Malta's Blenheims attacked enemy shipping and ranged against targets on the North African mainland, close to the coast. No.82 Squadron was followed by 10, 105, 107, 18 and 12 Squadrons, in turn, into February 1942. Losses were heavy, averaging one crew per day.

Operation Crusader was launched in the Western Desert with pre-emptive airstrikes starting on November 15, 1941. Blenheims, often heavily escorted, mounted close air support and airfield attack missions. The Japanese offensive in the Far East saw Desert Ari Force lose four of its nine Blenheim squadrons, with 45, 84, 113 and 211 departing for Sumatra and Burma in January and February 1942, leaving behind 8, 11, 14 and 55 Squadrons, plus the Free French 'Lorraine' unit. Free French, Hellenic and South African units all operated Blenheims in North Africa and the Middle East.

The Blenheim IV began to disappear from frontline service during the summer of 1942, with some units converting to the Martin Baltimore and Marauder (55 and 14, respectively) and others (15 SAAF and the Free French) to the Blenheim V. An exception was 11 Squadron, which continued with Blenheim IVs into August 1943. The Blenheim had all but disappeared from the Desert Air Force's front line by the time the Battle of El Alamein took place in October 1942, serving only with 15 (SAAF) and 11 Squadrons, and some coastal patrol and maritime reconnaissance units.

The Blenheim V would form the backbone of the army support force committed to

A Blenheim IV taking off from El Kabrit in Egypt during March 1943, by when the variant had left the front line squadrons.

Operation Torch, the Anglo-American invasion of Northwest Africa, which began with landings on November 8, 1942. No. 326 Wing, with 13, 18, 114 and 614 Squadrons, re-equipped in England before moving to Algeria. Without fighter escort, the Blenheim V was too unwieldy, poorly armed and badly protected to survive daylight bombing missions. By the spring of 1943, the aircraft was obsolete and replacement with Douglas Bostons in the close air support squadrons under way.

This left four coastal reconnaissance and ASW units operating the Blenheim in the Middle East, while 162 Squadron had some among its varied inventory for calibration. The last unit to use the Blenheim V as a bomber was 614 Squadron, which gave them up in December 1943. No.162 Squadron discarded its last Blenheims in January 1944, as did 8 Squadron, although 244 continued to fly them at Masirah off Oman until April 1944.

A flight of four 14 Squadron Blenheim IVs over North Africa in 1942. The squadron received Mk IVs in Sudan in September 1940 and retained them for two years, operating in Egypt, Libya, Palestine and Iraq.

SUBSCRIBE TODAY

TO YOUR FAVOURITE MAGAZINE!

SCAN ME

FlyPast is internationally regarded as the magazine for aviation history and heritage.

SIMPLY SCAN THE QR CODE OF YOUR FAVOURITE MAGAZINE AND SUBSCRIBE TODAY!

Order today from our online shop
shop.keypublishing.com
Call +44 (0)1780 480404 *(Mon to Fri 9am - 5.30pm GMT)*

THE DESTINATION FOR
HISTORIC & MILITARY ENTHUSIASTS

Visit us today and discover all our publications

Aeroplane is still providing the best aviation coverage around, with focus on iconic military aircraft from the 1930s to the 1960s.

Britain at War - dedicated to exploring every aspect of the involvement of Britain and her Commonwealth in conflicts from the turn of the 20th century through to the present day.

and subscribe to your favourite magazine...
/collections/subscriptions

Free 2nd class P&P on BFPO orders. Overseas charges apply.

Blenheims in the Far East

Nos 11, 39 and 60 Squadrons re-equipped with Blenheim Is in India by late 1939, while 34 and 62 Squadrons moved from Britain to the 'fortress' of Singapore. When Japan invaded Malaya on December 8, 1941, 27 Squadron was at Sungei Patani in Malaya with Mk IFs, 34 at Tengah in Singapore and 62 at Alor Star, while a detachment of 60 Squadron from India was at Kuantan, all with Mk I bombers.

Within two days all four units had been driven from their original bases with heavy losses; by December 9 around a dozen Mk Is and IVs remained at Kallang, Singapore. Six Blenheims attacked Japanese shipping at Singora, Thailand, that day, even though they did not have the range to return to base. One landed at Butterworth, while the other five crashed in the jungle, with 60 Squadron handing its survivors over to 27, 34 and 62 Squadrons and its airmen departing. Following the invasion of Singapore on February 8, the last aircrews headed for Sumatra in the Dutch East Indies, where 84 Squadron's Blenheim had arrived from Egypt on January 23.

By February 18, four days after Japanese paratroopers captured a Sumatran airfield, only six Blenheims remained, which were relocated to Kalidjati on Java. From here they mounted attacks on shipping and the approaching invasion force, hitting a submarine on February 23. With Kalidjati about to be captured, 84 Squadron destroyed its last Blenheims on March 1.

Blenheims of 62 Squadron off the coast of Malaya in 1940, shortly before the Japanese invasion. The unit used the code 'FX' only briefly before changing it to 'PT'.

Seven Blenheim squadrons would later defend the India frontier and fight in Burma. Typical of them was 113 Squadron, which had been rushed to Mingaladon, Burma, on January 7, 1941, to counter the Japanese advance. It later raided Bangkok in Siam and destroyed around 60 aircraft on Japanese-held airfields. The squadron retreated to Magwe at the end of February, then Akyab, before returning to India.

Blenheim units on the Burmese front initially flew Mk Is, which were later replaced by Mk IVs and eventually Mk Vs. They would cover the 14th Army as it pushed forward and retreated during the monsoon season in May 1943. The last five Blenheim V squadrons in the theatre all re-equipped with Hawker Hurricanes. Nos 11, 43 and 60 Squadrons received the fighter at Feni, Madras and Yelahanka, discarding their Blenheims by the end of July, while 13 Squadron at Feni flew its last sorties with the bomber on August 15 and 24 Squadron at Kumbhirgram retained them until October 1943. Blenheims would remain in service with second line units in India until the end of the war.

Blenheim I L1392 of 84 Squadron, the unit that deployed to Sumatra at the end of January 1941 to join the remnants of the squadrons fighting the Japanese. The unit's ground echelon was evacuated to India by sea at the end of February 1941 to re-equip with Blenheim IVs.

Blenheims for the World

The combination of the Blenheim's modern systems and high performance made it attractive to the air arms of many countries. This was underlined by the interest that the second Blenheim I – all gleaming metal and clean lines – generated during its exhibition at the Grand Salon Aéronautique in Paris in November 1936.

Both Finland and Lithuania expressed an early interest in the aircraft; both wanted the right to build the aircraft at their own factories and acquire an initial batch direct from Bristol. While Lithuania failed to sign on the dotted line, Finland did and became the first export customer. It would go on to play a significant role in the Blenheim story, taking new aircraft from the production line at Filton and receiving others from the RAF, as well as building its own examples. Finland's Blenheims were used against the Soviet Union and later Germany, as the country fought to survive, while its air force became the last to operate the aircraft. The second export customer was Turkey.

Blenheims were also built in Canada and Yugoslavia. The role played by Canada's Bolingbrokes during the war has received little attention, although within the Home War Establishment squadrons they patrolled its coast and were deployed to Alaska, as well as serving in many of the schools of the British Commonwealth Air Training Plan, one of the foundations of the Allies' eventual victory.

Canadian, as well as Australian, Indian, New Zealand and South African crews, also flew Blenheims in units that came under the operational control of the RAF. De Gaulle's Free French Air Force made use of the aircraft supplied from RAF stocks, as did a Hellenic squadron in exile, after those delivered at the start of the war were lost when Greece was occupied. Even the United States Army Air Forces had a handful, although for what purpose remains unknown.

Blenheims were also supplied to Romania during the war, partly to keep them out of the Axis camp – although it did not work. Portugal received the aircraft in exchange for basing rights in the Azores.

RAF Blenheims fell into the hands of both Germany and Japan during the war, while the Indonesians, keen to make use of what was available in their fight for independence, salvaged one left behind by the Japanese. Other countries acquired their examples from Yugoslavia while and after that country was being overrun by the Axis powers. Hungary's sole example was delivered by a Yugoslavian who defected during the fighting. After Yugoslavia was occupied, Germany passed the Blenheims to Croatia and Romania, while Finland bought other uncompleted aircraft.

Turkey acquired 30 Blenheim Is – including these examples – as well as a handful of Mk IV and 18 Mk Vs. It was a Blenheim operation between late 1936 into 1948.

Finland was the first export customer for the Blenheim after ordering 18 Blenheim Is, including BL-120. The aircraft was known as 'Pelti-Heikki' ('tin Henry') in Finnish service.

Australia

On February 12, 1937, Order O.I.550 was placed by Australia covering the procurement of 40 Bristol 149 Bolingbrokes, which were due to become A9-1 to -40. The order was later cancelled, but plans to build 50 Blenheim IVs in Australia were formulated in 1938, as part of a plan to expand the nation's aircraft industry to meet the needs of both the RAF and Royal Australian Air Force (RAAF). The aircraft was allocated the A8- serial prefix.

Australian interest in the Blenheim waned as development of the Bristol Beaufort progressed, and on July 1, 1939, an order for 180 was placed while the Beaufort Division was formed within the Commonwealth Department of Aircraft Production (DAP) to oversee production. At the same time plans for Blenheim production were dropped. A8- was later used for Australian-built Bristol Beaufighters.

A small number of Blenheims did see service with three RAAF squadrons during the war, although only relatively briefly. All three were Article XV units, which were squadrons formed with by graduates of the British Commonwealth Air Training Plan. The idea was that pilots from the Dominions would be assigned to Australian, Canadian or New Zealand units, but deployed as required, coming under control of 'a local air force', usually the RAF.

After forming on June 30, 1941, at RAF Valley on Anglesey in Wales, 456 Squadron was equipped with Boulton Paul Defiant I night fighters. From September 1941 it began the process of converting to the Beaufighter IIF. From August 1941 Blenheim I L4907 was used by the unit to help conversion to the aircraft, joined by L1371 in April 1942 and L1170 the following month, these two remaining with the unit until September and October 1942. L4907 stayed with the unit until June 1943, by when 456 Squadron had re-equipped with de Havilland Mosquitoes. It is unconfirmed if the Blenheims were radar-equipped IFs, but the subvariant was frequently used as a trainer for the equipment by the RAF, as the aircraft could accommodate an instructor and trainee, unlike the Beaufighter.

No.454 was raised mainly with British personnel at Blackpool in April 1942 without aircraft, and travelled via Egypt and Palestine to Iraq, settling at Qaiyara in Iraq. There, in November 1942, it received Blenheim Vs and ran a refresher course for other units on the aircraft. They remained with the squadron until January 1943, when a move to Gianaclis, Egypt, involved them being replaced by Martin Baltimore aircraft.

The third unit was 459 Squadron, a maritime patrol and bomber unit formed in February 1942 at Landing Ground 39, Burg-al-Arab South Airfield, with a pair of Lockheed Hudsons and four Blenheim Mk IVs. The Blenheims departed in May 1942 after additional Hudsons were received.

ROYAL AUSTRALIAN AIR FORCE BLENHEIM UNITS

Unit	Model	Code	Base	Dates
454 Sqn	Blenheim V		Qaiyara, Iraq	11/42-01/43
			Gianaclis, Egypt	01/43/-01/43
456 Sqn	Blenheim I	SA/RX	Valley	08/41-03/43
			Middle Wallop	03/43-06/43
459 Sqn	Blenheim IV	GK	LG39, Egypt	02/42-05/42

All the Blenheims operated by RAAF squadrons were RAF aircraft. The three squadrons that flew the aircraft only did so briefly before re-equipping with other types.

Canada

The Royal Canadian Air Force (RCAF) had the distinction of having the second largest fleet of Blenheims after the RAF – although most of its aircraft were not called Blenheims! The Canadian service used the locally built Bolingbroke, a variant of the Blenheim IV, in several versions, although the most important were the Mk IV and the Mk IV-T, the latter optimised for training. Outside the UK Canada also built the most aircraft of the four nations in which they were assembled. A total of 626 Bolingbrokes were produced in Canada by Fairchild Aircraft of Longueuil, Quebec, plus a further 51 as spare airframes, with production hitting 41 aircraft a month at its peak.

By early 1937 the RCAF wanted a new general reconnaissance aircraft and, observing developments on the other side of the Atlantic, where the long nose of the original Bolingbroke was incorporated onto the Blenheim to create the Mk IV, signed a contract with Fairchild Aircraft in November 1938 to build 18 under licence. The Blenheim IV 'prototype', K7072, was sent out to Longueuil to act as a pattern aircraft for Canadian production. The Canadians decided to retain the name Bolingbroke for its version of the Blenheim Mk IV; the first 18 became Bolingbroke Is, with the initial example flying on September 14, 1939. Six addition contracts were placed for Bolingbroke IV sub-variants, the last in June 1942.

Bolingbroke Is were first deployed operationally in December 1940 with 8 (BR) Squadron based at Sydney, Nova Scotia, operating alongside the unit's Northrop Deltas. The squadron was assigned to RCAF's Eastern Air Command and although designated a Bomber Reconnaissance (BR) unit, its main task was anti-submarine patrols off the Atlantic coast. Just after the Japanese attacked Pearl Harbor on December 7, 1941, not long after the Deltas departed from the unit, it was redeployed to Western Air Command, operating from Sea Island, British Colombia.

Fearing a threat to its Alaskan coastal communities, the United States asked Canada to supply combat squadrons to bolster defences. This resulted in the formation of two wings, each with a single bomber reconnaissance squadron and a fighter unit. No.8 (BR) Squadron was assigned to RCAF (X) Wing, alongside 111(F) Squadron, flying Curtiss P-40K Kittyhawks. The BR squadron, newly re-equipped with Bolingbroke IVs to replace its Mk Is (and the code worn on the aircraft changing from 'YO' to 'GA'), transited Annette Island, Juneau and Yakutat to land at Elmendorf Army Airfield near Anchorage, on June 8, 1942. Two days earlier the Japanese Vice-Admiral Boshiro Hosogaya had captured the Kiska and Attu islands in the Aleutians.

The Bolingbrokes of 8 (BR) Squadron flew anti-submarine patrols from Anchorage from early June 1942 into late February 1943. The unit also kept a detachment of three aircraft at NAS Kodiak on Kodiak Island during most of this period. Operating conditions were difficult, as spares were not readily available, the Bolingbroke's weapon shackles had to

		RCAF HOME WAR ESTABLISHMENT BOLINGBROKE SQUADRONS			
Unit	**Version**	**Code**	**Base**	**Dates**	
8 (BR) Sqn	Bolingbroke I/IV-W	YO	Sydney, NS	12/40-12/41	
			Sea Island, BC	12/41-06/42	
	Bolingbroke IV	GA	Elmendorf, AK	06/42-02/43	
			Sea Island, BC	02/43-08/43	
13 (OT) Sqn	Bolingbroke IV	AN	Sea Island, BC	10/41-06/42	
115 (F) Sqn	Bolingbroke I	BK	Patricia Bay, BC	08/41-12/41	
	Bolingbroke IV			11/41-04/42	
		UV	Annette Island, AK	04/42-06/42	
115 (BR) Sqn	Bolingbroke IV			06/42-08/43	
119 (BR) Sqn	Bolingbroke I	DM	Yarmouth, NS	08/40-08/41	
	Bolingbroke IV-W			08/41-11/41	
	Bolingbroke IV			11/41-01/42	
		DM/GR	Sydney, NS	01/42-06/42	
121 (C) Sqn	Bolingbroke IVTT	EN	Dartmouth, NS	08/42-09/45	
122 (C) Sqn	Bolingbroke IVTT	AG	Patricia Bay, BC	08/42-09/45	
147 (BR) Sqn	Bolingbroke I, IV	SZ	Sea Island, BC	07/42-03/43	
			Tofino, BC	03/43-03/44	
163 (AC) Sqn	Bolingbroke IV (PR)		Sea Island, BC	03/43-06/43	

Notes: Squadron codes were discontinued for security reasons within the RCAF Home War Establishment on October 16, 1942. Canadian province and territory codes: AB = Alberta; BC = British Columbia; MB = Manitoba; NB = New Brunswick; NS = Nova Scotia; ON = Ontario; PE = Prince Edward Island; QC = Québec; SK = Saskatchewan. AK is the US state of Alaska. RCAF unit codes: AC = Army Co-operation; BR = Bomber-Reconnaissance; C = Composite; F = Fighter; OT = Operational Training.

The first Canadian-built Bolingbroke was Mk I 702. After evaluation by the Test and Development Establishment, it served with 8, 116 and 147 (BR) Squadrons.

be modified as they were incompatible with US bombs, and the weather was generally poor. The decision was taken to replace the Bolingbroke squadron within the Wing, with another equipped with fighters, 14 (F) Squadron. This allowed 8 (BR) Squadron to return to Sea Island, where it re-equipped with Lockheed Ventura GR.Vs from May 1943.

Reformed on August 1, 1941, 115 (F) Squadron was equipped with Bolingbroke Is, replacing them with Mk IVs that November. The aircraft were equipped with a pack of four 0.303in (7.7mm) guns under the fuselage to act as fighters; they were considered to be nimble enough to deal with any intruding Japanese bombers, but in reality, crews spent their time patrolling off the coasts. The unit was later designated as the Bolingbroke component of RCAF (Y) Wing, to operate from Annette Island in Alaska. It arrived there on April 27, 1942.

On June 22 the squadron became a bomber reconnaissance unit. During its first mission, on May 13, a reported sighting of a submarine periscope turned out to be a floating log. However, on July 7 a 115 (BR) Squadron crew led by Flight Sergeant William E Thomas in Bolingbroke IV 9118, attacked a submarine just below the surface around 80 miles (130km) northwest of the Queen Charlotte Islands in the Pacific Ocean. Four 250lb (113kg) depth charges were dropped on the submersible. US Coast Guard, Royal Canadian and US Navy assets later searched the area; two days later the cutter USCGC *McLane* and patrol vessel USS *YP-231* claimed the vessel sunk, with credit being shared with the Bolingbroke crew. The identity of their victim has never been confirmed. Once believed to be a Japanese vessel, one theory is that it was a Soviet submarine (*Shch-138*) clandestinely collecting intelligence off the Canadian coast.

Other RCAF squadrons that flew Bolingbrokes were 163 (Army Co-operation), which briefly had Mk IVs equipped for photographic reconnaissance, alongside North American Harvard IIs, for three months in 1943. No.13 (Operational Training) Squadron used the aircraft, alongside a variety of other types, to train general (maritime) and bomber reconnaissance crews. Bolingbroke IVs modified for target-towing duties were flown by both 121 and 122 (Composite) Squadrons, assigned to Eastern and Western Air Commands, respectively. Both operated various types for a large range of duties,

including air-sea rescue, communications, radio calibration, short-range transport and photography. They disbanded on September 15, 1945.

Several other RCAF units operated Bolingbrokes. The Test and Development Establishment at RCAF Station Rockcliffe, Ontario, evaluated most of the different variants created, as well as developing the target-towing modification. Bolingbrokes were flown by the RCAF Central Flying School at RCAF Station Trenton, Ontario, from February 1940, while the sole Mk III floatplane was assigned to 5 (BR) Squadron at Dartmouth, Nova Scotia, for an operational assessment until February 1941. The Air Force Ferry Squadron, formed on the first day of 1942, was retitled 124 (Ferry) Squadron in mid-February 13. It ferried aircraft, including Bolingbrokes, across Canada.

BLENHEIMS IN BRITAIN

While nine Filton-built Blenheim IVs were earmarked for the RCAF, equipped with D/F radio, only four (P4856 to P4859) were completed with it, the other five having the standard RAF fit. All nine aircraft served with RAF units. Four RCAF squadrons did fly Blenheims, however, two of them very briefly and all from airfields in Britain. They were known as Article XV squadrons, after the clause in the British Commonwealth Air Training Plan that placed crews that graduated from the schools into units under the command of a 'local air force', according to operational needs.

No.404 Squadron was formed at Thorney Island, Sussex, on April 15, 1941, within RAF Coastal Command, moving to Scotland the following month. Equipped with Blenheim IVFs, it performed convoy escort and anti-shipping

CANADIAN ARTICLE XV BLENHEIM UNITS				
Unit	Version	Code	Base	Dates
404 Sqn	Blenheim IVF	EE	Thorney Island	04/41-06/41
			Castledown	06/41-07/41
			Skitten	07/41-10/41
			Dyce	10/41-12/41
			Sumburgh	12/41-03/42
			Dyce	03/42-08/42
			Sumburgh	08/42-09/42
			Dyce	09/42-01/43
406 Sqn	Blenheim IF, IVF	HU	Acklington	05/41-06/41
407 Sqn	Blenheim IV	RR	Thorney Island	05/41-07/41
415 Sqn	Blenheim IV	GX	Thorney Island	12/41-02/42

BCATP BOLINGBROKE UNITS		
Unit	Base	Dates
1 B&GS	Jarvis, ON	08/40-02/45
2 B&GS	Moss Bank, SK	10/40-12/44
3 B&GS	McDonald, MB	03/41-02/45
4 B&GS	Fingal, ON	11/40-02/45
5 B&GS	Dafoe, SK	05/41-02/45
6 B&GS	Mountain View, ON	06/41-[1]
7 B&GS	Paulson, MB	06/41-02/45
8 B&GS	Lethbridge, AB	10/41-12/44
9 B&GS	Mount Joli, QC	12/41-04/45
10 B&GS	Mount Pleasant, PE	09/43-06/45
31 B&GS	Picton, ON	04/41-11/44

Notes: Dates are those the school existed – the majority had Bolingbrokes for most of their existence as part of a mixed complement of types. [1] Absorbed into the post-war RCAF; Mountain View became the home of the Air Armament School.

Three Bolingbrokes of 119 (BR) Squadron in formation near Yarmouth, Nova Scotia, in August 1941.

sweeps over the North Sea. During much of 1942 it operated along the Norwegian coastline, re-equipping with Bristol Beaufighters that September. Two other units, 407 and 415 Squadrons, formed at Thorney Island in May and August 1941, the former with Blenheim IVs as interim equipment before receiving Lockheed Hudson in June. No.415 Squadron received Bristol Beauforts and Blenheim IVs, but it never became operational with them and in January 1942 re-equipped with Handley Page Hampdens.

A night-fighter unit within RAF Fighter Command, 406 Squadron was raised at Acklington, Northumberland, on May 5, 1941. It briefly had Blenheim IFs and IVFs to prepare the Canadians for radar-equipped Beaufighter IIFs.

No.8 (BR) Squadron personnel in front of one of the unit's Bolingbrokes in Alaska in 1942, while part of RCAF (X) Wing.

TRAINING FOR THE EMPIRE

Bolingbrokes played a major role in the British Commonwealth Air Training Plan (BCATP). It was designed to train 50,000 aircrew a year from the UK, Australia, Canada and New Zealand, with the first Canadian training course starting on April 29, 1940. At its peak in 1943 over 100 schools were running, covering the full gamut of training, from elementary to operational. The plan was extended and revised in a new agreement signed on June 5, 1942, which granted Canada increased control over the training programme and revised trainee quotas. The 1942 agreement was allowed to expire on March 31, 1945, after which the system was progressively dismantled. Operational training continued until the late summer of 1945.

The Bolingbroke was a stalwart of the Bombing and Gunnery Schools (B&GS) within the BCATP, alongside the Avro Anson and Westland Lysander. Fairey Battles were also operated by most of the schools, as bomber and gunnery trainers, as well as tugs. The Bolingbroke IV-T's Boulton Paul Type C turret, mounted on the rear upper fuselage, equipped with two Browning machine guns, and integral bombing capability made it ideal for the B&GSs.

Each B&GS needed a practice range to train over. Typically, these were about six miles (10km) wide and 18 miles (29km) long, preferably along a lake shore as it reduced costs and complications (caused by spent ammunition and munitions) of securing large areas of land. That used by 3 B&GS encompassed the southern part of Lake Manitoba, for example.

Within the BCATP, Operational Training Units (OTU) provided advanced training on service types in Canada, allowing pilots and crews to go straight overseas to an operational squadron, if they did not join a home-based unit. In practice, many attended a second OTU

Bolingbroke IV-W 9013 was one of 15 powered by Pratt & Whitney Twin Wasp Juniors. The variant served with both 8 (BR) and 115 (F) Squadrons.

Bolingbroke 9170 was delivered equipped as a target tug and was issued to 31 Operational Training Unit (OTU) at Debert, Nova Scotia. It crashed on April 5, 1944, but was repaired by February 1945, returning to the OTU, only to be written off on March 7 while with 7 OTU.

after arriving in Britain, and some an Advanced Flying Unit.

Bolingbrokes were used as support aircraft with at least five OTUs. For example, 5 OTU, which operated from RCAF Station Boundary Bay in British Colombia, and established a satellite at RCAF Station Abbotsford, from August 15, 1944, was a heavy bomber training unit. Crews trained on the North American B-25 Mitchell before progressing to the Consolidated B-24 Liberator (and Avro Lancasters just before the Japanese surrender in September 1945). Around six Bolingbrokes were used as target-tugs for the bomber's gunners to practice their skills, while some dozen Kittyhawks were used for fighter affiliation training.

CANADIAN OPERATIONAL TRAINING UNITS WITH BOLINGBROKES				
Unit	Main type	Base	Dates	Notes/'code'
1 OTU	Hurricane	Bagotville, QC	07/42-01/45	'UY'
5 OTU	Mitchell/Liberator	Boundary Bay, BC	04/44-08/44	
		Abbotsford, BC	08/44-10/45	
7 OTU	Hudson	Debert, NS	07/44-07/45	ex 31 OTU
8 OTU	Hudson	Greenwood, NS	07/44-	ex 36 OTU
31 OTU	Hudson	Debert, NS	06/41-07/44	'LR', to 7 OTU
34 OTU	Ventura	Pennfield Ridge, NB	06/42-05/44	'FY'
36 OTU	Hudson	Greenwood, NS	05/42-07/44	'EP', to 8 OTU

Notes: 3*-series RAF units, until transferred to RCAF and renumbered in mid-1944.

Croatia

An independent Croat state, the Nezavisna Država Hrvatska (Independent State of Croatia, NDH), had been declared on April 10, 1941, four days after Germany invaded Yugoslavia. The Zrakoplovstvo NDH (Croat Air Force) was formed on April 19, from assets and personnel of the Yugoslavian air force. The formation of the NDH triggered a brutal civil war, which would rage throughout the four years that the state existed.

In June 1941 the Germans began to pass on captured Yugoslav aircraft to the Croats, including five Blenheim Is and five Potez 25s. At the time the Croat Air Force had 95 aircraft, of which around 50% were serviceable. A further three were reportedly handed over by the Germans in the first half of 1942. Most of the presented aircraft needed to be overhauled, which was performed at the Wiener Neustadt works at Zemun, resulting in the last of them only being ready for service by 1943. The Blenheims, given the serial 1501 to 1508, were operated by the 8th Bomber Squadron of the 3rd Group.

In addition to supplying volunteers to fight with the Germans against the Soviet Union with the Croat Luftwaffen-Legion, the main task of the Croat Air Force was combating the partisans within the NDH and across Yugoslavia. Combat operations against their former countrymen were unpopular with many crews within the air force. In June 1943, and again in October 1943, Blenheim crews flew their aircraft (1502 and 1506) to neutral Turkey. By the end of the year the force was close to disintegration, plagued by desertion and, according to the Germans, a lack of fighting spirit. Blenheims 1504, 1505 and 1508 were destroyed on the ground by partisans in August 1943, using explosives supplied by the British. Another of the aircraft (1501) was also destroyed by sabotage, while 1503 was written-off by its own bombload.

This left just one Blenheim (1507) with the Croat Air Force, which remained in service until the end of the war. Along with several other Croat Air Force aircraft, it was flown to Klagenfurt in Austria on May 6, 1945, where its crew sought sanctuary from President Tito's Communist forces. It was later recovered for use by the Communist Partisans.

Blenheim I 1506 serving as a backdrop to a military parade at Zagreb in 1943. Later that year, the aircraft was flown by its crew to Turkey.

Finland

Of all the countries that operated the Blenheim, Finland had the longest association with the aircraft. It was the first export customer, built the aircraft under licence and was the last to fly them. Its aircraft saw considerable combat in the conflicts against the Soviet Union in the Winter and Continuation Wars, and the Germans in the Lapland War.

A five-year plan to re-equip and expand the Ilmavoimat (Finnish Air Force) to 11 combat squadrons began in 1937. In October 1936 Finland had ordered 18 Blenheim Is (c/n 8137 to 8154), which were built at Filton, outside Bristol. They were delivered as BL-104 to BL-121 from July 1937 into 1938, to equip Lentolaivue (LeLv, air squadron) 46 at Luonetjärvi, within a new aviation regiment with headquarters at Joroinen, Lentorykmentti (LeR) 4. The aircraft, which gained the nickname 'Pelti-Heikki' ('tin Henry'), were modified so that they could employ Swedish bombs of up to 800kg (1,764lb).

THE WINTER WAR

On November 30, 1939, the Soviet Union invaded Finland, marking the start of the Winter War. Finland had around 110 front line aircraft; Soviet troops were supported by 2,800, plus another 450 of the Baltic Fleet air forces. The Blenheims were initially used on long-range reconnaissance flights. It was found that the British Eagle IV cameras carried were prone to icing, so they were replaced by Zeiss RMK 20 and RMK 50 units. By the end of December the Soviet advance had been halted.

A further order for 12 Blenheims was placed, which was fulfilled by Mk IVs built by Rootes Securities (L9025, L9026, L9028, L9195 to L9203) and delivered as BL-122 to BL-133. Deliveries began on January 17, 1940, but BL-127 was lost when it ditched in the Gulf of Bothnia the following day, one landed in Norway and another was damaged prior to delivery and its arrival in Finland was delayed. The Mk IVs were delivered to LeLv 46, which handed over its Mk Is to LeLv 44, also part of LeR 4.

A further 12 former RAF Blenheim Is (including L1345, L1347, L1354 and L1362, all previously flown by 13 Operational Training Unit at RAF Bicester, Oxfordshire) were handed over on February 21, 1940, becoming BL-134 to BL-145. The aircraft were ferried from the

Skis could be fitted to the Finnish Blenheims for operations from snow. Blenheim I BL-104 was the first of its kind for the Finnish Air Force.

One of Finland's original Blenheim Is (BL-111) of Täydennyslentolaivue 17 landing at Luonetjärvi on March 28, 1944. The yellow wing and fuselage bands were adopted for the Continuation War as a recognition marking while operating alongside German forces.

The first of ten Blenheim IVs built by Valtion was BL-196. The sarja VI aircraft made use of major components built by Ikarus in Yugoslavia.

UK to Finland with civil registrations (with, for example, OH-IPD used for BL-137) by RAF crews in civilian clothing, a thin cover to avoid protests from the Soviet Union. Known as the Series IV aircraft, they were assigned to LeLv 42, which had formed under LeR 4 on January 16, 1940.

The additional Blenheims allowed raids to be undertaken in larger groups, rather than as single aircraft, as had been the case. On February 11, 1940, the Soviets launched a new offensive on the Karelian Isthmus front, but by the end of the month the Finns had stabilised the front between Viipuri (Vyborg) and Lake Ladoga. A Soviet army crossed the ice of the Gulf of Finland west of Viipuri on March 4 at the rear of the Finnish forces. This was countered during the next six days, with close air support missions flown by the Finnish Air Force during which three Blenheims (BL-122, -133 and -144) were shot down. The fierce resistance persuaded the Soviet Union to agree to an armistice, which was signed on March 13. Although Finland had lost considerable territory, it had survived. During the 105 days of the Winter War, the Blenheims flew 423 sorties and dropped 3,168 bombs. Their gunners claimed five kills, although seven of the Finnish Blenheims had been shot down and another five lost in accidents.

CONTINUATION WAR

The German occupation of Denmark and Norway in April 1940 isolated Finland from the west and surrounded it with more powerful and aggressive neighbours. Estonia, Latvia and Lithuania were annexed by the Soviet Union in June. Germany offered Finland war material from the states it had overrun.

In addition, Finland built its own arms. A licence to assemble Blenheims had been acquired in April 1938 and local assembly of the aircraft was undertaken by Valtion Lentokonetehdas (State Aircraft Factory) at Tampere, which would eventually build 45 of a variant of the Mk I (five of which were never assembled). The aircraft were known as Blenheim IIs by Bristol, with the first (BL-146) flying on June 14, 1941. The initial 15 aircraft (BL-146 to BL-160), all in service by the end of 1941, were known as sarja (series) II aircraft, the original examples delivered from Bristol becoming sarja I and those supplied by the RAF sarjas III and IV. They were followed by 30 sarja V Blenheim IIs (BL-161 to BL-190),

which were delivered between April and December 1943.

Finnish military leaders were informed of the German intention to invade the Soviet Union on May 25, 1941. Three days after the launch of Operation Barbarossa, the German assault east on June 22, Soviet aircraft bombed several targets in Finland, starting the Continuation War. Around 500 Soviet aircraft were available on the Finnish front.

The Finnish aim was to regain territory lost in the Winter War, with Finnish troops advancing from July 10. Blenheims were used to harass the Soviet transport systems, but the fighting took its toll. On July 15 LeLv 46 was declared non-operational,

Blenheim II BL-167 was one of 30 sarja V aircraft delivered by Valtion Lentokonetehdas between April and December 1943. The aircraft survived the war only to be damaged beyond repair on June 20, 1948, just before Pommituslentolaivue 41 gave up the Blenheim bombers.

One of the 12 Rootes Securities-built Blenheim IVs delivered to Finland in early 1940. British-built aircraft were delivered without the spinners fitted.

having lost most of its aircraft – Blenheims and captured Ilyushin DB-3Ms – in combat. LeLv 44's Blenheims repeatedly attacked Soviet air bases on the Karelian Isthmus during August. By early December 1941, favourable defensive positions had been reached between Lake Onega and the White Sea. From that point the fighting became one of attrition. The Blenheims were used to attack trains on the Leningrad to Murmansk railway, among other targets. They were sent out on the night of April 15, 1942, to repel a Soviet attack against Finnish forces along the River Svir. The raid was a disaster, as three Blenheims (BL-154, -157 and -159) exploded while attempting to drop their bombs when securing pins failed to release them.

The Finnish Air Force was reorganised into groups responsible for defined territorial areas on May 3, 1942. However, the Blenheims of LeLv 42 and 44 remained under LeR 4, as the Finnish bomber force would be deployed to cover all regions as required. In addition to the Blenheim squadrons, LeR 4 controlled the Dornier Do 17-equipped LeLv 46 as well as LeLv 48, which operated captured Soviet types. What did change was that the regiment flew larger daylight raids that involved nearly all its aircraft, with the bombers escorted by fighters. On February 20, 1943, LeLv 44 handed its Blenheims over to LeLv 42 while its crews headed for Germany to train on the Junkers Ju 88A-4. It became operational on the German bomber on May 30. LeLv 48 passed its Soviet aircraft to LeLv 46 and began conversion to sarja V Blenheim IIs on November 15 as they were delivered from Tampere. The squadron was declared operational on the aircraft on December 29.

At the end of January 1944, the Soviet army was able to lift the siege of Leningrad, freeing up forces for other fronts. In an attempt to remove Finland from the war, three night-bombing raids were launched against Helsinki. LeR 4 organised counter raids, following the retreating Soviet bombers back to their well-lit bases. On March 9 at least ten enemy bombers were destroyed by 21 Finnish aircraft, while on April 3 Kähy airfield near Leningrad was attacked by 34, the Finns claiming 17 aircraft on the ground. Role prefixes were added to Finnish squadrons on February 14, 1944; both the Blenheim air squadrons became Pommituslentolaivue (PLeLv, bomber squadron).

A major Soviet offensive on the Karelian Isthmus was launched on June 9, 1944, but it was brought to a halt on July 12 after the Finns gave up ground. LeR 4's bombers were used to attack troop concentrations, tanks and artillery with formations typically comprising 35 bombers and 16 escorting Messerschmitt Bf 109Gs. The escort was effective; no bombers were lost to Soviet fighters during the 1,232 sorties flown in 36 missions during the campaign.

Additional Blenheims were delivered to the Finnish Air Force in the second half of 1944, comprising ten Blenheim IVs built by Valtion as BL-196 to BL-205, known as sarja VI aircraft. These aircraft were started by Ikarus AD in

FINNISH BLENHEIM UNITS

Unit	Assigned	Base	Date	Notes
LeLv 42	LeR 4	Luonetjärvi	03/40	
		Siikakangas	02/44	to PLeLv 42
LeLv 44	LeR 4	Joroinen	?/39-?/?	
		Siikakangas	02/43	to Ju 88
LeLv 46	LeR 4	Luonetjärvi	?/39-07/41	
LeLv 48	LeR 4	Onttola	11/43-02/44	to PLeLv 48
PLeLv 41	LeR 4	Naarajärvi	12/44-01/45	
		Luonetjärvi	?/45-09/48	
			08/51-12/52	
PLeLv 42	LeR 4	Siikakangas	02/44-?/?	
		Naarajärvi	12/44	to PLeLv 41
PLeLv 43	LeR 4	Luonetjärvi	?/45-?/46	
PLeLv 45	LeR 4	Luonetjärvi	01/45-09/48	
PLeLv 48	LeR 4	Onttola	02/44	
		Vesivehmaa	12/44	to PLeLv 45
TLeLv 12	LeR 1		?/?-09/44	
T-LLv 17	LeR 4	Luonetjärvi	?/?-09/41	
			03/42-12/44	
HämLsto		Luonetjärvi	01/57-04/58	ex 1. Lennosto
KoeLtue		Kuorevesi	?/45-?/48	
			05/57-05/58	
1. Lennosto		Luonetjärvi	12/52-01/57	to HämLsto

Abbreviations: HämLsto (Hämeen Lennosto, Hämeen Air Command); KoeLtue (Test Flight); Lennosto (Air Command); LeR (Lentorykmentti, Aviation Regiment); LeLv (Lentolaivue, Air Squadron); PLeLv (Pommituslentolaivue, Bomber Squadron); T-LLv (Täydennyslentolaivue, Replenishment [ie training] Squadron); TLeLv (Tiedustelulentolaivue, Reconnaissance Squadron)

A Blenheim I being towed out of the forest around October 1941 during the Continuation War. Finnish Blenheims fought in three distinct conflicts with both the Allies and Axis powers during World War Two.

Zemun in Yugoslavia as B.4s, but had not been completed before the German invasion of the country. Ikarus was taken over by the Wiener Neustädter Flugzeugwerke and in October 1941 Finland made a deal to buy the components for 15 aircraft and some Bristol Mercury engines. The first flew on May 15, 1944, and the ten were issued to PLeLv 42 and 48. The other five were not assembled.

By early August 1944, all fronts were stationary and talks for a ceasefire under way. This was implemented on September 4, 1944, and a truce signed 15 days later. Finland had to withdraw to the 1940 Moscow Peace Treaty borders and all flying was banned, except when approved by the Allied Supervision Commission.

During the Continuation War, Blenheims conducted 2,768 sorties and claimed three Soviet aircraft. The cost to the fleet was high, as around 40 Blenheims had been destroyed to enemy action and in accidents. The signing of the ceasefire resulted in construction of another five Blenheim IIs (sarja VIIs BL-190 to BL-195) being cancelled.

THE LAPLAND WAR

Under the terms of the ceasefire, German forces in the north of Finland had to leave. Finland declared war on Germany on

September 15, but operations against its former ally began on October 1 in what became known as the Lapland War. The LeRyhmä Sarko (Air Group Sarko) was formed on October 6, including the Blenheims of PLeLv 42 and 48, plus other types of PLeLv 6, 44 and 46, for a total of 39 bombers, plus 55 fighters of other regiments. By the end of the month Finnish forces had advanced to the 68th parallel, leaving small German units in the extreme north and northwestern corner of the country.

LeRyhmä Sarko disbanded on November 16, replaced by LeR 2 to continue operations in Lapland; LeR 4 came under its control for missions against the final German positions. This situation lasted until December 3, when LeR 4 was placed in sole command of Lapland operations. The next day, as part of the truce terms, PLeLv 48 disbanded and PLeLv 42 was redesignated PLeLv 41. The last Blenheim unit had 12 aircraft at Luonetjärvi, while another 15 were based at Kemi with other air assets flying combat missions. The Blenheims flew 157 sorties during the Lapland War, the last a strafing attack on a German garrison on January 2, 1945. German forces withdrew to northern Norway on March 27, 1945, and the final Finnish Air Force sorties in the conflict were flown on April 4.

AFTER THE WAR

Under Soviet pressure, Finland removed the traditional blue and white 'swastika' from its aircraft on April 1, 1945, replacing it with the white, blue and white roundel. Around 37 Blenheims had survived the various wars, with 31 assigned to PLeLv 41 and 45, the latter having replaced its captured Soviet types. The Allied Supervision Commission ban on flights continued until August 1, 1945.

Blenheims remained in service until September 15, 1948, when Finland ratified the terms of the peace treaty. Under its provisions, Finland was not allowed to operate bombers, so PLeLv 41 and 45 disbanded and the 13 survivors – nine had crashed or been damaged beyond repair post-war, and others withdrawn – were placed into storage.

In 1951 two Blenheims were 'overhauled' by Valmet Oy (successor to Valtion) for second line duties. Effectively they were new-built aircraft, which adopted existing serials to avoid paying a licence fee to Bristol. The centre section and landing gear of BL-106 was used, the aircraft having been scrapped after a force landing on June 8, 1944. The nose of Mk IV BL-197 formed the second, mated to a new centre and rear fuselage, wings and tail surfaces. The other three were Mk II BL-173, and Mk IVs BL-199 and BL-200, all refurbished by 1955.

They were originally powered by Mercury XVs, but Mk VIIIs were later installed, with some aircraft flying with one of both versions. Later it is possible Mercury 25 and 30s were used.

Blenheim I BL-106 was used as a multi-engine and navigation trainer, operated by 1.Lennosto (the air regiments having been replaced by groups – Lennosto – on December 1, 1952) at Luonetjärvi, which became the Hämeen Lennosto on January 1, 1957. It was damaged beyond repair on March 20, 1957. Aerial surveys were performed by BL-197. It became the highest-time Finnish Blenheim, with 1,137hrs 10mins, at the time it was retired on October 6, 1957.

Blenheim II BL-173 of the Hämeen Lennosto suffered a landing accident at Oulunsalo on September 13, 1957, during which its wing tip was damaged. It was repaired and continued to fly until April 10, 1958. BL-200 was retired in June 1957, while BL-199 completed the last flight by an operational Blenheim, on May 20, 1958. It had accumulated a total of 707hrs 5mins, flight time.

France

The Forces Aériennes Françaises Libres (Free French Air Force – FAFL) was formed in June 1940 under the control of General Charles de Gaulle. Flying aircraft carrying the Cross of Lorraine, several of its units flew Blenheim IVs in combat. Although most had been withdrawn from frontline operations by late 1942, Blenheims continued to be flown by the FAFL and its successors in second-line roles into 1945.

Groupe de mixte combat (GMC, mixed combat group) 1 was formed at RAF Odiham, Hampshire, on August 29, 1940, with sub-units manned by French personnel. It had a few Dewoitine D.520 fighters, an escadrille (squadron) with Westland Lysanders and Caudron C.270 Lucioles for reconnaissance and liaison, and another equipped with six Blenheim IV bombers. The group soon embarked on ships at Liverpool for Operation Menace, the unsuccessful attempt to rally Senegal in French West Africa to the Free French cause and take the port of Dakar from Vichy control. After Menace, GMC 1 went to Cameroon and participated in rallying Gabon to accept Free French authority in November 1940. The group disbanded on December 10, 1940.

The first FAFL unit with Blenheims had been Escadrille 'Topic', also formed at RAF Odiham on August 1, 1940, before taking its eight aircraft to RAF Andover, Hampshire. The unit left from Glasgow on October 18 heading for Takoradi in the Gold Coast, from where it proceeded to Maïdugari in eastern Nigeria.

Groupe réservé de bombardement (GRB, reserve bombing group) 1 was the first FAFL group formed, on December 24, 1940. It incorporated the two bomber squadrons originally formed at Odiham, the escadrille formed for Operation Menace (later based at Fort Lamy in Chad), and Escadrille 'Topic' at Maïdugari, both flying Blenheim IVs. During the advance on Koufra in the Tibesti Desert during February 1941 both squadrons provided support from Ounianga in northern Chad, 600 miles south of Koufra. Air attacks started on February 2, but two days later only one out

After being operated by 45 Squadron, Blenheim IV Z7633 was assigned to Groupe de bombardement 'Lorraine'. It survived its time with the FAFL to be returned to the RAF.

of four Blenheims dispatched on a bombing mission returned, having suffered problems with its engines on its way to the target. One of the four (T1867) – and the bodies of its crew – was not found until 1959. Koufra fell on February 25, but by then only four of the 12 Blenheims were serviceable.

In March 1941 GRB 1 was sent to Gordon Tree airfield in Khartoum, Sudan, having been attached to 203 Group of the RAF for operations over Eritrea. Operations started on March 24 and on May 13 a Blenheim shot down an Italian Fiat CR.42 Falco. The campaign

ended in July 1941, after which the squadrons returned to Damascus, Syria. There the group was retitled Groupe de bombardement 'Lorraine' on September 24, 1941, and the Escadrilles 'Metz' and 'Nancy'.

On October 16 'Lorraine' departed Damascus for Abu Sueir near Cairo, Egypt, moving out to the Libyan Desert on November 13 to support the British offensive. Instead of dispatching small numbers of Blenheims to hit targets, larger flights participated in raids, during which a crew recorded the group's second aerial victory

As Blenheim IV N3622 was delivered to the FAFL after use by the RAF Fighter Flight in Sudan, it is likely to have been flown by Groupe réservé de bombardement 1.

Free French Air Force Blenheim IVs, probably of Groupe de bombardement 1/17 'Picardie', at an airfield in Syria. The aircraft carried both the Cross of Lorraine and RAF roundels under the wings.

by shooting down a Messerschmitt Bf 109. By the end of January 1942, the group had to be withdrawn from the fighting after losing eight Blenheims and 13 killed, settling at Rayak in Syria.

During April 1942, Escadrille 'Metz' was attached to the Aircraft Delivery Unit, Middle East, ferrying aircraft around the region, while Escadrille 'Nancy' operated under RAF control as a general reconnaissance unit based in Palestine,

augmenting its Blenheim IVs with Mk Vs. From the winter of 1942, the group's FAFL personnel departed for England, with 342 Squadron FFAF 'Lorraine' forming on April 7, 1943, at RAF West Raynham, Norfolk, flying Douglas Bostons.

The Groupe de bombardement 'Bretagne' formed in Chad on January 1, 1942, with Escadrille 'Rennes', equipped with Lysanders based at Moussoro, and Escadrille 'Nantes' with Martin Marylands at Fort-Archambault. It supported French forces advancing on Tripoli in Libya from airfields at Douar and Wour during March 1942, before returning to its bases in Chad. In December 1942, prior to Operation Fezzan II, 'Nantes' was reinforced with six Blenheims. The group operated from Zouar, with Uigh-el-Kebir used as an auxiliary airfield, before moving to Sebba. Tripoli fell on January 23, 1943.

The Blenheims left behind in Syria by the departure of 'Lorraine' were used to form the Escadrille de surveillance de Syrie (Syrian surveillance squadron) at Damascus in December 1942, tasked with coastal patrol missions over the eastern Mediterranean. Another flight, based at Hassetché in northern Syria, flew Potez 25s. The two merged to form the Groupe de bombardement 1/17 'Picardie' on October 16, 1943, with three escadrilles operating from Damascus, Palmyra and Rayak. The group continued to fly Blenheim IVs and Vs until they were replaced by Baltimore Vs at the end of 1944.

Germany

The fall of Belgium, France and the Netherlands saw British forces evicted from continental Europe, leaving behind much of its equipment. This included several Blenheims damaged in the fighting, plus the wrecks of others shot down. It is highly likely that the Luftwaffe was able to recover and repair at least one RAF Blenheim, as a Mk IV in German markings with the code '5+5' was noted in May 1941. The aircraft is understood to have been used to teach Luftwaffe fighter pilots methods of shooting down the aircraft.

The Luftwaffe was also able to evaluate a Finnish Air Force Blenheim IV (BL-130) in late 1940, after the end of the Winter War but before the start of the Continuation War. Somewhat ironically, the aircraft was a former RAF example delivered to Finland at the start of that year.

Blenheim IV '5+5' was active with an unidentified Luftwaffe unit in mid-1941.

The World's Fastest Growing Aviation Website

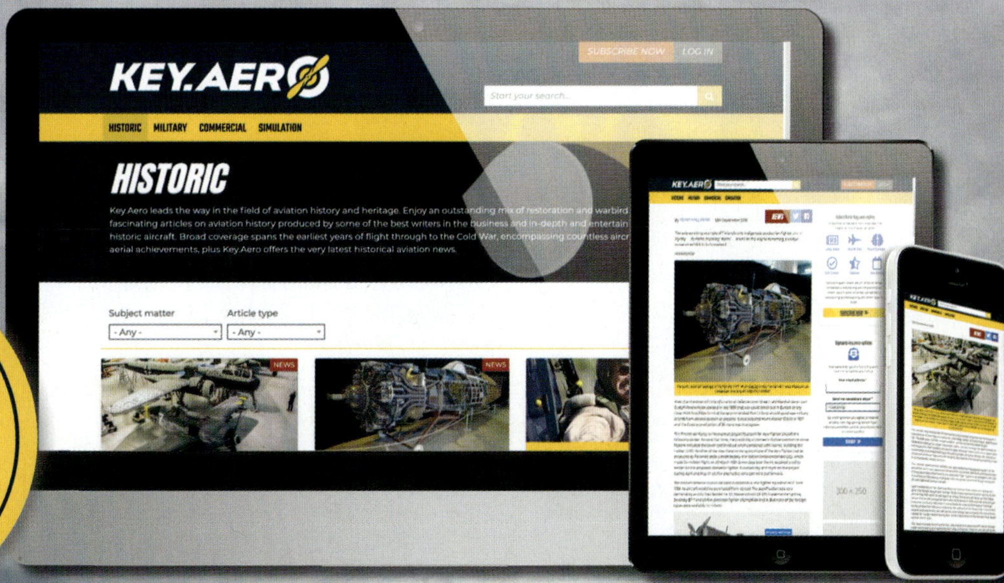

Join us online

GREAT REASONS TO SUBSCRIBE

- In-depth articles, videos, quizzes and more, with new material added daily
- From historic and military aviation to commercial and simulation – *Key.Aero* has it all
- Exclusive interactive content you won't find anywhere else
- A fully searchable archive
- Access to all the leading aviation magazines
- Membership to an engaged, global aviation community
- Access on any device – anywhere, anytime

www.key.aero

Subscribe FROM JUST £5.99 for unlimited access

Greece

A total of 12 Blenheim IVs were ordered for the Ellinikí Vasilikí Aeaporía (EVA, Royal Hellenic Air Force). The aircraft were built at Filton outside Bristol and were fitted with different equipment to Blenheims destined for the RAF. They were P4910, P4911, P4915, P4916, P4921, P4922, P6891, P6892, P6897, P6898, P6903 and P6904 (c/n 9392, 9393, 9397, 9398, 9403, 9404, 9416, 9417, 9422, 9423, 9428 and 9429), which were registered G-AFXD to -AFXO for their ferry flights via Hungary between October 13, 1939, and February 1940.

They were delivered unarmed and without the bomb aiming sight, bomb rails, crew intercommunications and radio; the start of the war meant many systems were in high demand or reserved for domestic use, rather than export. Many of the missing parts were either created or installed after the aircraft entered service with 32 Mira Vomvardismou (32 Bombing Squadron) at Larrisa. They received the markings B251 to B262.

On October 28, 1940, Italy invaded Greece from occupied Albania. The EVA was heavily involved in the conflict. Three Blenheims attacked the forward Italian airbase at Koritza (now Korçë) on November 1, although they caused little damage. Another three returned the next day, destroying a Fiat CR.42 Falco.

Two days later, the first RAF Blenheims arrived in Greece, when eight Mk I/IFs of 30 Squadron landed at Eleusis. They were later augmented by Blenheim Is from 84 Squadron and, by the end of November, 211 Squadron. A Greek Blenheim was lost after crash-landing after a raid on Kalpaki on November 10, while another was shot down by CR.42s the next day.

Blenheims supported the Greek counteroffensive launched on November 14, with the EVA bomber force (that also included a squadron of Fairey Battles and another of Potez 633s) striking Koritza and Argyrokastron airfields on that day, for the loss of a Blenheim and a Battle from anti-aircraft artillery. Later that afternoon, Falchi shot down a pair of Blenheims attacking targets around Koritza. By November 23 Hellenic forces had restored the pre-war border in Epirus and captured Koritza, and continued to advance into Albania until early January 1941. From the 6th of that month the front stabilised.

Six Blenheim Is (including L6658 and L6670, previously with 211 Squadron, and L8384 and L8385, former 39 Squadron aircraft) were handed over to Greece from RAF stocks to reinforce 32 Bombing Squadron, making good the losses suffered during operations fighting the Italians on the Albanian border. Sources state the aircraft were handed over in January or February 1941, although official RAF documents are dated April 1. The aircraft became B263 to B268 in Greek service but retained the Desert or European schemes applied by their former owner.

No Hellenic Blenheims escaped the German invasion of Greece, which was launched on April 6, 1941, following a failed Italian offensive

Greece received its Blenheims after the war had started, with all 12 allocated British civil registrations for delivery. Originally ordered as P9416, G-AFXG is understood to have become B254 in Hellenic service.

One of the original 12 Blenheim IVs delivered to the Royal Hellenic Air Force, B261 is being prepared for a mission in late 1940. The aircraft were delivered unarmed, with bomb shackles added by 32 Bombing Squadron personnel upon delivery.

in March. The Germans reached the southern shoreline of Greece on April 30. Most of the 18 are understood to have been destroyed, although at least one survived in reasonable condition after the Axis take over.

In June 1941 the 13th Light Bomber Squadron was reformed within the Royal Hellenic Air Force at Dekhelia, Egypt, as part of the RAF's 201 Group, equipped with five Avro Anson Is that had escaped the overrun of the country by German forces. In November 1941 it moved to Mariyut near Alexandria and the Ansons were replaced by Blenheim IVs, which continued to wear British camouflage and markings but had the Hellenic blue and white roundel. The squadron primarily operated in the convoy escort role and on anti-submarine patrols in the Eastern Mediterranean. At least 19 Blenheim IVs served with the unit, but they were replaced by Mk Vs from November 1942, with the final Mk IV leaving in January 1943. By then, the squadron's aircraft retained the RAF roundel. At least 33 Blenheim Vs were operated by the unit (BA106, BA165, BA167, BA290, BA294, BA304, BA323, BA324, BA384, BA395, BA399, BA403, BA429, BA454, BA487, BA544, BA580, BA581, BA593, BA847, BA848, BA850, BA882, BA912, BA929, BA934, BA937, BA948, EH316, EH319, EH336, EH338 and EH405), which was generally known as the 13 (Hellenic) Squadron by 1943. It re-equipped with Martin Baltimore aircraft in September 1943.

Blenheim I B268 was one of the aircraft transferred from RAF stocks in early 1941. Intriguingly, just above the rear fuselage is the tail of a Luftwaffe aircraft, indicating that the aircraft fell into the hands of the Germans following the Axis occupation in April 1941.

Hungary

Hungary became the assembly area for German troops heading for Yugoslavia in April 1941. Hitler asked for active Hungarian participation in the invasion of its neighbour, with Yugoslav aircraft bombing Hungary's railway stations and airfields from April 6. Six days later, a Yugoslav pilot of Hungarian extraction flew his Ikarus-built Blenheim I to Hungary. The aircraft involved is understood to be c/n 3516 (but has also been stated to be 3528). It was retained by the Magyar Királyi Honvéd Légierő (Royal Hungarian Air Force) as J-104 (also reported as L-104), which removed all armament and used it as a light transport.

On August 9, 1944, Ferihegy airfield, outside Budapest, was attacked by US Army Air Force Consolidated B-24 Liberators. The Hungarian Blenheim was destroyed in the raid.

The Hungarian Blenheim soon after its arrival in the country, still wearing the Yugoslavian Air Force fin flash.

India

The Indian Air Force Volunteer Reserve (IAFVR) was established in 1939 to create a reserve of personnel for the defence of India in case of war. As a result of the recommendation by the Expert Committee on the Defence of India of late 1938, chaired by Admiral Alfred Ernle Montacute Chatfield (the 'Chatfield Committee'), the IAFVR authorised five coastal defence flights to protect major ports. The flights used a wide variety of aircraft, including Armstrong Whitworth Atalantas, de Havilland Dragon Rapides and Tiger Moths, and Westland Wapitis, while one would go on to operate Blenheims.

No.3 Coastal Defence Flight was raised at RAF Dum Dum, Calcutta, on August 1, 1940, equipped with Wapiti IIAs. In December 1941 the biplanes were replaced by six Blenheim Is. On April 1, 1942, the unit was redesignated 103 (Coastal Defence) Flight, but it disbanded at the start of June and was absorbed into 353 Squadron, RAF.

Mechanics working on the Mercury VIII of a 3 Coastal Defence Flight Blenheim I.

Indonesia

In November 1945 a group of Indonesians decided to salvage a Blenheim IV abandoned at Semarang, Java. The previous month the Tentara Keamanan Rakyat (TKR, People's Security Army) had been formed, with an aviation arm. The Blenheim was taken to Maospati airfield (Iswahjudi Air Force Base from late 1960) near Madiun in East Java, where a group of engineers, led by Sergeant Sajad (also reported as Sadjad), set about restoring it to airworthy condition. TKR Aviation became the Angkat-an Udara (Indonesian Air Force) on April 9, 1946.

The Mercury engines were substituted with Japanese Nakajima Ha115 (Sakae) 14-cylinder, air-cooled engines, rated at 950hp (708kW), taken from Nakajima Ki-43 Hayabusas. Japanese instruments were also installed, taken from the available stocks of abandoned Japanese aircraft. The Blenheim was also fitted with an aerial camera, so that images could be taken of the Dutch fleet blockading Indonesia during the War of Independence.

On November 13, 1946, the Blenheim was rolled out of the Maospati Aircraft Maintenance Centre (previously the People's Security Army Aircraft Workshop) for engine tests, which confirmed that the work was sound. Later that day test pilot 'Suhanda', a former Japanese Army pilot who had taken a new, Indonesian name, and Sajad, were aboard for the first test flight. The aircraft reached a height of around 330ft (100m), but after lining up to land, power was lost. 'Suhanda' completed a belly landing outside the airfield; along with Sajad, he escaped the incident without a scratch.

Indonesia's one and only Blenheim IV on November 13, 1946, the day of its sole flight. *Key Publishing*

Japan

The Imperial Japanese Army Air Force is understood to have operated some of the Blenheims abandoned by the RAF. The RAF had four squadrons, 27, 34, 60 and 62, flying the aircraft against Japanese forces after they invaded the Malayan peninsular. A Blenheim, along with other captured aircraft, was evaluated by the Japanese Institute of Technical Research of Military Aviation in Singapore soon after the conquest of the territory.

Exactly how many Blenheims fell into Japanese hands has not been confirmed, but the hulks of at least four aircraft were noted at Semarang in Java in Japanese markings at the end of the war. They included three Blenheim IVs and a Mk I. They were painted in Japanese camouflage and wore the Hinomaru (the red roundel) on the fuselage and wings.

Evidence that some of the captured aircraft were modified by the Japanese was also noted on the hulks at Semarang. At least one of the Blenheim IVs had four windows installed each side of the cabin. Another is understood to have had its Bristol Mercury engines replaced by Nakajima Sakaes. One of the hulks at Semarang was salvaged after the war by Indonesian forces (*see above*).

The dump at Semarang in 1947. At least three Blenheims are visible at the rear, including the fuselage of a Mk IV on the right, with what appears to be windows along the cabin.

New Zealand

No Blenheims were delivered to the Royal New Zealand Air Force (RNZAF) and the aircraft was never allocated a RNZAF serial, but one of its squadrons did briefly fly the aircraft in England. No.489 (NZ) Squadron was formed at RAF Leuchars, south of Edinburgh, on August 12, 1941, under RAF Coastal Command. It was an Article XV unit of the British Commonwealth Air Training Plan manned largely by New Zealanders, but with personnel from other countries. Wing Commander J A S Brown was commanding officer of the squadron; he, along with both initial flight commanders, Squadron Leaders B Sandeman and D Evans, were British.

It was equipped with Bristol Beaufort torpedo bombers that carried the code 'XA', but its work-up was slow; only four aircraft had been delivered by October. In January 1941 Blenheim IV and IVFs began to arrive to replace the Beauforts, most of which had briefly previously been assigned to 143 Squadron based at RAF Aldergrove in Northern Ireland. That squadron had

The High Commissioner of New Zealand, Sir Wiliam Joseph Jordan (in civilian attire), stands with officers and air men of 489 (NZ) Squadron in front of one of the unit's Blenheim IVs.

effectively served as an operational training unit for crews to be posted overseas, but had fully re-equipped with Bristol Beaufighters.

The Blenheims were always viewed as interim equipment by 489 (NZ) Squadron,

before another type could be sourced. They were replaced by Handley Page Hampden Is from March 1942 and the squadron became operational in the following month.

A 489 (NZ) Squadron Blenheim IV in front of one of the hangars at RAF Leuchars, Scotland, in the second half of 1941. The aircraft lacks the gun pack and its bomb bay is open, making it a 'straight' Mk IV rather than a IVF.

Portugal

The Blenheim had a relatively short career in Portugal, although it served with both the army and naval air arms. The country received 21 former RAF Blenheim IVs and a pair of Mk Vs in August to November 1943, under the terms of the Azores Treaty. In addition to granting the Allies access to facilities on the Azores, the treaty stated that serviceable Allied aircraft that landed in Portugal could be retained and would be provided with spares, although their crews would be repatriated. Portugal had originally requested the supply of Bristol Beaufighters.

Prior to the treaty, several RAF aircraft flying between the UK and destinations in the Middle East had sought sanctuary in Portugal after they had encountered trouble south of the Bay of Biscay. Upon diverting into Portuguese airfields, they were impounded as the country was neutral in the conflict that raged around it.

Among them were at least three Blenheims, including Mk IV Z7366 previously of 105 Squadron, which landed on the beach at Cabo de Santa Maria near Faro on July 17, 1941, after becoming short of fuel after an auxiliary pump broke on its way to Gibraltar from RAF Portreath, Cornwall. The nose was badly damaged and the two propellers bent, slightly on the right engine and, more noticeably, one blade on the left engine. One year later it had been moved to the workshops of the OGMA company at Alverca for repair. Two Blenheim Vs also force-landed in Portugal in June and November 1942. Other examples of the aircraft came down in Portugal, including Mk V BB166, which crashed into the sea on January 24, 1943, and was washed up on the beach near Comporta.

All of the treaty Blenheims had very high flight hours and had seen extensive use with the RAF. Most, if not all, of the aircraft identified for transfer to Portugal were delivered to 301 Ferry Training Unit at RAF Lyneham, Wiltshire, which trained crews to ferry overseas. The A Flight there dealt with Bristol twin-engined designs. The actual deliveries were performed by 1 Overseas Aircraft Despatch Unit based at RAF Portreath. A 22nd Blenheim Mk IV, L8837, did make it to Portugal, but force-landed at Cintra on September 9, 1943.

A total of 14, including the pair of 'new' Blenheim Vs equipped with dual controls,

PORTUGUESE NAVY BLENHEIMS		
Port Serial	RAF Serial	Notes
B-1	AZ986	Mk V, to Portugal 30/08/41
B-2	AZ987	Mk V, to Portugal 15/09/41
B-3	R2775	to Portugal 01/09/43
B-4	V5429	to Portugal 30/08/43
B-5	V5434	to Portugal 30/08/43
B-6	Z5762	to Portugal 30/08/43
B-7	Z5760	to Portugal 30/08/43
B-8	Z6030	to Portugal 30/08/43
B-9	N3600	to Portugal 17/09/43
B-10	R3623	to Portugal 17/09/43
B-11	V5729	to Portugal 15/09/43
B-12	Z6341	to Portugal 16/09/43
B-13	Z5736	to Portugal 29/11/43
B-14	Z6035	to Portugal 29/11/43

were allocated to the Aviação Naval Portuguesa (Portuguese Naval Aviation) and entered service with Esquadrilha B das Forças Aéreas da Armada (Flight B of the Naval Aviation) at Lisbon Airport in Portela de Sacavém.

Most of the Mk IVs for the navy were delivered with the under fuselage four-gun pack, but the armament was in poor condition and not used in Portuguese service, with the gun packs - if not the individual weapons - usually removed from the aircraft. Portugal's Blenheims received little in the way of maintenance in service and were stored primarily outdoors, as Lisbon Airport lacked the proper shelters for the work to be undertaken. Dust and dirt were a constant problem.

From March 1945, the first of 16 new Beaufighter TF.Xs began to arrive at Lisbon

The first Blenheim 'delivered' to Portugal was Mk IV Z7366, which force-landed on a beach near Faro on July 17, 1941. The aircraft became an attraction, until it was dismantled and transported by road to Alverca and repaired in 1942. It became 262/'ZE-B'. The middle aircraft is a Mk V, possibly 'ZE-A', which should make it 261, the interned BA829.

Portugal used four Blenheim Vs, with two going to both the air force and navy, this example belonging to the former. The aircraft retains the bomb racks under the rear fuselage.

MILITARY AVIATION BLENHEIMS

Port Serial	RAF Serial	Notes
261	BA829	Mk V, force-landed and interned 17/11/42; crashed 11/08/44
262	Z7366	force-landed Faro and interned 17/07/41
263	BA288	Mk V, crash-landed Portella 21/06/42
264	N3544	to Portugal 01/09/43
265	R2781	to Portugal 01/09/43
266	R3830	to Portugal 01/09/43
267	V5883	to Portugal 30/08/43
268	T2431	to Portugal 17/09/43
269	T2434	to Portugal 17/09/43
270	V5501	to Portugal 15/09/43
271	V6395	to Portugal 15/09/43
272	Z7492	to Portugal 15/09/43

Institute of Engineering) at Lisbon, along with a pair of Beaufighters, as instructional airframes. It is not known if the airframe was delivered to the college.

Under Army command, the Aeronáutica Militar (Military Aviation) received the other nine Blenheim IVs delivered in 1943. They had earlier taken on the three interned aircraft, after they had been returned to airworthy condition, which entered service with the Esquadrilha ZE at Base Aérea 2, Ota.

Portuguese squadrons had been identified by the codes applied to their aircraft since the winter of 1940, with the Blenheims all carrying 'ZE' and an individual letter either side of the roundel. (Photographic evidence has 262 as 'ZE-B' and 267 as 'ZE-G', probably indicating that 261 to 272 were '-A' to '-L').

On the morning of August 11, 1944, eight of the aircraft were airborne over the Tagus River. Two of the aircraft collided, resulting in 261 crashing, killing the commander of Esquadrilha ZE, Captain Ribeiro Ferreira. The accident effectively ended the operation of Blenheims by the squadron.

for Esquadrilha B, while a small number of the naval Blenheims remained active for training purposes. By mid-1946 almost the entire unit was grounded because of a lack of pilots. The last flight of one of its Blenheims occurred in 1947. Around 1950, a single naval Blenheim was offered to the Instituto Superior Técnico (Technical

Blenheim IV 267/'ZE-G' of Esquadrilha ZE at Base Aérea 2, Ota, in 1944, head a line-up of three of the aircraft. Built in late 1940 by Rootes Securities as V5883 with the RAF, it had served with the 54 Operational Training Unit at RAF Charterhall on the Scottish borders, and was transferred to Portugal on August 30, 1943.

Romania

The June 1936 re-equipment plan for the Aeronautica Regalã Românã (Romanian Air Force) covered the procurement of 406 new aircraft. Among the total were 39 Blenheim Is diverted from RAF orders. They were L6696 to L6708 (13), L6713 to L6718 (six), L8603 to L8608 (six), L8619, L8620, L8622 (three), L6824 to L6830 (seven), L8632 (one) and L8652 to L8654 (three), which became 1 to 40, excluding 13. They were dispatched to Romania between May 17 and June 26, 1939, but two aircraft were lost during delivery.

Once in Romania, they were issued to five reconnaissance-bomber squadrons, known as escadrille de recunoastere-bombardament, which had a standard establishment of eight aircraft each. Their primary role was long-range reconnaissance, but the units had a secondary bombing capability.

During the summer of 1940, Romania was forced to cede large swaths of its territory, with Bessarabia and Northern Bukovina passing to the Soviet Union, Northern Transylvania to Hungary and Southern Dobruja to Bulgaria. The Blenheims were used to clandestinely observe the changes in the border. One aircraft was lost during a mission over Northern Transylvania in September 1940, crashing into the Carpathian Mountains. That month a coup brought Marshal Ion Antonescu to power and in November 1940 the country joined the Axis powers.

By 1941 a further Blenheim had been lost, with the 35 aircraft shared between escadrille de recunoastere-bombardaments 1 to 4. The squadrons were assigned to flotile de informatie ('information fleets'). Escadrila 1 recunoastere-bombardament of Flotila 2 informatie operated from Cluj, Transylvania; Escadrila 2 and 4 were based at Iasi, Moldavia, with Flotila 1 informatie; under Flotila 3 informatie was Escadrila 3, covering Wallachia and Dobruja from the airfield at Galatia. In early 1941 Escadrila 2 disbanded.

A total of 28 Blenheims, plus three unserviceable aircraft, remained in service with the three units on June 22, 1941, the day Romania began operations against the Soviet Union alongside the Germans. Escadrila 1 recunoastere-bombardament was assigned directly to the headquarters of the Gruparea Aerianã de Luptã (Air Combat Group), the ARR's main combat element, while Escadrila 3 came under the Aero Armata 4 Românã (Air Element of the Romanian 4th Army) and Escadrila 4 Aero Armata 3 Românã. A Blenheim of Escadrila 1 became the ARR's first combat loss of the war on June 22, the first of four lost that day. A total of ten had been destroyed by the end of the initial campaign, July 26, and a lack of spare parts was becoming problematic.

In September 1941 the Germans handed over three former Yugoslavian Blenheim Is. German sources stated that an additional three aircraft followed in 1942, but this was not confirmed by Romanian sources. By the end of August 1942 just 27 Blenheim were operational. Six of the aircraft were with the Escadrila 1 recunoastere indepãrtatã (1st Long-Range Reconnaissance Squadron), under the Grupul 1 recunoastere indepãrtatã (1st Long-Range Reconnaissance Group), which also had units flying Dornier Do 17Ms and Potez 63s. The group arrived in the Stalingrad area in September 1942 and the Blenheims operated in the area until the squadron was withdrawn back to Romania at the end of the year.

By then, the Blenheims were becoming unreliable. Escadrila 1 recunoastere indepãrtatã continued to operate them over the northern and eastern areas of the Black Sea, but their pilots tried to stay as close to land as possible in case of equipment failure.

Romania signed an armistice with the Allies on August 23, 1944. On that day six Blenheims remained with Escadrila 1 recunoastere indepãrtatã at Ciocârlia airfield, although one was shot down three days later by 'friendly' anti-aircraft fire and another captured by Soviet forces at Ciocârlia. In early September 1944, three Blenheims, plus four Junkers Ju 88Ds, were assigned to Escadila 1/2 recunoastere of the Corpul 1 Aerian Românã, subordinate to the Soviet 5th Vozdushnaya Armiya (5th Air Army). Unreliability of the Blenheims meant they were soon relegated to the transport role, with the last remaining in service into 1948.

South Africa

egotiations by South Africa to acquire a squadron's worth of Blenheims began in 1937. Nearly two years later, this resulted in the supply of Blenheim I L1431, handed over for evaluation in December 1938.

The aircraft was tested at Waterkloof, outside Pretoria, in March 1939, the results reinforcing the South African Air Force's desire to acquire the type for squadron service. This was frustrated by the RAF's re-equipment plans, however, as production for the British service had priority over the needs of the dominions, especially as the likelihood of war in Europe increased.

South Africa declared war on Germany on September 6, 1939, at which point the Blenheim was still in the union. During that October and November, the aircraft participated in the hunt for the German 'pocket battleship' *Admiral Graf Spree* in the South Atlantic. It would remain with the South African Air Force (SAAF) until returned to the RAF on August 29, 1941. A new marking, AX683, was allocated to the aircraft, making it the only Mk I with a 'double letter' identity.

Three SAAF squadrons flew Blenheims during World War Two. No. 15 Squadron re-equipped with Blenheim IVs in Egypt in early 1942 as a light bomber unit, operating in North Africa with the Desert Air Force. A detachment was established at the Kufra oasis in the Libyan Desert during April, to which Blenheims T2252, Z7513 and Z7610 arrived on the 28th. A familiarisation flight from Kufra was launched early on May 4, each of the three aircraft carrying a fourth person, an

The wreck of a 15 Squadron Blenheim V. The aircraft continued to be known as the Bisley within the SAAF.

armourer, in addition to the standard crew. High winds and communication failures meant that the three aircraft got lost, and after an engine in T2252 began to malfunction, the order was given to land in the desert. All three successfully came down, but while three further flights were undertaken by two of the crews to try and find Kufra, each time they returned without finding it. The next day, two further flights were undertaken in Z7513 to locate Kufra, and as it failed to return from the second, the other nine survivors thought its crew had been successful and rescue was on its way. On May 6, with water supplies nearly exhausted, Z7610 took off before returning. Only three people remained

alive by May 8. The next day a Wellington crew located Z7513 and its three deceased occupants, while two days later, on May 11, the same aircraft located T2252 and Z7610 and a sole survivor. While T2252 and Z7610 were later recovered to Kufra, Z7513 was abandoned in the desert.

No.15 Squadron received Blenheim Vs from July 1942 and its role changed to flying convoy protection patrols along the Egyptian coast, later moving to Cyprus. On February 17, 1943, Blenheim V 'W' of the unit assisted the Royal Navy destroyer HMS *Paladin* attack the Type VIIC U-boat U-205 off the north-west African coast. While the crew abandoned the U-boat and opened the sea vents, it remained afloat and was taken in tow, although it later sank. Martin Baltimore aircraft began to replace the Blenheims in May 1943.

After flying operations against the Vichy French in Madagascar, 16 Squadron moved to Kenya and converted from Bristol Beauforts and Martin Marylands to Blenheim Vs in November 1942. The squadron flew patrols off the Kenyan coast during the winter of 1942-43 before being transferred to Egypt in April for more of the same. In mid-1943 it gave up its Blenheims and once again received Beauforts.

The last SAAF unit to receive Blenheims was 17 Squadron, which had reformed at Zwartkop in Centurion, South Africa, on October 8, 1942. It moved to Aden, where it received Blenheim IVs, at the start of 1943 to fly anti-submarine patrols. In May 1943 it moved to Bilbeis in Egypt, where its Blenheims were handed over to other units.

SOUTH AFRICAN BLENHEIM SQUADRONS				
Unit	**Type**	**Code**	**Base**	**Dates**
15 Squadron	Blenheim IV	ZP	Amriya, Egypt	02/42-03/42
			LG98, Egypt	03/42-07/42
	Det		Kufra, Libya	04/42-11/42
	Blenheim V		El Ballah, Egypt	07/42-07/42
			Maryut, Egypt	07/42-01/43
			Cyprus	01/43-07/43
16 Squadron	Blenheim V		Kilifi, Kenya	11/42-04/43
			LG91, Egypt	04/43-05/43
			Misurata West, Egypt	05/43-06/43
17 Squadron	Blenheim V		Little Aden, Aden	01/43-05/43
			Bilbeis, Egypt	05/43-05/43

Blenheim I G-AFFZ (c/n 8166), the last of the original 12 for Turkey, in the United Kingdom in June 1938 prior to delivery. It is understood to have become 2512 in Turkish service.

Turkey

In April 1936 Turkey ordered 12 Blenheim Is, becoming the second overseas customer for the aircraft after Finland. The aircraft were built at Filton, outside Bristol, as c/n 8155 to 8166 and were allocated the British civil registrations G-AFFP to -AFFZ. The first pair were sent by ship to Turkey in October 1937, but the other ten were ferried across Europe between March and June 1938. They became 2501 to 2512 once in Turkish service.

A further 18 (c/n 9222 to 9239) were ordered, registered as G-AFLA to -AFLS, and were delivered between November 1938 and February 1939. These aircraft became 397 to 408 and 485 to 490, but were later re-serialled as 2513 to 2530. On September 21, 1939, another ten former RAF Mk Is (L1483, L1485, L1488, L1489, L1493, all previously flown by 211 Squadron, L4826 ex 113 Squadron, and L4821, L4824, and L4828 without RAF service, plus one) which became 2531 to 2540.

Turkish pilots converted to the Blenheim at 12 (Pilots) Advanced Flying Unit at RAF Grantham (Spitalgate) and its relief landing ground at RAF Harlaxton, both in Lincolnshire.

The Blenheims were assigned to units of the 3. Hava Alayi (3rd Air Regiment) based at Gaziemir in Izmir, which came under the Ikinci Hava Tugayi (2nd Air Brigade) with headquarters at Güzelyali. They served with four aircraft squadrons (Tayyare Bolugu) of two battalions (Tabur), 23. and 24. Tayyare Bolugu of XII. Tabur and 25. and 26. Tayyare Bolugu of X. Tabur.

Although Turkey maintained a strict neutrality throughout the war, by April 1941 it was surrounded by the Axis powers. In order to gather intelligence on the activities of these neighbours, especially any preparations to advance into Turkish territory, daily reconnaissance flights were conducted along the border and over Bulgaria, Greece and the islands in the Aegean Sea, the Italian occupied Dodecanese Islands, and the Soviet Union. Blenheims are understood to have been employed on these long-range reconnaissance flights.

The Turkish air arm was reorganised in 1943. The Air Brigades became Air Divisions, with 3. Hava Alayi coming under the Ikinci Hava Tumeni (2nd Air Division) of Izmir. The battalions and squadrons flying the Blenheims were renumbered, with I. Tabur having the 1. and 2. Tayyare Bolugu, and II. Tabur the 3. and 4. Tayyare Bolugu. Turkey also acquired some Blenheim IVs, reportedly between three (2541 to 2543) and five. Known examples are T1996, previously with 105 Squadron RAF, and Z7986, ex 107 Squadron. They operated alongside the Mk Is within 1. Tayyare Bolugu.

On March 31, 1943, Turkey received 18 Blenheim Vs from the United Kingdom,

A line up of six Blenheim Is of the 3. Hava Alayi (3rd Air Regiment) based at Gaziemir. Turkey would operate the aircraft as bombers throughout the war, eventually symbolically joining the Allies in February 1945.

The Blenheim V served with two torpedo bomber squadrons under direct navy command, as well as the aviation school. This example appears to have been withdrawn.

comprising former 113 Squadron aircraft BA137, and BA292, BA495, BA591, BA613, BA614, BA713, BA827, BA854, BA855, BA887, BA910, BA922, BA925, EH320, EH326, EH341 and EH372. At least the EH3** examples were assigned to 301 Ferry Training Unit at RAF Lyneham, Wiltshire, which trained crews to ferry overseas, before being flown to Turkey by 1 Overseas Aircraft Despatch Unit, based at RAF Portreath, Cornwall. The others reportedly came from RAF stocks held in the Middle East.

The Blenheim Vs were issued to the 1. and 2. Tayyare Bolugu of the 105. Torpil Grubu (105th Torpedo Group) at Köceköy, which was controlled by Naval Aviation Command at Güzelyali. The Command reportedly directly to naval headquarters.

On January 31, 1944, the Hava Kuvvetleri Komutanlığı (Air Force Command) was formed

UNITED STATES OF AMERICA

A small number of Blenheim Vs were supplied from RAF stocks to the US Army Air Forces in Northwest Africa on October 1, 1943. They include two former 13 Squadron aircraft (EH347 and EH458), one that had previously served with 614 Squadron (BB179) and another (EH443) from an unknown unit. Exactly what use was made of the aircraft, or how long they were operated by the US Army Air Forces, remains unknown.

as a separate branch of the Turkish Armed Forces, unifying logistic support previously under the Air Undersecretariat and operations and training under the Turkish General Staff.

The Blenheim Vs of the 105. Torpil Grubu were augmented from March 1944, when Bristol Beauforts were delivered from surplus RAF stocks in the Middle East. The group's second squadron continued to fly some Blenheims alongside the Beauforts, while 1. Tayyare Bolugu completely re-equipped with the new aircraft. This allowed some Blenheim Vs to go to the Hava Okulu (Aviation School) at Eskisehir, where they were assigned to the 2. Talim Bolugu (2nd Training Squadron) of the III. Talim Taburu (Training Battalion), which also had Avro Anson Is.

Turkish Blenheim I and IVs remained active into 1947, while the Mk Vs continued to fly into the next year. 

Eight of the original Blenheim Is bound for Turkey. A total of 40 of the variant was delivered.

Yugoslavia

The Kingdom of Yugoslavia sought a licence to produce 50 Blenheim Is at the Ikarus AD factory at Zemun, close to Belgrade. Two pattern Blenheim Is (G-AFCE and 'CF, c/n 8814 and 8815) were supplied by Bristol Aeroplane Company and delivered from Filton, Bristol, in November 1937, becoming 160 and 161 (later 3501 and 3502). One of the two later became the personal aircraft of General Dušan Simović, Chief of the Yugoslav Armed Forces. The licence was finally granted in April 1938, following procrastination by both governments over the deal. The first Blenheim built at Zemun flew in March 1939.

The Blenheim I entered service with the Vazduhoplovstvo vojske Kraljevine Jugoslavije (Royal Yugoslav Army Air Force) initially assigned to the 1 Bombarderski puk (BP, Bomber Regiment) based at Novi Sad, which had the subordinate 61 and 62 Grupas (Groups). The groups controlled 201, 202, 203 and 204 Eskadrilas (Flights). A second bomber unit, the 8 BP at Zagreb, was later formed, with the 215, 216, 217 and 218 Eskadrilas under the 68 and 69 Grupas.

By 1939 Ikarus had completed around 23 airframes, but supplies of Bristol Mercuries from the UK did not keep up with production; only 52 engines were delivered from the original manufacturer. In order to overcome this problem, other powerplants were investigated, resulting in Alfa Romeo 126 RC.34K engines being fitted to Blenheim 3529, although it made the aircraft slightly slower. The Italian radial was not adopted for the fleet. An alternative source of Mercury engines was located in Poland, where PZL built it under licence, and in mid-1940 Germany agreed to supply enough to complete another 14 Blenheims. While all 40 Mk Is are understood to have been completed by Ikarus (3503 to 3542), only 18 may have been delivered.

Ikarus-built Blenheims were armed with Italian 12.7mm (0.5in) Breda-SAFAT machine guns instead of the British 0.303in (7.7mm) weapons. Some of the aircraft had additional examples of the Italian machine-gun added to improve defensive capabilities, at the cost of increasing the aircraft's weight.

Local production was augmented by 20 Mk Is diverted from an RAF order in February 1940, comprising L6813, L6814, and L6817 to L6834. All the aircraft were built by A V Roe at Chadderton, outside Manchester, and were collected together at RAF Aston Down, Gloucestershire, for preparation by 20 Maintenance Unit. They became YU-BAA to -BAT (probably not in serial order) for the delivery flights, after which they were allocated the serials 3543 to 3562. The aircraft were delivered in lieu of Blenheim IVs originally requested by Yugoslavia in August 1939. The additional aircraft allowed two Eskadrilas, 21 and 22, to be formed in 1940, which reported to the 11 Grupa of the 11th Independent Long Range Reconnaissance Group (SDGI). The unit was based at Veliki Radinci.

Yugoslavian interest in the Blenheim IV resulted in the conversion of an Ikarus-built Mk I with the nose of the Mk IV. The aircraft (which became 3563) was delivered to the 11th SDGI. A contract for an additional 20 aircraft, to be built at Zemun as Ikarus B.4s, was signed on March 25, 1941.

By the time the Axis powers invaded Yugoslavia on April 6, 1941, only 16 Ikarus-built aircraft and the 20 from the UK had entered service, shared between ten flights. The Blenheims flew bombing missions against enemy airfields and advancing tank columns during 11 days of fierce fighting. The Royal Yugoslav Army Air Force was outnumbered and the Blenheims suffered heavy losses during the campaign. One aircraft was flown to Hungary by a defecting pilot on April 12, where it remained.

Yugoslavia was forced to surrender on April 17. Around 24 aircraft on the production line at Zemun were badly damaged to stop them falling into German hands. Components for ten additional, incomplete aircraft were captured, however, along with the operational examples that had survived the fighting. Eight were presented by the Germans to the Zrakoplovstvo Nezavisna Drazava Hrvatska (Croat Air Force) of the 'puppet' Croatian state in June 1941 (five) and the first half of 1942 (three), which became 1501 to 1508. Romania also received three former Yugoslavian Blenheims, via the Germans, in September 1941. Parts of 15 incomplete Ikarus B.4s, plus Blenheim I spares, were sold to Finland, along with tooling and jigs from the Zemun factory.

The last surviving Croat Blenheim I (1507) was flown to Klagenfurt in Austria on May 6, 1945. It later became the only one of its kind to serve with the post-war Jugoslovensko Ratno Vazduhoplovstvo (Yugoslav Air Force), remaining in service into 1947.

Blenheim I G-AFCF prior to delivery to Yugoslavia as a pattern aircraft for local production.

Last of the Many

It is largely thanks to Canadian farmers that the current generation can see a member of the Blenheim family in a museum in Europe and North America. While the Blenheim all but disappeared, many of its Canadian cousins escaped the post-war smelters to sit on farms across the prairies. As time and climate took its toll on the airframes, no one would have placed odds on ever seeing a Blenheim back in the air.

n August 1973 Ormond Adare Haydon-Baille acquired two Bolingbroke IV-Ts (9893 and 10038) from the multiple examples held in open store at Hartney, Manitoba, owned by Wes Agnew. Along with a huge cache of spares, came 23 Bristol Mercury engines, acquired for his Haydon-Baille Aircraft and Naval Collection. The whole lot was shipped to Britain, arriving at Harwich docks in 1974, around the time Haydon-Baille was relocating his collection from Southend, Essex, to Duxford, Cambridgeshire. Unfortunately, Haydon-Baille was killed flying a Cavalier Mustang in Germany on July 3, 1977.

BOLINGBROKE TO BLENHEIM

The two Bolingbrokes were bought by Graham Arthur Warner of the British Aerial Museum at Duxford, with the plan of returning one to flight. The fuselage of 10038 was selected and received the registration G-BLHM on March 4, 1982, which was changed 22 days later to the more appropriate G-MKIV. Work to complete the aircraft took eight years, at the end of which the Bolingbroke was painted as Blenheim IV 'V6028', 'GB-D' of 105 Squadron, the aircraft flown by Wing Commander Hughie Idwal Edwards, VC. He received his Victoria Cross during a daylight raid on Bremen, Germany, flying V6028.

Only one member of the Blenheim family is flying today, G-BPIV, seen in its early incarnation as a Mk IV. A dedicated team devoted countless man-hours of hard work to get a Blenheim back into the air – three times – undertaking extensive rebuilds of two airframes. The result is a fitting tribute to all those who flew the type across the globe.

The Spirit of Britain First meets the Spirit of Great Britain, both civilian operated bombers. Just 17 years separated the maiden flights of the Type 142M and the Avro Vulcan. Although the Vulcan last flew in October 2015, G-BPIV remains active on the airshow circuit. David Willis

During its time as a long-nosed Mk IV, G-BPIV carried three schemes, one each from Bomber, Coastal and Fighter Commands. Between 1996 and 2000 it represented L8841 of 254 Squadron, one of the 'Trade Protection' units transferred from Fighter to Coastal Command.

On May 22, 1987, John Lacombe, with John Romain in what became known as the 'engineer's seat' in the aircraft, performed the first flight of a 'Blenheim' for nearly three decades. Less than a month later, on June 21, the aircraft crashed during an unscheduled touch-and-go at Debden in north Essex. While all three onboard survived, significant damage resulted in G-MKIV having to be written-off.

Three days later, Warner announced another Bolingbroke would be restored to fly. At the time the Strathallan Aircraft Collection at Strathallan (Auchterarder) in Perth and Kinross, Scotland, was winding down and sold Bolingbroke IV-T 10201 to the British Aerial Museum. It arrived at Duxford on January 28, 1988, and The Aircraft Restoration Company was formed by Warner and Romain. The identity G-BPIV was registered for the project on February 15, 1989.

It took 'just' five years before the aircraft was ready to fly, completed as all-black 'Z5722' of 68 Squadron, Wing Commander Max Aitkin's aircraft with the code 'WM-Z'. On May 18, 1993, 'Hoof' Proudfoot, with Romain again in the right-hand seat, lifted the aircraft off the runway at Duxford. Ten days later, in front of invited guests, the aircraft was named *Spirit of Britain First* by Viscount Rothermere, in homage to his grandfather's Type 142 *Britain First*. Also present was Lady Violet Aitkin, who had married Sir Max in January 1951.

From the 1996 season G-BPIV was painted in 254 Squadron colours as 'L8841/QY-C', and in late 1999 it became 'R3821/UX-N' of 82 Squadron. After a display at Somerley Park, Hampshire, on August 18, 2003, the aircraft was badly damaged making an emergency landing at Duxford, after the starboard Mercury stopped due to fuel starvation. It hit the embankment short of the threshold, slid up it and turned through 90°, before coming to rest. A landing gear leg was torn off and the other shoved into the wing but, thankfully, both onboard walked away without injury.

A new company, Blenheim Duxford Ltd, was formed in October 2003 to restore the aircraft. The opportunity was taken during the rebuild to replace the long nose with that of Mk IF L6739. The short nose section had been converted as an electric car after the war by former Bristol employee Ralph Nelson, who had the foresight to retain all the parts, which were also donated to the project. Blenheim IF L6739 was a Battle of Britain veteran, flying with 23 Squadron.

On June 4, 2014, G-BPIV was rolled out as Blenheim IF L6739, with the 'YP-Q' code it carried during its time with 23 Squadron. The aircraft reflew on November 20, 2014. Since then, it has delighted crowds at airshows across the UK. Although in legal documents G-BPIV is still listed as a Bolingbroke IV-T, for all intents and purposes it is a Blenheim IF.

ON DISPLAY IN THE UK

In addition to being the home of the only airworthy member of the Blenheim family, several others are displayed at museums in the British Isles. Bolingbroke IV-T 10001 was taken on charge by the Royal Canadian Air Force (RCAF) on October 20, 1942, serving with 3 Bombing and Gunnery School (B&GS) at McDonald, Manitoba, and them possibly with 5 B&GS at Dafoe, Saskatchewan. After accumulating 905 flying hours, it was struck-off charge on May 15, 1946. It was acquired for CAD200 by a farmer and taken to his farm at Portage La Prairie, Manitoba.

When the RAF Museum began looking for a Blenheim, it identified 10001 as a suitable candidate for restoration and offered to buy its hulk in April 1966. The RCAF provided transport facilities, in exchange for which the RAF Museum gave it Beaufighter TT.10 RD867 from its store at Henlow, Bedfordshire. The Bolingbroke arrived there in crates in 1969 and

It is highly unlikely that Bristol had electric cars in mind when it designed the Blenheim. Yet one of its former employees modified the nose of a Mk IF as such a vehicle post-war. It was donated to the restoration project (seen here at Duxford in September 1998), opening the possibility of modifying G-BPIV as a short nose variant, an option taken after the 2003 accident. *David Willis*

Sir William Roberts' Bolingbroke IV-T 9940 at Strathallan in March 1977. The museum was somewhat off the beaten track for tourists, which reduced visitor numbers, resulting in most of the collection's aircraft being auctioned off in June 1981. The Bolingbroke was acquired by the (then) Museum of Flight at East Fortune, East Lothian.

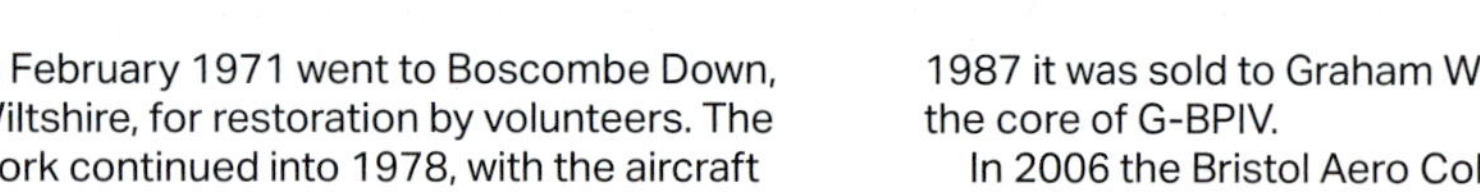

Unlike other Bolingbrokes on display in the UK, the National Museum of Flight Scotland at East Fortune finished the restoration of its Mk IV-T by painting it in the colours it would have worn during its time as a trainer in Canada. Jim Winchester

in February 1971 went to Boscombe Down, Wiltshire, for restoration by volunteers. The work continued into 1978, with the aircraft painted to represent Blenheim IV L8756 'XD-E' of 139 Squadron. On July 17, 1978, it was transported to Hendon in north London and placed on display in the Battle of Britain Hall at the RAF Museum.

When the fabulous Battle of Britain exhibition was revamped into the RAF First 100 Years display, which opened in 2018, the Bolingbroke moved into the main halls at Hendon. It was relocated to RAF Museum Midlands at Cosford, Shropshire, by May 2023.

Avid aircraft collector Sir William Roberts acquired Bolingbroke IV-T 9940 in Canada, with the airframe arriving at his Strathallan Aircraft Collection during December 1972. The aircraft was sold at an auction of the museum's collection on June 14, 1981, and was acquired by the Museum of Flight at East Fortune, south of Edinburgh, where it arrived on August 8, 1981. There it was restored in the colours it wore during its time with 5 B&GS.

In 1984 Sir William acquired a second Bolingbroke IV-T (10201) from Canada via Wes Agnew, plus the wings of 9073. Although work started to return it to flying condition, in late 1987 it was sold to Graham Warner, becoming the core of G-BPIV.

In 2006 the Bristol Aero Collection Trust acquired Bolingbroke IV-T 9048, which was placed in store at Kemble, Gloucestershire, prior to moving to Filton, when the Aerospace Bristol museum was established. The aircraft is currently being restored.

Bolingbroke IV-T 9048 came from a store of the type at Nashville, Tennessee, having previously been at Chino, California, and with the 1st Composite Group at Apple Valley and Chiriaco Summit Airport in the same state beforehand. Between 1972 and 1999 9048 was at Chino, first with David Tallichet then, from 1981, the Yankee Air Corps Museum. Tallichet had recovered the airframe from Wes Agnew's farm at Hartney, Manitoba. It had served with 8 (BR) Squadron, 3 and 7 B&GSs before being struck-off charge by the RCAF on August 21, 1946.

SURVIVORS IN THE UNITED KINGDOM		
Version	**Serial**	**Location/Notes**
Bolingbroke IV-W	9019	Manx Aviation and Military Museum, Isle of Man AP; cockpit
Bolingbroke IV	9048	Aerospace Bristol, Filton
Bolingbroke IV-T	9893	IWN, Duxford
Bolingbroke IV-T	9940	National Museum of Flight Scotland, East Fortune
Bolingbroke IV-T	9980	Lincolnshire Aviation Heritage Centre, East Kirby
Bolingbroke IV-T	10001	RAF Museum Midlands, Cosford; 'L8756'
Bolingbroke IV-T	10073	Lincolnshire Aviation Heritage Centre, East Kirby
Bolingbroke IV-T	10201	ARC, Duxford; 'L9739'/G-BPIV as Mk I; original nose also at Duxford
Bolingbroke IV-T		Kent Battle of Britain Museum; 'L9446'/BAPC.603, composite (fuselage, centre section and wings of 9893, nose, other parts possibly from 9980)

The first restored 'Blenheim' to go on display in England was Bolingbroke IV-T 10001, lovingly rebuilt at Boscombe Down, Wiltshire, for the RAF Museum. It was one of the exhibits of the Battle of Britain Hall at Hendon in north London, where it is seen in May 2016, and is currently displayed at the RAF Museum Midlands at Cosford, Shropshire. *David Willis*

The cockpit of Bolingbroke IV-W 9019 is on display at the Manx Aviation and Military Museum at Isle of Man Airport. It arrived at the museum in June 2004, having previously been part of a large cache of Bolingbrokes at Nanton in Alberta.

The fuselage, centre section and outer wings of 9893 arrived at Hawkinge from Duxford for the Kent Battle of Britain Museum on December 6, 2017. The cockpit of a Mk IV-T and other elements were sourced from Canada in 2019 and used to complete the airframe, which was painted as 'L9446/LA-N' in the colours of 235 Squadron.

On November 14, 2022, components of Bolingbroke IV-T 9980 arrived at the Lincolnshire Aviation Heritage Centre at East Kirby, home of Avro Lancaster *Just Jane*. There it joined parts of 10073, which had arrived in November 2018, having previously been used by the Pima Air & Space Museum at Tucson, Arizona, as a source of spares for its own restoration. It had been at Chino, California, beforehand.

HOME OF THE BOLINGBROKE

At the end of the war the RCAF had large numbers of Bolingbrokes that were surplus to requirements, with the majority being struck-off charge in 1946. The aircraft were offered for sale, with many acquired as a source of metal or even for the fuel remaining in their tanks. Large numbers were towed away from storage depots to farms and other private properties. Many of them remained there, slowly being robbed of parts and deteriorating over the years. It was from this pool of derelict airframes, scattered across the Canadian countryside, that most of the Bolingbrokes displayed in museums across Canada, Europe and the United States were sourced.

As interest in historic aircraft grew in the 1960s, museums began to approach many of their owners to acquire what remained of the Bolingbrokes. In the 1960s into the 1970s, Wes Agnew of Harney, Manitoba, acquired or brokered at least 19 airframes (9048, 9059, 9073, 9893, 9895, 9904, 9911, 9940, 9947, 9980, 9983, 9987, 9989, 10038, 10070, 10073, 10076, 10078 and 10201) sourced from farms across Canada. Many of these formed the basis of restorations in the years to come, most of which included parts from several airframes.

In 1962 George A Maude donated Bolingbroke IV-T 9892 to the RCAF. It was dismantled and trucked in May 1963 from his property at Salt Spring Island, British Columbia, to Alberta for restoration. The Bolingbroke was completed in the colours of 8 (BR) Squadron as 'YO-X' and was officially handed over by Maude during a ceremony on June 6, 1964 – Air Force Day. It was placed on display at the National Aviation Museum at Rockcliffe, Ontario. In May 2010 the name of the collection changed to the Canada Aviation and Space Museum. As of 2025, the Bolingbroke is understood to be in the museum's reserve facility and not on display.

The Commonwealth Air Training Plan Museum at Brandon, Manitoba, has Bolingbroke IV-Ts 9059 and 10107. The museum also displays Mk IV-T 9883, which sits next to the Comfort Inn in Brandon as '9944'. The collection is planning to put a Bolingbroke back into the air. To further this aim, the remains of another Bolingbroke discovered near the helicopter training areas near Portage la Prairie Southport Airport, was donated to the museum by the RCAF in March 2024.

At Hamilton International Airport at Mount Hope, Ontario, the Canadian Warplane Heritage Museum is restoring a Mk IV-T to ground running condition, work having started in 1986. It was originally hoped to fly it, but these plans changed in September 2019. The aircraft is a complex composite, using parts from at least eight other Bolingbrokes salvaged from Manitoba in the mid-1980s. Parts from at least 9889, 9937, 9949, 9981, 10040 (the nose of this aircraft went to Melun-Villaroche) and 10184, and possibly 10078, last reported at Uxbridge, Ontario around 2004, are being used. (Some of the aircraft, including 9981, were destroyed in a hangar fire on February 15, 1993). Registered C-GBLY, the bulk of the fuselage is understood to be from 10117, although 10040 was

Finished in 8 (BR) Squadron colours, Bolingbroke IV-T 9892 belongs to the National Aviation Museum at Rockcliffe, Ontario. It was the first Bolingbroke to be restored and put on display in a Canadian museum.

SURVIVORS IN CANADA

Version	Serial	Location/Notes
Bolingbroke IV	9059	Commonwealth Air Training Plan Museum, Brandon, MN
Bolingbroke IV	9104	British Columbia Aviation Museum, Victoria, BC
Bolingbroke IV-T	9869	Royal Aviation Museum of Western Canada, Winnipeg, MN
Bolingbroke IV	9883	Commonwealth Air Training Plan Museum, Brandon, MN
Bolingbroke IV-T	9887	James Armstrong Richardson International, MN
Bolingbroke IV-T	9892	Canada's Aviation and Space Museum, Rockcliffe, OT
Bolingbroke IV-T	9896	Canadian Museum of Flight Association, Langley, BC
Bolingbroke IV-T	9897	Bomber Command Museum of Canada, Nanton, AB; fuselage
Bolingbroke IV-T	9904	Reynolds Museum, Wetaskiwin, AB
Bolingbroke IV-T	9978	Bomber Command Museum of Canada, Nanton, AB; fuselage
Bolingbroke IV-T	9987	Bomber Command Museum of Canada, Nanton, AB; fuselage
Bolingbroke IV-T	9989	Bomber Command Museum of Canada, Nanton, AB; 'R3662'
Bolingbroke IV-T	9990	Reynolds Museum, Wetaskiwin, AB
Bolingbroke IV-T	9997	Greenwood Military Aviation Museum, Greenwood, NS
Bolingbroke IV-T	10040	Canadian Warplane Heritage, Hamilton, ON; rest to fly, composite
Bolingbroke IV-T	10107	Commonwealth Air Training Plan Museum, Brandon, MB
Bolingbroke IV-T	10117	Canadian Warplane Heritage, Hamilton, ON; composite
Bolingbroke IV-T	10120	Reynolds Museum, Wetaskiwin, AB
Bolingbroke IV-T	10121	Montreal Aviation Museum, St-Anne-de-Bellevue, Montreal, QC
Bolingbroke IV-T	10122	Readlyn, SK
Bolingbroke IV-T		Commonwealth Air Training Plan Museum at Brandon, MB

Notes: Several other Bolingbrokes are believed to survive in Canada, along with major components of many more (see main text). Canadian province and territory codes: AB = Alberta; BC = British Columbia; MB = Manitoba; NB = New Brunswick; NS = Nova Scotia; ON = Ontario; QC = Québec; SK = Saskatchewan.

originally due to be used; major parts of that aircraft eventually went to Melun-Villaroche, France. The completed Bolingbroke will be painted as Mk I 714 'DM-L' of 119 (BR) Squadron.

Plans for Bolingbroke IV-T 10121 of the Montreal Aviation Museum (known as the Canadian Aviation Heritage Centre until 2016) at St-Anne-de-Bellevue in Montreal, Québec, originally included restoration to airworthy condition, but it will be completed for static display. The aircraft is due to be completed as '9066'.

Bolingbroke IV-T 9104 is displayed at the British Columbia Aviation Museum at Victoria International Airport, British Columbia, in the colours of 3 Operational Training Unit based at RCAF Patricia Bay, with the code 'BK-L'. It is a composite, using parts of 9093 and 10163, restoration having been completed in 1996.

The Canadian Museum of Flight Association at Langley Regional Airport, British Columbia, has Bolingbroke IV-T 9896. Until December 2014, the Royal Aviation Museum of Western Canada, Winnipeg, Manitoba, was known as the Western Canada Aviation Museum. It owns Bolingbroke IV-T 9869.

The Bomber Command Museum of Canada at Nanton, Alberta, was known as the Nanton Lancaster Society until 2010. On display is Bolingbroke IV-T 9989 as 'R3662', with the codes 'WV-L' of 18 Squadron. The museum also has, or had, 9897, 9978, 9987 and 10074, plus major sections of 9041, 9874, 9897, 9978, 9994 and 10074.

In 1988 Bolingbroke IV-T 9904 joined the Reynolds-Alberta Museum at Wetaskiwin Regional Airport, Alberta, where it was joined in 1988 by 10120 and 9990 in 1991. The collection also donated Mk IV-T 9997 to the Greenwood Military Aviation Museum at CFB Greenwood, Nova Scotia. Restoration began in April 2009 and the aircraft will be completed as Blenheim IV 'EE-H' of 404 Squadron, RCAF, during its time with RAF Coastal Command.

Bolingbroke IV-T 9887 arrived at James Armstrong Richardson International, Manitoba, in October 2013 for restoration by personnel of the co-located CFB Winnipeg. Also present in 2007 was the fuselage of 10209, while 9869 (later to the Royal Aviation Museum of Western Canada) and 10182 then at Winnipeg/St Andrews may have supplied parts for the project. Another Mk IV-T (10122) was reportedly under restoration to static condition at Readlyn, Saskatchewan, although nothing has been heard of the project for at least two decades.

Bolingbroke IV-T C-GBLY under restoration at the Canadian Warplane Heritage Museum at Hamilton International Airport, Ontario, in October 2014, when the plan was to fly the aircraft. This changed partly because of the time needed to receive approval for materials used in the project. Jim Winchester

The Canadian Warplane Heritage Museum collected at least eight Bolingbrokes to support its plan to put one back in the air. They included 9889 from St Andrews, Manitoba, acquired in December 1985. The aircraft later went to Uxbridge in Ontario and was exported to Melun-Villaroche in France in June 2009.

BLENHEIMS AND BOLINGBROKES IN EUROPE

As the last country to fly Blenheims operationally – and use it in three conflicts between 1939 and 1945 – it was logical for the Finns to save one for posterity. The aircraft would become the last, whole Blenheim built in Europe.

The Blenheim involved, BL-200, was a sarja (series) VI Mk IV built at the Valtion Lentokonetehdas (State Aircraft Factory) at Tampere in 1944, and was one of the five revived for service in the early 1950s. It was last flown on June 5, 1957, and from June 1960 sat on block as a memorial at Tikkakoski air base, the Air Force Academy. Often covered in snow, it suffered in the harsh Finnish climate but remained outdoors until 1970, when it was moved to the Keski-Suomen Ilmailumuseo (Aviation Museum of Central Finland), Luonetjärvi air base, before going on loan to the Tampereen Teknillinen Museo of Tampere. Between 2005 and 2008, the Blenheim was thoroughly restored, having its turret and bomb bay refitted, before going on display inside the new museum building at Tikkakoski. The museum also has a pair of Blenheim noses in store; one from an unidentified Mk I or II, while the other is a spare built at Tampere but never fitted to a Blenheim.

Although BL-200 is Europe's only complete Blenheim, the substantial wreck of a Bristol-built example can be found in Greece. No.203 Squadron moved to Heraklion in Crete on April 24, 1941, following the German invasion of Greece. Four days later, L9044, flown by Flying Officer Peter Gordon-Hall, with navigator Sergeant Cliff Poole and air gunner/wireless operator Sergeant Ivor Oultram, took off at 0620hrs heading for the island of Melos. It was one of three Blenheims due to rendezvous with a convoy around 120 miles (193km) off Crete. Despite signalling the colours of the day and on the agreed approach vector, the warships fired on the aircraft. The starboard Mercury of L9044 was hit and caught fire, although it was extinguished after fuel was cut to the powerplant.

Gordon-Hall set course for Crete. Although the crew jettisoned what they could, the Blenheim could not maintain 1,000ft (305m) and, in sight of the coast, the aircraft had to ditch into the sea. All the crew got into their dinghy while the Blenheim disappeared beneath the waves and after paddling towards the coast, a Greek soldier swam out near Retimon and towed them ashore.

In 1996 the Hellenic Air Force recovered the hulk of the Blenheim from the seabed. It was transported to Tatoi-Dekelia Air Base, where it was conserved, layers of marine life being removed from the airframe. Although most of the cockpit was gone, much of the rear fuselage survived. The starboard wing and Mercury engines of Mk I L1434 of 113 Squadron, recovered from Lake Prespa in 1993, were included in the airframe, which was placed on display at the Ellininki Aeroporia Mousion (Hellenic Air Force Museum) at Tatoi-Dekelia.

The only Bolingbroke on display in Europe is in the heart of the Belgian capital at the Musée Royal de l'Armée et d'Histoire Militaire/Koninklijk Museum van het Leger en de Krijgsgeschiedenis (Royal Museum of the Armed Forces and Military History), housed in the impressive Parc du Cinquantenaire/Jubelpark. The museum has a large collection of aircraft, including Mk IV-T 9895 in the colours of 139 Squadron as 'L9416', with the codes 'XD-A', the 'real' aircraft having been posted as missing on May 12, 1940.

The aircraft was acquired by the museum in 1971 from the stock of Bolingbrokes held by Wes Agnew. It underwent restoration at St Trond air base using parts from many other aircraft between 1988 and 1996, before being moved to Brussels and going on display.

Three Bolingbrokes are kept within the Musée de l'Aviation de Melun Villaroche, although it is understood the collection is only available to be inspected on special

		SURVIVORS IN EUROPE
Version	**Serial**	**Location/Notes**
Blenheim I/II		Keski-Suomen Ilmailumuseo, Tikkakoski, Finland; nose, store
Blenheim II		Keski-Suomen Ilmailumuseo, Tikkakoski, Finland; spare nose, never fitted to aircraft, store
Blenheim IV	BL-200	Keski-Suomen Ilmailumuseo, Tikkakoski, Finland
Blenheim IVF	L9044	Ellininki Aeroporia Mousion, Tatoi-Dekelia AB, Greece; wreck
Bolingbroke IV-T	9889	Musée de l'Aviation de Melun Villaroche, Melun-Villaroche, France
Bolingbroke IV-T	9895	Musée Royal de l'Armée et d'Histoire militaire, Brussels, Belgium; 'L9416'
Bolingbroke IV-T	10040	Musée de l'Aviation de Melun Villaroche, Melun-Villaroche, France (see under Canada)
Bolingbroke IV-T	10184	Musée de l'Aviation de Melun Villaroche, Melun-Villaroche, France

For more than a decade, Europe's last surviving Blenheim was outside at Tikkakoski air base in Finland, often covered by a thick blanket of snow. Built by Valtion, BL-200 was later fully restored and is currently displayed at the Aviation Museum of Central Finland.

The remains of Blenheim IVF L9044 on display at the Hellenic Air Force Museum at Tatoi-Dekelia in Greece. The wreck is all that survives of all the Blenheims built in Britain. Visible below the tip of the propeller is the ventral gun pack fitted to fighter variants of the aircraft. David Willis

Bolingbroke IV-T 9895, finished as 'L9416' of 139 Squadron lost during the Battle of France, is displayed within the cavernous hall of the Brussels Air Museum. The aircraft was one of many that passed through the hands of Wes Agney before arriving in Belgium in 1971. *David Willis*

SURVIVORS IN THE UNITED STATES OF AMERICA		
Version	**Serial**	**Location/Notes**
Bolingbroke IV	9073	Fantasy of Flight, Polk City, FL; dismantled
Bolingbroke IV-TT	9983	Fantasy of Flight, Polk City, FL; dismantled
Bolingbroke IV-T	10070	Springfield, MO
Bolingbroke IV-TT	10076	Pima Air & Space Museum, Tucson, AZ; '9118'

open days. When the Association des Mécaniciens Pilotes d'Avions Anciens (AMPAA) at Melun-Villaroche dissolved in May 2021, it ended its plans to return a Bolingbroke to the air. The three airframes it owned were inherited by the Musée de l'Aviation de Melun Villaroche at the airfield. Major parts of 10040 and 10184, including the cockpit sections, had been acquired by AMPAA, having donated parts to the Canadian Warbird Heritage Museum's planned airworthy restoration. In June 2009 they were joined by 9889.

The only other example in France was Mk IV-T 9947, which joined the Musée de l'Air et l'Espace collection at Le Bourget, outside Paris, from the Eric Vormezeele collection at Brasschaat, Belgium, in August 1985. Unfortunately, it was destroyed on May 17, 1990, by the fire that claimed many historic aircraft in the museum's Dugny facility, the opposite side of the airfield to its display halls.

AMERICAN BOLINGBROKES

Only a single Bolingbroke is on display in the United States. Mk IV-TT 10076 was trucked from Chino, California, to the Pima Air & Space Museum in Tucson, near Davis-Monthan AFB, Arizona, around 2003, where it underwent restoration using parts from many other aircraft. It went on display as 'Z9592' in RAF North African camouflage, but in 2015 was repainted as '9118' of 115 (BR) Squadron of the RCAF, with the code 'BK-V'.

Kermit Weeks has a pair of dismantled Bolingbrokes at his facility at Polk City in Florida, among his many projects. Other Bolingbrokes are believed to survive in the United States. Mk IV-T 10070 was at Springfield, Missouri, from 1976, where it was joined by parts of 9991 and 10223 in 1991. However, they were last noted there two decades ago and may have moved on in one form or another.

David Tallichet kept Bolingbroke IV-T 10073 at Chino, California (as seen here) from 1972. The aircraft included parts from three aircraft. In 2003 it went to the Pima Air & Space Museum at Tucson, Arizona, where it is believed to have donated parts to 10076. What remained went to East Kirkby, Lincolnshire, in 2022.

The Bristol Story Part Two
Blenheims to Concorde

Jim Winchester concludes the story of the Bristol Aeroplane Company and its subsidiaries, from its wartime expansion through to the consolidation of the British aerospace industry.

Bridging the gap between wartime requirements and civil needs, the Bristol 170 Freighter became the company's first successful post-war product. Although it became famous for carrying cars across the English Channel, many were operated by air arms.

Bristol grew several times over during the war and dispersed its production away from Filton. Including Blenheims built before September 1939 and Beaufighters after September 1945, the company assembled nearly 12,000 aircraft used by the RAF, Royal Australian Air Force, Royal Canadian Air Force, US Army Air Forces, and several other air arms in all combat theatres.

DISPERSED PRODUCTION

Under a system established from 1935 by the Ministry of Aircraft Production, 'shadow factories' were established to expand the output of fighters, bombers, engines and aircraft components by utilising existing facilities and their workers, particularly from within the motor industry. With large Blenheim orders, Bristol had opened two more lines to increase production for the anticipated war with Germany. In 1936 Rootes Securities Ltd, parent company of Hillman, Talbot and Sunbeam cars, built a shadow factory at Speke, near Liverpool. It was designed for an output of 40 Blenheims a month, but by the end of the war was producing 60 four-engined Handley Page Halifaxes every 30 days. A second Rootes plant, at Blythe Bridge in Staffordshire, built Blenheims from 1941 to 1943. In May 1940 a site at Oldmixon, near Weston super Mare, was chosen for a shadow factory. By 1943 it was producing 80 Beaufighters per month, rising to 100 a month by the end of the year; it would eventually build 3,335 Beaufighters. Another site at nearby Banwell assembled the last 250 Beauforts.

In the pre-war expansion programme, the Bristol Engine Company was contracted to manage the first shadow engine group. By 1937 it had been confirmed that parts from Bristol and contractors could be combined with no adverse consequences. Rover produced rods, pistons, valves and springs, while Austin at Longbridge in Birmingham were responsible for crankshafts and reduction gears, as well as assembly and testing of half of the Bristol engines.

FILTON UNDER ATTACK

By 1940 Filton and its associated plants had become the biggest aircraft manufacturing centre in the world and, consequently, a prime target for attack by the Luftwaffe. Several night raids targeted the Bristol area. While none of them did much actual damage to the main site, component factories were not so lucky and they did kill or make homeless Bristol Aircraft workers. From May 1940 Filton was protected by barrage balloons. This had the unfortunate

Cyril Frank 'Papa' Uwins was the chief test pilot for Bristol, completing the first flights of 58 types of aircraft up to the Type 170 Freighter. He later became deputy chairman of the company.

side-effect of hindering operations at the airfield, particularly at night and during periods of poor visibility.

Fighters were also detached to Filton on a temporary basis to provide local defence. On July 4 two Hawker Hurricanes of 92 Squadron scrambled from the airfield and shot down a Heinkel He 111 that had bombed the company's Rodney engine plant, located on the North Gloucester Road.

The Filton site was bombed in daylight on September 25, 1940. Although most bombs fell on the airfield, eight aircraft were destroyed and 92 workers killed, most of them when two air raid shelters took direct hits. The factory's gun defences shot down three of the attacking He 111s. The Beaufighter line was disrupted for ten days. Soon after, all design staff and non-production workers were relocated to other sites around Bristol. Work on small components was dispersed to locations including a chocolate factory, a cider mill and a bus garage, while the flying school at Filton moved to Staverton, Gloucester. Another Bristol-run school at Yatesbury, Wiltshire,

would train 18,500 radio operators for the RAF during the war.

Thousands of women worked on Bristol's assembly lines alongside the men. A training school in Bristol city also instructed large numbers of women as inspectors for the Aeronautical Inspection Department (AID), which signed off materials and components as they arrived and the completed aircraft as they left.

FEDDEN'S DEPARTURE

While the Bristol Aircraft Company had gone public in 1935, its board consisted of White family members; Sir George's two sons and two cousins. By 1942 the company's payroll had increased to more than 52,000 people at Filton and the shadow factories. During that year, one of its most famous employees, engine designer Roy Fedden was both knighted by the King and sacked by Bristol. The circumstances of his dismissal were discussed in the House of Lords. Lord Brabazon of Tara stated it was a tragedy that such a parting had occurred, going on to note that Sir Roy's engines accounted for more than half of those in RAF service. Lord Sempill added that the total power output of his engines built to date exceeded 75 million horsepower; he went on to say he hoped that people on the financial side of business would stop making war against those on its technical side.

At the root of Sir Roy's departure appears to have been a disagreement concerning over-optimistic forecasts for his projects and poor cost control. By the time he left, his only communication with the company was via solicitors. Fedden went on to serve various roles for the government, but he never designed another aeroengine. His assistant, Leonard Frederick George 'Bunny' Butler, was overworked and passed away from a heart attack at Paddington Station on September 3, 1943. The rest of the engine design team gradually dispersed and development of engines suitable for post-war civil use was neglected.

In 1944 the company had created a helicopter division under the Austrian émigré

Raoul Hafner, inventor of the Rotabuggy flying jeep. It was not to bear fruit until 1947, when the Type 171 flew. Cyril Uwins, by now in his late 40s, continued to undertake the maiden flights of all new Bristol designs, although he had a team of ten test pilots for development work.

AFTER THE WAR

Bristol's plants and shadow factories in Britain rolled out 3,725 Blenheims, 1,121 Beauforts and 5,564 Beaufighters. Production in Canada and Australia increased the total of these wartime types to 11,807 aircraft, while approximately 71 additional Blenheims were completed in Finland and Yugoslavia.

Throughout the conflict, Bristol was busy building its own designs and had little capacity to assemble those of other manufacturers. The exception was a batch of 50 Hawker Tempest IIs assembled at Banwell at Locking, near Weston super Mare, but orders for a further 250 were cancelled when the war ended.

The last Beaufighter, TF.X SR919, departed the works at Oldmixon on September 21, 1945. The factory then turned to making aluminium

The Beaufighter was the most numerous Bristol aircraft produced during World War Two. This example, a post-war TT.10 target-tug conversion, was among the last batches built.

The two prototypes of the Bristol Brabazon – of which only the first flew – under construction at Filton in the hangar purpose-built for the project. At the time it was the world's largest aircraft, but airlines baulked at the prospect of finding enough passengers to justify operating it.

bungalows for the temporary housing programme. Later, in 1955 it became the home of the Helicopter Division of Bristol Aircraft.

Post-war the company continued the line started with the Blenheim with the Buckingham bomber and Brigand strike fighter, which would become Bristol's last combat aircraft. Filton moved into the civil sector, although its most successful post-war aircraft, in terms of numbers built, started as a military transport before becoming a moderately successful vehicle and cargo carrier for civilian use. The Bristol 170 Freighter flew in December 1945 and 214 were built in six major versions.

As part of the government's plans for civil aviation development, Bristol built the giant Brabazon to meet the Brabazon Committee's requirement for a 100-seat transatlantic airliner. The largest aircraft in the world at the time it first flew in September 1949, it failed to secure an order from the national carrier and the project was suspended in early 1952, and cancelled outright in mid-1953.

The smaller turboprop Britannia achieved more success, although development was plagued by problems with its Bristol

The prototype Britannia 101 G-ALBO outside the Brabazon hangar at Filton, prior to its first flight on August 16, 1952. The future of the airliner had looked promising, but by the time it was ready for service, turboprops were passé.

The Bristol Type 188 was notoriously hard to build, thanks to difficulties machining the stainless steel used in its construction. It was subsequently delayed, while its de Havilland Gyron Junior engines failed to power it to the speeds required to investigate the high temperatures it had been ordered for.

Proteus engine and, although it first flew in August 1952, it only began carrying passengers with British Overseas Airline Corporation in February 1957. By then the airlines were looking to acquire their first jets, limiting production to just 85 aircraft, including deliveries to the RAF.

Bristol's dalliance with rotary-wing aircraft produced the Sycamore (178 built) and the twin-rotor Type 173 (three built), which was developed as the Belvedere, of which 26 were delivered to the RAF.

CONSOLIDATION

The experimental Type 188 was a supersonic research aircraft constructed largely of stainless steel. The first of the two built flew in April 1962. Three additional Type 188s had originally been planned, but they were cancelled after the release of the infamous 1957 Defence White Paper, which incorrectly predicted that missiles would soon be able to undertake many of roles performed by manned combat aircraft. The Paper had a significant effect on the British aircraft industry, triggering a wave of consolidation and mergers. Vickers, English Electric and Bristol formed the British Aircraft Corporation

(BAC), while de Havilland joined with Hawker to become Hawker Siddeley. The new chairman of BAC was Sir George Edwards of Vickers. Cyril Uwins had retired from test flying in 1947 and was appointed to the company's board. When Bristol Aircraft became a subsidiary company in 1956, 'Papa' Uwins was made its chairman.

Bristol's engine business merged with Armstrong-Siddeley to become Bristol-Siddeley, which later subsumed de Havilland and Blackburn's engine businesses. Although the Type 188 was the only one pure jet Bristol aircraft to fly, Bristol-Siddeley engines were widely used on other manufacturer's aircraft, including the Avro Vulcan bomber (Olympus), Fiat G.91 (Orpheus) and P.1127/Harrier (Pegasus). Bristol-Siddeley merged with Rolls-Royce in 1966 although engine work continued at Filton.

The Bristol Helicopters division was sold to Westland in 1959, after pressure from the government to concentrate all helicopter manufacturing within one firm. Its legacy continues today, under the Leonardo Helicopters name, at Yeovil, Somerset.

A lesser-known facet of Bristol's work was on space rockets and satellites.

Bristol's Guided Weapons department developed the Skylark, a high-altitude sounding rocket, which was first launched in 1957. It created the Black Arrow rocket and Prospero satellite combination, which was launched in 1971, as was the Ariel 4 science satellite. Other Filton space products included the Intelsat IV F-4 communications satellite (1972), the science satellites GEOS and GIOTTO in the 1970s and 1980s, and the solar panels used on the Hubble Space Telescope.

In the early 1960s contracts for complete airframes were few and far between, but between 1963 and 1966 Filton built wings for the Short Belfast – based on those of the Britannia – which were shipped to Northern Ireland for final assembly. This was the beginning of a wing construction business which continues to this day. To keep Filton operating, some work on the Vickers VC10 airliner and development of the two-seat English Electric Lightning fighter was transferred to the plant. Filton would go on to build 20 Lightning T. Mk. 5s. The Bristol Aircraft Company name would finally disappear in 1966 as the company was absorbed within BAC.

The first product of Bristol's helicopter division was the Type 171 Sycamore. Sycamore HR.14 XG504 was one of the last in RAF service, operated by 32 Squadron into the early 1970s.

The Bristol Type 204 of 1957 was a supersonic tactical strike and reconnaissance aircraft to meet the requirements of Operational Requirement OR.339. What became the TSR.2 was to fulfil the requirement, with development of that aircraft central to the industry consolidation that saw Bristol become part of BAC. David Willis

CONCORDE

With the creation of BAC, Filton inherited, in July 1960, the task of modifying Fairey Delta 2 WG774 to support research into a future supersonic transport (SST), which had originally been allocated to Hunting. First flown in 1954 as a supersonic research aircraft and a previous holder of the world air speed record, it was transformed with an ogival delta wing, emerging as the Type 221. It would become the last aircraft with a Bristol Type Number to fly, and was allocated the Sequence Number (as Bristol termed its constructor's numbers) 13521. It flew in its new form at Filton on May 1, 1964, in the hands of Godfrey Auty and would go on to make 273 research flights at Royal Aircraft Establishment (RAE) Bedford.

Of course, the last aircraft associated with the Bristol name and its Filton birthplace was Concorde. In 1956 the Ministry of Supply formed a Supersonic Transport Advisory Committee (STAC), which recommended the development of two SSTs. France had similar aspirations and the two nations' projects would merge, but not before Bristol had

Filton was responsible for modifying one of the two Fairey Delta FD2s to support research for a supersonic transport. The aircraft became known as the BAC 221, the designation combining its Bristol Type number and the name of the new, merged conglomerate.

The Belvedere HC.1 was the last rotary-wing designed by Bristol, with pre-production examples first flying on July 5, 1958. The helicopter served with the RAF between 1961 and 1969.

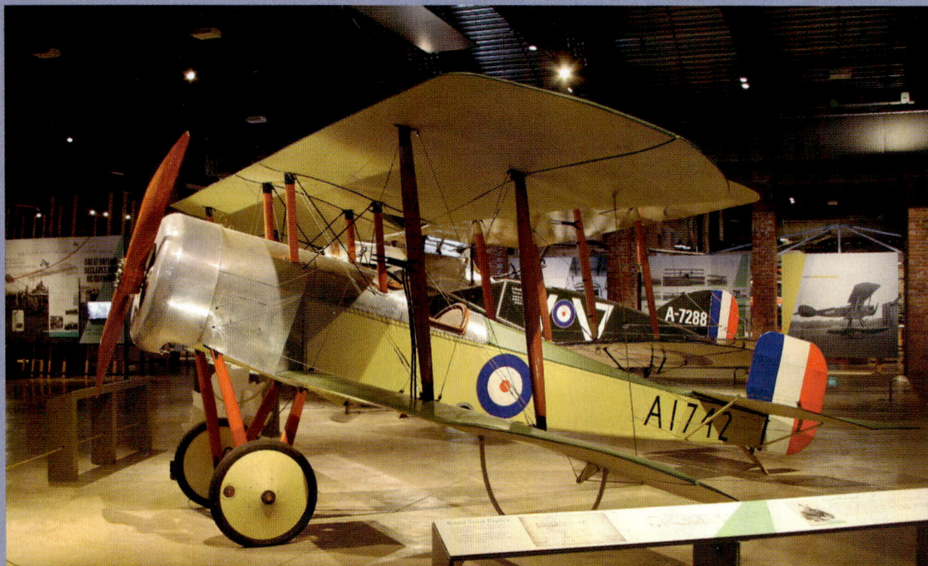

Filton is home to the Aerospace Bristol museum that celebrates the history of the company and the site. Bristol Scout replica 'A1742' (BAPC.38) is one of the many exhibits within its halls. David Willis

proposed its Type 198, offered in 'M-winged' or delta-wing form, and the Mach 3.0 Type 213. The Type 223, drawn up by Bristol's Archibald Edward Russell, was very close to the Sud Super Caravelle, and by late 1962 an agreement was drafted for signature by the two governments for co-operation on the project that the British called Concord until 1967.

Many companies on both sides of the Channel contributed to the technical success of the project. Bristol-Siddeley led engine development on a 60-40 basis with French aircraft engine manufacturer SNECMA. The Olympus 593 was the only suitable engine; SNECMA developed the afterburner, nozzle, thrust reverser and other parts aft of the core. Thousands of hours of ground running of the engines took place at Filton, conducted by the test pilots who gained much experience in the aircraft systems long before the first flight.

The second prototype Concorde, 002, took flight on April 9, 1969, with a crew comprising Brian Trubshaw, John Cochrane, and Brian Watts. After completing a few test points, the aircraft landed at RAF Fairford in Gloucestershire, where most of the flight test programme would be conducted until late 1976, making Filton a much quieter place. A much-reduced test department, then part of British Aerospace (BAe), would relocate to Filton.

Ten Concordes would be assembled at Filton in the Brabazon Hangars. The last of them, G-BOAF, flew on April 20, 1979, marking the end to production of complete aircraft at the site. That same aircraft would make Concorde's last ever flight, returning to its birthplace on November 26, 2003. There it joined the Bristol Aero Collection, which opened the Aerospace Bristol museum on the north side of the airfield in October 2017.

FILTON FINALE

Following the end of Concorde production, aviation activity at Filton continued for another European collaboration programme. BAC had become part of BAe in April 1977, an Airbus partner in 1979, transferring Filton to the consortium. Wing construction for the Airbus A300 moved from the BAe facility at Hatfield when that site closed. BAe became BAE Systems in 1999 and departed the civil aviation sector. Its share in Airbus was sold to European Aerospace and Defence Systems (EADS) in 2006. EADS in turn sold Filton to GKN for £136m in 2008. Airbus undertook the design of the wing structure, fuel systems and landing gear integration for Airbus airliners at Filton and made some structures there, while final assembly was conducted at Broughton, Cheshire. To move wings between the sites, the company used A300-600ST Beluga outsized transports, which were frequent visitors to Filton until BAE Systems, which still ran the airfield, decided it was no longer economically viable and sold it for development. The last fixed-wing aircraft flights from the historic airfield were undertaken by specially charted Airbus A380 giving local rides to employees, plus a few light aircraft relocating to the Bristol Aeroclub's new home at Kemble. The airport closed on December 21, 2012, ending 101 years of flying from the site.

The runway was dug up and is now a suburb, along with a golf course. The Brabazon hangars are being converted into a multi-purpose entertainment centre. Wings for the Airbus A400M military airlifter are still made on site, but now are taken by road to Avonmouth for onward transport by ship. BAE Systems and Airbus still retain a presence, the latter employing nearly 3,000 staff, who provide design, engineering and support for Airbus wings, fuel and landing gear systems. Other departments work on aerodynamics research, development and testing, including for the ZEROe future zero-emissions programme. Airbus also opened a Wing Technology Development Centre at Filton in mid-2023.

The last Concorde built at Filton about to touch down back where it was assembled on November 26, 2003, at the end of the last flight by the type. The aircraft is currently displayed at the museum on the site of the former airfield. David Willis